PRELIMINARY DESIGN OF BOATS AND SHIPS

PRELIMINARY
DESIGN
of
BOATS *and* SHIPS

BY

CYRUS HAMLIN, N.A.

CORNELL MARITIME PRESS

A Division of Schiffer Publishing, Ltd.
Atglen, Pennsylvania

Published by Schiffer Publishing, Ltd. 2010

Preliminary Design of Boats and Ships was originally published by Cornell Maritime Press in 1989

Copyright © Cornell Maritime Press in 1989

Copyright © Cyrus Hamlin 2010

Calligraphy by Cecile Bayon.

Library of Congress Control Number: 2010920963

Schiffer Books are available at special discounts for bulk purchases for sales promotions or premiums. Special editions, including personalized covers, corporate imprints, and excerpts can be created in large quantities for special needs. For more information contact the publisher:

Published by Schiffer Publishing Ltd.
4880 Lower Valley Road
Atglen, PA 19310
Phone: (610) 593-1777; Fax: (610) 593-2002
E-mail: Info@schifferbooks.com

For the largest selection of fine reference books on this and related subjects, please visit our web site at
www.schifferbooks.com
We are always looking for people to write books on new and related subjects.
If you have an idea for a book please contact us at the above address.

This book may be purchased from the publisher.
Include $5.00 for shipping.
Please try your bookstore first.
You may write for a free catalog.

In Europe, Schiffer books are distributed by
Bushwood Books
6 Marksbury Ave.
Kew Gardens
Surrey TW9 4JF England
Phone: 44 (0) 20 8392 8585; Fax: 44 (0) 20 8392 9876
E-mail: info@bushwoodbooks.co.uk
Website: www.bushwoodbooks.co.uk

ISBN 978-0-87033-621-8

Printed in China
First edition; third printing, 2010

To the memory of
my mother and father

Charlotte and Marston

who gladly nurtured my compulsion
to design boats

Contents

Naval architecture: part art, part science; the role of the naval architect; air/water interface; the design spiral

PART I : GROUNDWORK

1. Tools of the Trade : 9

The sketch designer's tool kit: drawing paper, pencils and pens, measuring devices, triangles, and straight edges; methods of reproduction; sources of information

2. Sketching : 14

Sketching explained; freehand drawing; hints on successful sketching; laying out a sketch; your first sketch

3. Vessel Geometry : 22

Showing the hull shape: models, drawings; lines drawing: profile, plan, sections, buttocks, waterlines, diagonals; DWL (design waterline); displacement; form coefficients; making a pickle model

4. Calculations : 36

High school level math helpful; exponents and space; reference axes: X, Y, Z; relativity and similitude; measurement of areas and centers; moments; use of graphs; curves of form

Figures

Tables

Preface

When I was 12 years old, and already sure of my naval architecture vocation, my parents gave me a small blue book, *The ABC of Yacht Design,* by Charles G. Davis. As my first introduction to the mysteries of small craft design, this tiny 68-page volume was a wonder. Indeed, the insight I gained from Davis's work may have been a contributing factor to my lasting 50 years in this fascinating profession.

As my need for knowledge outgrew the "ABCs," I turned to the only other comprehensive reference available at the time, *The Elements of Yacht Design,* by Norman L. Skene. The jump from Davis to Skene was too great for a 14-year-old. After all, Skene was to be found on the drawing boards of just about every designer in the business. Although I puzzled out large chunks of it and it was my constant companion for many years, I have always felt there was a need for something between the utter simplicity of Davis and the overwhelming complexity of the many professional treatises now available. My effort to answer that need resulted in this volume, which I hope will be of interest to all who have a vocational or avocational interest in watercraft—fishermen, tugboat skippers, research vessel crews, yachtsmen, vessel owners and managers, boatbuilders, even naval architects.

Absorbing all the information in this book won't make you a naval architect, but it will allow you to discuss the details of small vessel design knowledgeably. It also will enable you to make a sketch that a naval architect can translate into a finished design. The delight of seeing your brainchild take form and do its job can be yours.

I want you to find this book interesting and fun. I want it to be browsable, but I also hope it will have enough substance to encourage thought and study. I suggest you start by leafing through the book, going back later to study those portions that intrigue you. Sources for deeper delving can be found in the Bibliography.

Although you will encounter mathematics, fluid (air and water) dynamics, hydrostatics, mechanics, and other technologies, don't let this awe you. Most of it is just plain common sense wrapped up in fancy language. My aim will be to explain the fancy language so that your common sense will have full play.

Most books on naval architecture are somewhat specialized, dealing in planing craft, fishing vessels, or sailing yachts. But the same fundamental principles apply in all watercraft, so why not cover all these types of craft in a single book? I think you will find the great diversity of craft covered in this work fascinating, even though your primary interest may be in a specific type like racing catamarans, pilot boats, or RO/RO vessels.

All the illustrations in this volume are drawn freehand—in contrast to the beautiful drafting exhibited by Chapelle, Kinney, and others in naval architecture works. Using sketches emphasizes the creative, preliminary, and conceptual phase of naval architecture described in this book. The flow of ideas must be just as fluid on paper as in your head; when you start putting in a lot of time on "pretty" drawings, the creative phase begins to grind to a halt. Use the illustrations as guides and examples of what you can do with a little practice.

The use of sketches, and especially freehand curves on the graphs, also emphasizes the dangers of "the arrogance of significant figures." My students in the yacht design program at the Landing School of Boatbuilding and Design at Kennebunkport, Maine, start out being enamored of putting down all the numbers shown on the screens of their calculators. This leads to calculations giving a length on the waterline of 45.6930213 ft. The unfunny part of using such numbers is that the user begins to feel he actually is working to this accuracy; this is clearly ridiculous when one considers that .01 ft equals $1/8$ in, a tolerance to which few boats of that size have been built. Data should be presented using only three or four significant figures.

The first few chapters of this book lay a groundwork, explaining some of the physical, mechanical, and mathematical concepts you will need in order to comprehend the discussions. The groundwork also includes detailed definitions of some of the important general terms used; more specialized terms will be defined in the pertinent sections of the book. A glossary is included at the back of the book. Don't worry if the meaning of some terms eludes you the first time around; I'll direct you back to the basics at the appropriate spots in the story so that you can have another go at understanding them when you need them.

Subsequent chapters go from the general to the specific, dealing with specific vessel types and design factors. Each specialized vessel chapter allows you to sketch a boat as you study, referring to the background chapters when necessary. Having completed your sketch design you will know something about the challenges facing the naval architect, and should be able to work out solutions to many of them.

So study, think, plan, and sketch as you follow this book into one of the most fascinating of occupations.

People pass through three phases of life: learning, producing, and teaching. I am now in the teaching phase, and I consider it my responsibility to impart to the coming generation whatever wisdom I have picked up in the 50 years since I got my first job designing boats. Having reached this stage of life does not mean that I am wiser or smarter than others, just that I have lived longer, have been exposed to more experiences, and have thought about them more hours and days. What I have to impart may be useful or useless, smart or stupid, right or wrong—each reader must make that determination. Obviously, since it is impossible to create a book without making some errors or omitting some salient step or vital piece of information, I will be grateful to any readers who spot such departures from correctness and inform me of them through the publisher.

While I am tempted to run through a long list of those who contributed to this volume, instead I am giving credit to the hundreds, perhaps thousands, of people who, by imparting their wisdom to me, have made me what I am and, consequently, have made this volume what it is. In writing this book I feel an obligation to be a pipeline for bringing their contributions to those who are fascinated by everything that floats.

Much credit also must go to the yacht design program of the Landing School of Boatbuilding and Design. Teaching there for nine years has forced me to straighten out my own thinking so that I can explain the concepts of naval architecture to my students, and has exposed me to the searching questions of over a hundred bright young, and not so young, students, often finding me embarrassingly wanting in answers. (Never again will I try to give a lecture on galvanic action!)

There are two persons, however, whose contributions must be singled out. One of these is Cecile Bayon of Kennebunk, whose calligraphy has added elegance to my simple sketches. The other is my wife Jean. Not only has she put up with my crotchets and fed and clothed me, but she has illuminated the text with her skill as a technical editor.

PRELIMINARY DESIGN OF BOATS AND SHIPS

Introduction

Naval architecture has often been described as half art, half science. This characterization has remained remarkably true to the present day, despite the fantastic advances in technology and the increase in knowledge of the marine environment achieved since World War II.

The art component of naval architecture is manifest when one is watching a gorgeous sailing yacht beat into a harbor in a fresh, crystal-clear northerly. It is equally important, though, in the more mundane and hidden elements of a vessel, especially those relating to a smooth flow of water about the hull, the minimizing of wake waves, and the mysteries of seaworthiness.

Yet art and science are not two separate components of a vessel, such as the propeller and the anchor windlass. Both qualities are inextricably melded together throughout the entire vessel. The curve of a vessel's sheer, which at its best can be one of the purest art forms, is also functionally designed to keep water off the decks, to provide adequate freeboard yet keep the deck weights as low as possible, and, as in the beautiful Gloucester schooners, to facilitate the launching and retrieving of dories.

Combining art and science, and making the many compromises necessary for a successful design, gives naval architecture a special quality the reader should keep in mind all through his creation of a sketch design. While most engineering is pretty much a linear process—one starts with the requirements and step by step develops the various elements of the structure, Element 1———▸ Element 2—naval architecture may be described as "indeterminate engineering," that is, a good deal of empiricism and subjective decision making go into synthesizing all the conflicting conditions and relationships into a good vessel design.

The indeterminate nature of naval architecture requires that the design process be done in a number of iterations. Graphically, this can be thought of as taking the ordinary engineer's straight task line and bending it around into a spiral. The resulting spiral, called the "design spiral" by naval architects and shown in figure I-1, provides a clear concept of the task path for creating a vessel design. Starting at the outside with his original concept, the architect works his way around the spiral; each time he crosses a task line he checks that task against the work he has done since his last crossing, and makes changes that will bring it closer to conformity with the other tasks. At some point, the architect is able to get all the way around the spiral without making any changes, at which time it is safe to assume that the major design decisions have been made.

While experienced naval architects are accustomed to working with the design spiral concept, in my experience neophytes have some problems with it. I have even seen a student complete a set of lines before fully determining the displacement of the craft or working out the arrangement plan. Invariably the premature lines plan must be discarded, with consequent wasted time and frustration.

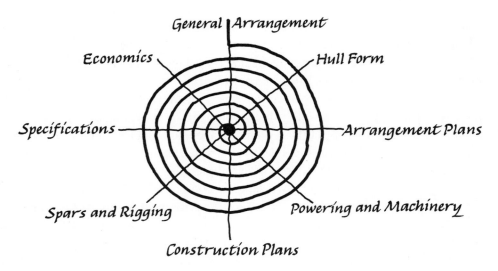

Fig. I-1. The design spiral

Every user of this volume seeking guidance in creating a sketch design of the ideal vessel should keep the design spiral clearly in mind. He should develop the philosophy that nothing he commits to paper is sacred—any of it can be changed. This freedom to change will go a long way toward ensuring the best possible design.

The naval architect you engage to complete your design will ensure the artistic and scientific integrity of your vessel, but in preparing your preliminary design you must keep in mind that the start you give him must also be artistically and functionally sound. The naval architect can't make a silk purse out of a sow's ear, or make sound something that is inherently unsound.

As you proceed through the steps outlined in this book, you should have fun. Let your fancy have free rein. Try out ideas—on paper as well as in your head—that you may have harbored for years. Be critical of them, but try them. Incorporating those you find worthwhile in a design will be a very rewarding experience.

Approaching the completion of your sketch design, you will find yourself becoming more down-to-earth and pragmatic. In seeking the answers to the practical questions of vessel design, the learning process can be as fascinating as the free-ranging creative phase. Is that beautiful curve from the stemhead down to the rudder heel practical and efficient? Will there be space enough in the head to sit down? Are the leads for the trawl warps fair and easy on the wire? Are the fuel tanks located so that trim will be minimized as fuel is consumed? Is the hull shape actually a good one for the purpose intended?

An important set of questions has to do with safety. The results of system failures on boats and vessels can be almost as serious as in aircraft. So develop the habit of studying whenever possible the causes of marine accidents, and how the design of the vessel systems is related to the cause and the outcome.

These are the types of questions you must address as you develop a final conceptual design. It is then up to the naval architect to solve other crucial problems, such as ensuring that the vessel will float on her waterline, that there is the required stability, that the vessel will perform under power as expected, and that the total structure and its component parts are adequately strong.

Finally, keep in mind that a major function of the designer is to communicate. If he can't express his ideas well, either by drawings, by text, or by equations and graphs, then they cannot be accurately transformed into reality, and all his brilliant work is pointless. So, as a conceptual designer, develop your communication skills, especially sketching and drawing, so that when your work is transformed into the real thing it accurately reflects what you had in mind at the start.

What will you need in personal qualities and in hardware to get yourself through this volume? Not a great deal, considering the complexity of vessel theory, design and construction. In addition to patience and a willingness to think and work hard at times, the only real requirements are a fair acquaintance with algebra and a passing knowledge of trigonometry. Wherever understanding beyond these levels is required, I have tried to explain the principles in the simplest possible terms. If the explanation misses the mark for you, work around it and come back later; frequently you will find that the matter has straightened itself out in your head without your being aware of it.

The mathematics, while not difficult, is often tedious. Having worked for many years with a slide rule and tables of logarithms, I am now never far from a pocket calculator. A $20 scientific calculator is adequate, and not a great loss if it should drop overboard; it should have variable power and root (exponential) capabilities, as well as trigonometric functions.

If you have a computer, don't use it. Even if you own some of the great number-crunching software so dear to the the naval architect's heart, do everything by hand as described in this book before using the software. If you try to use your computer you will inevitably waste a lot of time learning how, and the mechanical process of operating the computer will get in the way of your creative thinking. Computer aided design (CAD) is for the professional (and not always for him).

Symbols can often be confusing. Symbols and nomenclature used in this volume are generally those of the Society of Naval Architects and Marine Engineers and the Fishing Vessel Division of the Food and Agriculture Organization of the United Nations (FAO-UN), with an occasional original one to meet a unique need. The symbols are defined in the back of the book.

A significant element of naval architecture is artful compromise because the number of conflicting factors in a vessel is awesome. Once upon a time (as other fairy stories start out) I thought that, if I listed all the factors and relationships that affected sailing yacht performance, I could apply logical techniques to unravel their mysteries. By the time the list had 40 items in it, I realized that the only computer that could adequately synthesize those, through compromises, into an above-average design was the human brain. So the only computer you will need is that wonderful one between the ears and behind the eyes, which empties into the mouth and makes the hands do the right things.

So get under way—and enjoy it!

PART I

GROUNDWORK

1. Tools of the Trade

THE design of a vessel has the purpose of communicating to the builder how the vessel is to be built. Prepared by the naval architect, the design is made up of a collection of drawings, written specifications, and backup material such as catalogs. The most expressive and important of these are the drawings, or plans, prepared by the architect's own hands. This book will help you prepare sketches that communicate your ideas clearly, even though the skills of da Vinci are not required for your sketch design. It begins with a description of useful tools of the trade.

For most of the work described in this book the tools you will need are relatively few, simple, and easily obtained. Of course it is possible to expand your tool kit to include the more expensive and esoteric tools common to a naval architect's office, but I suggest you start small, working up if the mood moves you.

There are several categories of tools you will need: drawing paper or film; marking instruments, including pencils and pens; erasing devices and materials (you will find great need for these!); drawing instruments; drawing edges, such as triangles, curves, and splines; measuring devices, such as tapes, rulers, and scales; furniture; and miscellaneous items.

Drawing paper or film: These are either opaque or translucent. The opaque materials can only be reproduced on photocopiers, the translucent on both photocopiers and diazo (blueprint) machines. Translucent film can be used for making a new drawing by tracing from an old one, as well as being the base for original plans. Whatever the material, a rather smooth finish works best; if there is much "tooth," or roughness, it quickly wears down a sharp pencil point and tends to become rather dirty. These materials come in pads measuring 8½" × 11" (22 cm × 28 cm), 8½" × 14" (22 cm × 36 cm), or 9" × 12" (23 cm × 30 cm); cut sheets in multiples of 24" × 36" (60 cm × 90 cm); or rolls 24" to 42" (60 cm to 107 cm) wide.

Opaque—This material is available as ordinary lined pads, 8½" × 11" (22 cm × 28 cm); photocopier paper, 8½" × 11" and 8½" × 14" (22 cm × 28 cm and 22 cm × 36 cm); 18" × 24" (46 cm × 60 cm) cut sheets; pads of 8½" × 11" or 8½" × 14" (22 cm × 28 cm or 22 cm × 36 cm) graph paper, 10 divisions to the inch, every inch accented (5 divisions to the cm, every 2 cm accented), light blue lines. There are books available of every conceivable graph paper for reproduction on photocopiers (see the Bibliography). Photocopy machines that will accept roll stock (any length) in widths to 36″ and above are now common.

Translucent—There are two types, a parchmenty material known as "vellum" and a "foil," usually of Mylar. Vellum is inexpensive, fairly strong, fairly stable dimensionally, and will yellow after a number of years unless protected from light and moisture. Foil is several times as costly as vellum, very strong, completely stable dimensionally (well within the tolerances used in drawing), and essentially a permanent material. Except for smooth-surfaced foil, both materials will take pencil and ink equally well. You will not need a translucent material, but if you want to experiment with blue-line prints I suggest you purchase a 10-yard × 24″ (10 m × 60 cm) roll of good quality, medium-weight vellum.

Marking instruments: You will not need drawing pens so, unless you are familiar with them, I suggest you stick to pencils. If you do use pens, only ink the construction, or grid, lines; the design itself should be sketched in pencil.

For initial rough sketching, a plain dime-store wooden pencil with #2 grade of lead (or #2½, which is somewhat harder) is entirely satisfactory. As you get into more refined and detailed sketching, the click-type mechanical pencils will be much more convenient. I find it handy to have one of each lead diameter: 0.3 mm for delicate work, 0.5 mm for ordinary work, and 0.7 mm for daily use. Architectural lead grading goes from the hardest, 6H, through HB to the softest, 6B. My preference for sketching is HB or H, but you can experiment a bit to determine which combination of paper and lead best suits you. Remember that a sketch or drawing with fairly dark firm lines is much more impressive than one with wispy light lines, so lean toward the softer leads rather than the harder.

Erasing materials: Never hesitate to erase! No line you ever draw is sacred! Plastic erasers are excellent as are rubber ones called "Pink Pearl." Several types are available in very convenient plastic tube holders. There is no need for an electric eraser until you become a professional.

Drawing instruments: These are the intriguing pieces nestled in black velvet in handsome cases—compasses, dividers, ruling pens, even a tiny screwdriver. You will not need them.

Drawing edges: When sketching, it is well not to use any drawing edges, but to do all your drawing freehand. However, a natural desire for order and regularity in most people compels them to draw both straight lines and curves with some kind of device. If you must, these are the ones available.

Triangles—Conventionally these come in two configurations, 30-60-90 degrees and 45-45-90 degrees, and are made of clear plastic. You might like to have two of each, in 4″ (10 cm) and 8″ (20 cm) sizes.

Straight edges—These can be very precise steel or less precise wood-and-plastic, all plastic, or aluminum. If you feel the need for one (you will if you use large-size paper), I recommend for starters a 24″ (60 cm) aluminum. You may wish to lacquer it to keep the aluminum from dirtying the paper.

French curves—Plastic, available in assorted shapes, mostly with small-radius curves (as opposed to sweep curves), these are useful for final drawings but not for sketches.

Ship curves—These are long, easy sweeping curves of plastic in sets of 56 curves or singly. I've never had more than half a dozen, with which I have been able to draw all the different curves I wanted. Fun to look at, but don't buy any yet.

Splines, or battens—These are long, thin pieces of plastic or wood used for carefully crafting the longitudinal curves in a boat design. Splines are held in place by "ducks," whale-shaped pieces of lead with a point sticking out the head end which fits into a groove in the spline. Drawing the long sweeping curves that define a vessel's hull is a time-consuming art to learn; your naval architect will use them in the later stages of design.

Measuring devices: In addition to the tapes and rules a naval architect might use in the field, there are measuring instruments for the drawing table. The most important is the architect's scale rule, 6″ (15 cm), 12″ (30 cm), or 18″ (45 cm) long, with several of the most commonly used scales marked on it. In the English measurement system, scale is usually given as the number of inches or parts of an inch which, on the plan, equals one foot. When a scale is given as one-quarter inch, it means that each foot on the full-size vessel measures ¼″ on the plan. (In the metric system, scale is given as a proportion. A scale of 1:20 means that the vessel on the plan is one-twentieth as long as the full-size vessel.) A triangular scale rule for the English measurement system will have 10 different scales plus the full scale (12″ = 1′), which is all one needs. Metric scales are full scale (1 cm = 1 cm), or in various proportions, such as 1:25, 1:50, etc. Flat scale rules are more convenient but have fewer scales marked on them.

The measurement of areas looms large in naval architecture. This can be done at the preliminary design level perfectly adequately and simply without instruments, but architects use one that you will no doubt hear about—the planimeter. Once this device is set up, its pointer is run around the periphery of the figure being measured and the area is read from a dial. These are quite expensive and have little use outside naval architecture or surveying, so my recommendation is not to buy one.

Calculating device: A $15-$20 scientific calculator is all you will need. Much of the calculation can be done in your head—a good skill to develop for the preliminary design phase—but you will have need to calculate roots and powers, and some trigonometric functions. Don't try using computer aided design (CAD) even if you know how; it will get in the way of the free flow of thought so important in the conceptual sketching of a vessel.

Furniture: It's well to have a good drawing board, about 18″ × 24″ (45 cm × 60 cm or so), which you can use in your lap or on a desk or table. You may prefer one of the small, folding, stand-up tables and a stool, but it is not necessary. Storage of letter and legal size paper is no problem; larger plans may either be rolled up and stood on end in a carton, or stored in an inexpensive corrugated cardboard drawing filing cabinet.

Miscellaneous: Drafting tape is used to hold plans down on the drawing board. Masking tape will do, but don't leave it down too long, especially in hot weather!

A soft cloth or brush can be used to clean off the board without smudging it with the oils in the skin.

Lighting of a drawing board should generally be from a line or plane source, not a point source. Work something out that avoids shadows on your pencil point, and is comfortable for you. I find "warm" fluorescent, or a mix of "cold" fluorescent and incandescent, lighting works best.

Recommendations: Among the tools and materials described above, some will be useful to the beginning sketch designer, and others are suitable only for more advanced work. Those I would recommend to the beginner are listed below. These items should be available in any shop carrying drafting and engineering supplies; many will also be found in a neighborhood stationery or variety store.

lined paper pads, $8\frac{1}{2}'' \times 11''$ (22 cm $\times$ 28 cm)

photocopier paper, $8\frac{1}{2}'' \times 11''$ and $8\frac{1}{2}'' \times 14''$ (22 cm $\times$ 28 cm and 22 cm $\times$ 36 cm)

graph paper pads, $8\frac{1}{2}'' \times 11''$ or $8\frac{1}{2}'' \times 14''$ (22 cm $\times$ 28 cm or 22 cm $\times$ 36 cm), 10 divisions to the inch, every inch accented (5 divisions to the cm, every 2 cm accented), light blue lines

wooden pencils, #2 grade lead

mechanical pencil, 0.3 mm, 0.5 mm, and 0.7 mm HB leads

plastic erasers, in a plastic tube holder if available

4" (10 cm) 30-60-90 degree triangle

8" (20 cm) 30-60-90 degree triangle

4" (10 cm) 45-45-90 degree triangle

8" (20 cm) 45-45-90 degree triangle

24" (60 cm) aluminum straight edge

6" (15 cm) or 12" (30 cm) architect's scale rule

triangular scale rule

drawing board, about $18'' \times 24''$ (45 cm $\times$ 60 cm or so)

drafting tape

soft brush

A most important tool of the trade is information. The characteristics of mahogany, the size and weight of stock fastenings, engine specifications, the effect of beam-draft ratio on vessel performance—all this information is out there waiting for you to use it. Use it! It's very depressing to find after your handsome conceptual design is completed that some important piece of information that was guessed incorrectly was readily available.

The Bibliography lists a good selection of basic texts that will give most of the technical answers if you wish to delve deeper than required by this book. Another great source of information is the manufacturers of the fittings, machinery, and gear required on a vessel; they are as eager as you are to see that their product is properly applied and installed so that it is satisfactory. In addition to using their fact-filled catalogs, don't hesitate to write to them for specific advice on the use of their products; I often will send plans and specifications to manufacturers or their agents showing the application of their product for their comment. There is also a vast quantity of professional journals and government publications which may on occasion be very helpful. To avoid missteps and backtracking, do all your information gathering and studying before you get deeply into your sketch design.

Perhaps the most complete sources of information on boat and ship designs are the periodicals and trade papers covering your particular sphere of interest. They publish plans, photos, and technical articles that can be of tremendous educational value. Copy these for your reference file, which you will find helpful at all stages of your work.

One way to start searching for information is to have your local, state, or university library carry out a computer data search for specific information—for instance, harbor tug operation. These organizations usually have access to huge computer bibliographies in this country and sometimes abroad. For little or no charge, you will receive a very comprehensive selection of abstracts of papers, articles, books, etc., on the particular subject you requested. From these abstracts you can pick out the most useful-sounding and obtain the original piece.

Above all, keep it simple. Don't saddle yourself with a bunch of fancy equipment and thick books. Figuring out how to use all this stuff will only tend to get in the way of your thinking about your design.

2. Sketching

Sketch, An outline or rough draft
or plan of any design.
—Webster's

THIS book is about making a "sketch design," the same process many naval architects employ in developing a new design concept. When your sketch design is completed, it will be suitable for use by a naval architect as the basis for preparing the design for construction purposes. Sketching therefore is essential to the successful use of this book.

The design you create as a result of this book will only have value if it is communicated to someone else—your wife, a friend, the naval architect who will translate it into reality. The name of the game is "communication." Most of what you will wish to tell the others is not communicable with words and numbers alone. Imagine, for instance, trying to describe only in words how to build a skylight.

A little thought will make it clear that naval architecture is essentially based on graphics; a design is a collection of drawings supplemented by words and numbers. This is not to say that words and numbers do not have an important place in the communication process, but even a small boat cannot be built without the pictographs ("pictures representing and expressing ideas") that we call plans or drawings.

It is neither feasible nor good design practice to sit yourself down at a drawing table and immediately start turning out finished plans for a vessel. The design spiral, which you met in the Introduction, makes it clear that a design begins very tentatively and experimentally. Only when all the major decisions are made through a lengthy, iterative process is it practical to begin the final drawings for the vessel.

It will be an advantage to begin working out the design with the simplest and easiest of pictographs—the freehand sketch. This early planning stage should be filled with changes, revisions, corrections, erasures, as well as fundamental conceptual changes on the part of you, the creator. The less time and effort one has invested in a picture, the easier it is to change it or discard it and start over.

Sketches therefore have an essential place in the design process. They make it possible to try out new ideas, perfect concepts, and develop important details, all without a discouraging investment in fancy drawings. In fact, it is possible to prepare a complete design in sketches of sufficient accuracy as to require no important corrections as they are transformed into a set of working drawings.

Some readers will state most emphatically that they have never been able to sketch and cannot begin now. If they have totally convinced themselves of that, there is nothing that can be done for them, but in my experience there has never been anyone who was inherently incapable of making acceptable sketches. With a "can do" attitude, the hints I will give you, and some pleasurable and interesting practice, the "nonsketcher" can learn to make pleasing sketches of acceptable accuracy; that's all that's necessary.

Get in the habit of making sketches of ideas as they occur to you. It often helps to doodle a sketch or two to get one's ideas squared away before making the presentation, or working, sketch. Enough of talk! Let's do it! Right from the beginning.

We will start by drawing a straight line freehand. This is surprisingly difficult to do, but some hints and a bit of practice should enable anyone to draw an adequate one. Place a piece of plain letter size paper in front of you on a clear desk or tabletop. Clasp both hands on top of the paper in a comfortable position; relax there for a moment until all tension has left your muscles. Move the paper until your clasped hands are centered on the top edge, and your drawing forearm lies along the center of the sheet. Relax again, keeping your nondrawing arm anchoring the paper. Pick up your pencil and make two dots on the paper about an inch in from each edge and halfway up from the bottom. To connect those two dots with a straight line, while still relaxed and without thinking much about it put your pencil on the left-hand point (for right-handed people) and draw your line to the other point by gently sliding your forearm sideways.

Still look kind of funny? Don't despair. Put a couple more dots about an inch below the first two. If you found yourself tightening up before or during the previous effort, try changing the position of the paper, your arms, your head, your whole body, until you feel comfortable. Now this time, when you draw the line vibrate your hand a little so that the line has tiny wiggles in it; don't ask me why, but this maneuver helps keep the line straight. Also, before starting out from the departure dot think in your mind where the target dot is; this helps you to aim straight for it.

Continue practicing drawing straight lines as long as you want to, but certainly not after you have begun to tense up. It's not the most exciting occupation in the world, but after a couple of sessions you'll be able to astonish your friends with your skill.

For a variation, turn the paper 90° and draw a few lines as nearly as possible at 90° to the earlier lines. Using a triangle or other square edge, check to see how nearly at right angles the two sets of lines are. You will find this ability to draw lines square with each other very helpful as you progress.

There are four basic types of lines you will use: construction lines, centerlines, ghost or invisible lines, and hidden lines. These are shown and explained in figure 2-1.

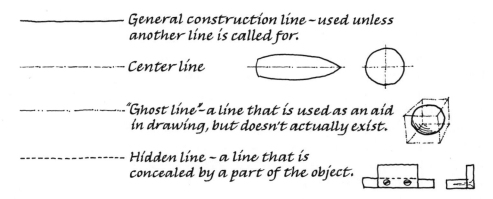

Fig. 2-1. Four basic types of lines

Just for fun, after you have drawn your last straight line, draw a sweeping curve across the top of the paper, holding the pencil steady and using your forearm like a compass with your elbow being the center point. This will start you drawing the curves, such as sheer lines, that are so important in naval architecture.

Now try other types of curves: arcs of circles, short sharp curves, long almost imperceptible curves, curves in which the degree of curvature varies along its length. These shouldn't be *of anything in particular,* just nicely shaped curves drawn randomly on the paper. These exercises with drawing curves will prove that you can do it, so when the time comes you will be able to draw a stem profile with reasonable confidence.

For any regular sketching it is well to settle on a standard format, paper size, and identification. A standardized format for your sketches, regardless of their size, not only looks professional but simplifies the filing, finding, and use of your plans. Figure 2-2 suggests a format for the border and for the title block, a most important element of every plan. For a sail plan the paper would be the tall way, but the title block is always at the lower right-hand corner.

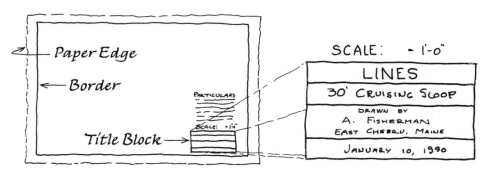

Fig. 2-2. Typical plan format

There is no limit to *what* can be drawn—boats, people, trees, houses, construction details. Anything goes, but for starters we will try something simple, say a binocular box. At this point we won't try drawing it to scale, but will dimension the sketch for the builder to work from.

On a letter size piece of paper, sketch a border and put in the title block with whatever information you want to include. The sketch of the binocular box is shown in figure 2-3; don't hesitate to incorporate any changes in format or actual design of the box that appeal to you. When the sketch is completed, you can put in the appropriate dimensions and specifications measured directly from your own binoculars.

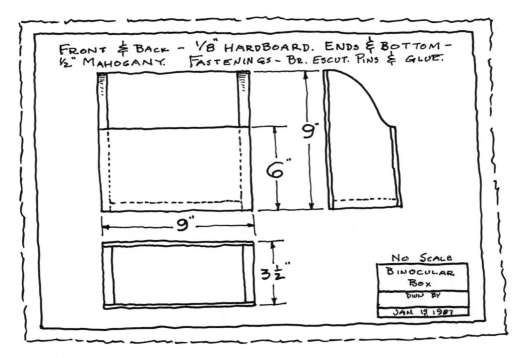

Fig. 2-3. Detail sketch of a binocular box

The most important element of a design is the hull form. Upon the shape of the hull depends the performance, cost, structural requirements, and a host of other characteristics of the finished vessel.

Depicting on a piece of paper the shape of a boat hull (called the lines plan) differs from any other type of engineering drawing because the architect must clearly and completely portray in only two dimensions a three-dimensional shape composed almost entirely of curves. The reader of a lines plan must transpose in his mind the two-dimensional representation back into three dimensions in order to fully understand it. After sketching a couple of hulls, you will begin to understand the subtleties of this two-dimensional (technically called orthogonal) picture of the hull form. These subtleties are further explained in chapter 3.

Unlike the exterior of the hull as shown on the lines plan, sketches of the interior of a boat are considerably easier to interpret because the objects can be portrayed in a representational fashion. The stove can look like a stove, and the bunks like bunks. But drawing such plans still requires thinking in three dimensions, even if they are drawn in only two.

Once the major dimensions of the vessel have been definitely fixed, it is time to start sketching to scale. This is still a preliminary stage, during which the elements of the design are refined, so the sketch should be rather quick and simple. Do it all freehand, saving the hard edge instruments for later. Cross-section (graph) paper is often useful here, with each square representing a specific dimension (such as ¼″ square = 1′), but it is by no means necessary; I often make scale sketches on any old piece of paper, using a carpenter's tape for dimensioning.

Because of the complexity of vessel designs, a few practices have been adopted down through the years to simplify the design process and to make comparisons between designs simpler and more useful. Figure 2-4 illustrates these conventions. Note the following in particular:

1. The bow is always to the right.

2. The designed waterline (DWL) is divided into 10 equal spaces, marked by 11 stations numbered from 0 to 10 starting at the forward end of the DWL. Therefore, when comparing the shape of station 2 of one boat with station 2 of another, it is immediately known that they occur at the same position in the two designs.

(Note: You will find variations to these standards, such as the stations being numbered 0 to 20 instead of 0 to 10, station 0 being at the after end of the water plane, bow to the left, or other departures. Whatever system you adopt, it should be consistent and in accordance with local practice.)

3. The body plan is composed of a half-section drawn for each station, sometimes with a few extra ones for added detail. The forebody sections for station 0 to and including station 5 are drawn to the right of the vertical centerline, the afterbody sections, starting at station 6, to the left of it.

4. The plan layout shown is standard, with the profile at top left, the body plan at top right, and the plan (top) view at the bottom. Note that the DWL of the profile is the same as for the body plan, that the stations in the plan view line up with those in the profile, and that the plan view centerline and the DWL are parallel to each other.

You will sometimes see a funny symbol above station 5, a circle intersected by back-to-back Cs. This identifies the midsection, or largest section, and may also be a symbol for dead flat. In large vessels there is often a portion in the middle of the vessel where all sections are the same size and shape; this is called the parallel mid-body. It would be a waste of time and paper to draw this dead flat so it is often omitted. But the station at which the parallel midbody occurs is identified by the dead flat symbol. Vessels of the size we are apt to be interested in normally do not have parallel midbodies, but the symbol still occasionally identifies the largest station, usually station 5.

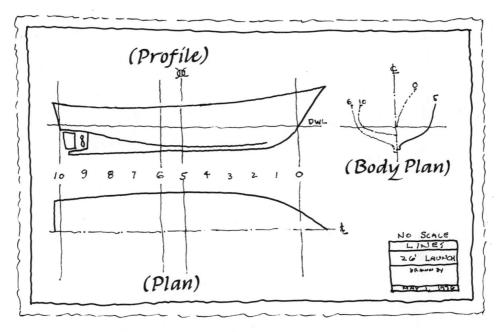

Fig. 2-4. Conventional layout of boat and ship plans

For a fun exercise, let's take 15 minutes to rough out a design, using the sketching hints we have learned so far. We won't scale anything, but will still try to have proportions that are realistic and pleasing. This first time follow figure 2-4 and the steps listed below; later you can do it any way you wish.

1. Decide what type of boat you will draw and what its approximate size will be. This can be taken out of your head or out of a magazine or other source.

2. On a letter size sheet of paper, lightly lay out a grid consisting of the DWL, plan view centerline, body plan centerline, and stations 0, 5, and 10. Arrange the grid on the paper so it will be well centered and have some white space around it. (A sketch that is uncentered, or too small or too large, relative to the paper it's on, is unattractive and loses something as a communicator.) When the positioning is all

right, darken in the grid lines, doing it all freehand, of course. Add the title block; a border also helps to isolate the sketch from distracting externals.

3. Sketch in the profile lightly until it suits you. Transfer the stem and stern of the profile view down onto the centerline for the plan view, and sketch in the plan view. Then transfer the heights of sheer, bottom of keel, and half-beam of station 5 from the plan view onto the body plan. The reason for roughing these lines in lightly

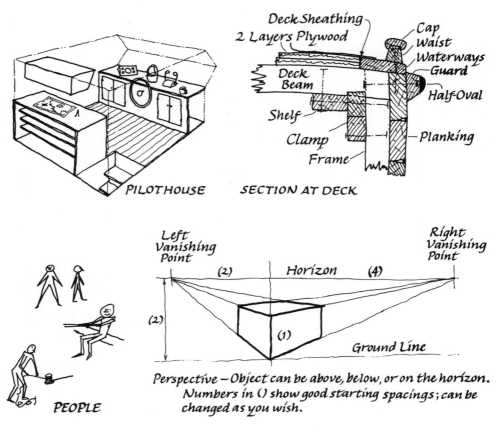

Fig. 2-5. Examples of freehand sketching

is that you will be changing them several times before they satisfy your conception of what you are trying to portray, and correspond properly with each other as described above.

4. When all is pleasing to you, darken the lines, add the title block and a border, and after pinning the sketch to the wall for a few days to allow the inevitable minor dissatisfactions to develop, file it away for future reference. Corrections will be made on the next sketch!

Other nice things can be done with sketching. Figure 2-5 shows some of them, but the list is limited only by your imagination. People, construction details, tanks, cockpit arrangements, anything physical can be sketched. So get in the habit of sketching. I keep a few 3″ × 5″ (7.5 cm × 13 cm) index cards in my pocket for the purpose and a 6½″ × 9 ½″ (16.5 cm × 24 cm) spiral notebook is never far away, so I'm able to transfer anything from my mind's eye to paper on the spot.

The secret to learning to sketch easily and with satisfying results is to *do it!* If subjects for sketching don't appear magically in your head, choose subjects from life. Or figure out some widget your boat needs and make a sketch of it; maybe you will end up building it. But once you become comfortable with sketching, you will discover it is a great source of pleasure and satisfaction.

3. Vessel Geometry

THE delineation of a complex three-dimensional shape like a vessel's hull is not an easy thing. Undoubtedly the earliest shipbuilders built vessels by eye, without any design aids. This method is still used with great skill by the Indonesian builders of the large and handsome pinisi and lampa cargo ketches, and by the builders of the beautiful dhonis in the Maldives (see figure 3-1). Their procedure is first to set up the keel with the stem and sternpost attached. The vessel is then planked, the planks edge-fastened with wooden pegs (trunnels or tree nails in the west). No forms or molds are used; the shape of the vessel is determined by the curvature the master builder gives to the planks. Once the planking is completed or well along, the frames are shaped to fit the planking.

Fig. 3-1. *Left,* Indonesian pinisi ketch; *right,* dhoni of the Maldive Islands

The next development seems to have been the use of half-models. After the model block had been shaped by eye to the desired form of hull, it was cut up or taken apart and the sections so exposed were used for shaping the frames and

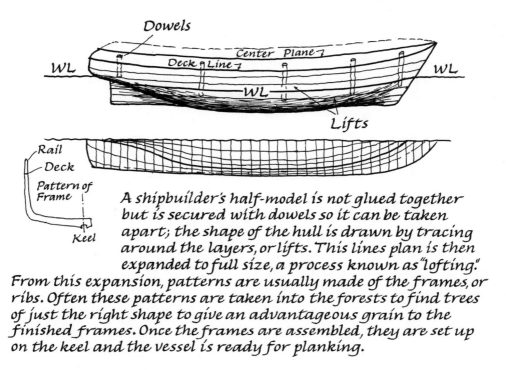

Dowels

Center Plane

Deck Line

WL

WL

WL

Lifts

Rail

Deck

Pattern of
Frame

Keel

*A shipbuilder's half-model is not glued together
but is secured with dowels so it can be taken
apart; the shape of the hull is drawn by tracing
around the layers, or lifts. This lines plan is then
expanded to full size, a process known as "lofting."
From this expansion, patterns are usually made of the frames, or
ribs. Often these patterns are taken into the forests to find trees
of just the right shape to give an advantageous grain to the
finished frames. Once the frames are assembled, they are set up
on the keel and the vessel is ready for planking.*

Fig. 3-2. Shipbuilder's half-model, used by the shipbuilder not only for
designing the hull shape but also for building the hull to that shape

backbone. Half-models provided the builders with a good historical record of
past vessels, which must have materially enhanced the evolution of improved
hulls. Also, the builder could examine various hull shapes using quickly made
half-models instead of building full-size vessels. Figure 3-2 describes one way
in which shipbuilders used half-models; this method is still in use by many
artisanal boatbuilders.

The modern way of drawing vessel hulls, the orthographic projection that we
met in the previous chapter and in figure 2-4, has been in use for about 300 years.
The use of plans developed when calculations entered the increasingly refined art
of vessel design. This permitted sister ships to be built in different shipyards. With
the half-model method most of the design resided in the master builder's brain, but
this technique would obviously not suffice in a widespread shipbuilding industry
such as the navies of the western powers depended upon.

Delineating a surface of complex curvature like the hull of a boat or vessel is
done by passing a number of planes through the hull, at various angles and locations
as shown in figures 3-3 and 3-4. The designer massages the intersections of these
planes with the hull surface until he has achieved the shape he wishes. But, once the

grid (the system of straight lines representing the basic planes) has been drawn, he begins with some important boundary lines. Most visually noticeable is the sheer, which is more precisely identified as "top of deck at side" because "sheer" can mean the top of the rail cap, the underside of the deck, a paint line, or anything else the user has in mind. Notice that the sheer is drawn both in the profile and in the plan (top) view. The second line completes the delineation of the side view; known as

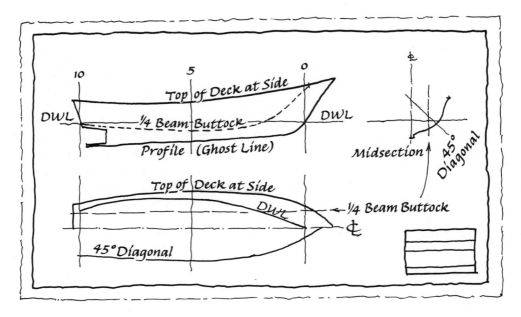

Fig. 3-3. The lines required to roughly, but quite completely, delineate the hull form of a vessel

the profile, or sometimes the ghost line, it runs from the deck at one end to the deck at the other end, by way of the stem, bottom of the keel, rudderpost, and stern. And finally there is the midsection, conventionally cut through at station 5; it is generally assumed to be the largest section in the hull although that is usually at about station 5½. Half of the midsection is drawn on the body plan to the right of the centerline. Secondary lines include the following: the design waterline on the plan view; a buttock line approximately ¼ of the beam out from the centerline, shown on the profile; and the 45° diagonal drawn below the plan view.

Although your architect will use many more waterlines, buttocks, and diagonals in his final lines plan to ensure precise duplication in full size of the craft he has shown on paper, the lines enumerated above will describe the hull shape with more than enough accuracy for your purposes.

Orthographic representation of the hull shape is based on the use of planes cutting the body at various angles and positions. Since a plane can be represented two dimensionally on a flat surface, then if the body is cut with enough planes the shape of the object can be precisely defined in two dimensions. By means of this process it is possible to locate in space any point on a hull's surface. As previously pointed out in figures 3-3 and 3-4 the naval architect uses a

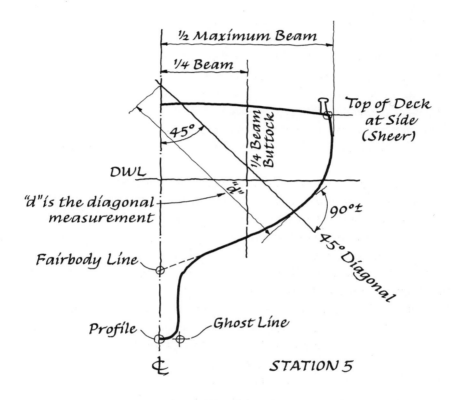

Fig. 3-4. Midsection, station 5, showing the important
lines and points described in the text

variety of planes to portray the complex and subtle curves of a vessel's hull. To more fully understand these, we will go to the vegetable bin. For help in picturing these definitive planes we will build an instant model of a hull. I use a straight, firm cucumber for the purpose, but a zucchini is also fine. A pickle will do, and it can be consumed at the end of the demonstration. Cut it in half lengthwise, and you will have two "models," not very stylish but, like all good designs, suitable for our purpose, which is to demonstrate how the hull is cut by planes for delineating the hull form. From here on, each time a slice or cut is made, the shape revealed is traced onto a piece of paper.

Stand one of the hulls on its keel, with the *deck up;* cut it lengthwise down the middle, giving us two half-models. When we lay the last-cut surface on the paper and draw around it we have traced the profile, or center plane. Stand the half-hull on its keel with the deck up and make a vertical cut lengthwise, parallel to the center cut and halfway out to the side; lay the outer portion of the model down on the center plane outline, with deck lines coinciding and the piece located properly fore and aft, and draw around it. This line is the quarter-beam buttock.

Now lay the second half-model *deck down* on the paper, and draw around it. The straight line is the centerline, the curved line is the outline of the deck in plan view. Lay the model on its center plane and slice it lengthwise approximately parallel with the deck and about halfway between deck and keel. Lay this newly cut surface on the plan view with its centerline on the centerline drawn earlier and bow to bow and stern to stern, and draw around it. This represents the DWL, design waterline.

Next, holding the two pieces of the waterline model together, lay it on its center plane and cut it into 10 thick slices with a nubbin at each end. The first and last cuts will be made at the ends of the water plane, and the rest will be evenly spaced between. Each cut represents a station, numbered from 0 forward to 10 aft. On a piece of paper draw two lines perpendicular to each other; the vertical line will be the centerline, the horizontal line the waterline. Divide the slices into two groups at station 5, the middle cut. Lay the cut surface of station 5 on the crossed lines, to the right of the centerline and with the model center plane and waterline corresponding with the drawn centerline and waterline; draw around it. Do the same with the rest of the stations 0 to 4, and with stations 6 to 10 to the left of the centerline. You have now drawn a cucumber body plan, which shows the sectional shape at each station.

Cut the other model into two half-models, and lay one on its center plane. Holding the knife at about 45° to the tabletop, make a straight cut from bow to stern. Make sure the point of the knife follows a straight line, parallel to the waterline, and that the knife where it emerges from the cucumber is about 90° to its surface. Lay this cut surface on the same drawing as the plan view, but on the other side of the centerline, and draw around it; this line represents the 45° diagonal.

Now try to cut the remaining half-hull with all the planes you have cut on the other three. If you can manage it, you will see that the model is well covered with a network of cuts which, if all transferred to paper, would nicely delineate the shape.

Anybody for cucumber salad?

It was easy making this plan when starting with an existing shape, such as our cucumber. But our task is to imagine a shape, and to transfer it by means of the various planes and lines we have just explored.

With the help of the cucumber and figures 3-3 and 3-4, you should have a pretty good understanding of the major construction lines by which the naval architect delineates the hull form of a vessel. This information is gathered together in figure 3-5 which shows a sailing yacht hull sketched as you will do for your sketch design. The terms we have been using are illustrated in figure 3-4 and defined below.

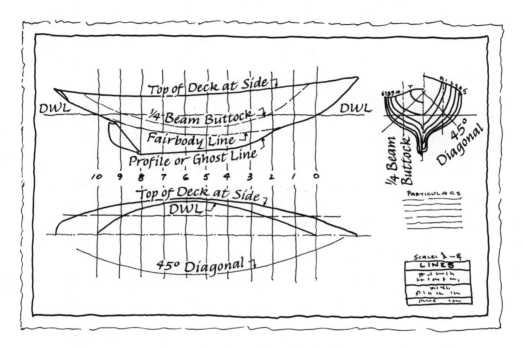

Fig. 3-5. A sailboat hull, sketched using the lines described in this chapter

The *top of deck at side* (the term "sheer" is indeterminate because it can mean the top of a bulwark, the top of the deck, the underside of the deck, or even a paint line on the hull; always define the upper edge of the hull as the top of deck at side, which can't be misunderstood) and the *profile* define the limits of the hull and are of major importance in determining the shape, function, and appearance of the finished product. The profile is sometimes called the *ghost line* because it may not actually exist on the boat, as illustrated in figure 3-4.

The *designed waterline,* DWL, is the line formed by the intersection of the hull surface with the water plane at which the architect estimates the vessel will be floating. The precise location of the plane of flotation when the vessel is in service may be other than the DWL because of changes during design, small errors in calculating the weight of the vessel, differences in loading, etc., but the designer endeavors to keep the actual plane of flotation as close to the DWL as possible.

The *sections* that make up the body plan are the shapes of the hull at each of the stations.

As the shape of the hull takes form, I like to lay in the *45° diagonal.* This not only helps "fair" in the sections (when the sections are fair, a plank bent around them will have a smooth curve with no bumps or hollows), but it also is the closest of the lines to the actual flow of water around the hull when the vessel is in motion. The projection of the diagonal is laid out below the plan view, the measurement at each station being taken out and down from the centerline; "d" is the measurement at station 5 on figure 3-4. Locating the ends of the diagonal is a bit tricky but extreme accuracy at the ends is not necessary at this phase of design.

The *buttock* is a useful line to show the fore-and-aft shape in a vertical plane away from the center plane. For uniformity, which helps in comparing hulls and in drawing a hull that is a development of another, I locate this buttock about 1/4 × beam out from the centerline.

When the lines plan is completed, the entire system of lines must be consistent; that is, wherever lines cross each other, they must intersect on the surface of the hull; one cannot be above or below the other. (Go back to the cucumber to see what a pickle it would be if they did *not* intersect.) For instance, the buttock must cross the DWL at the same point in both the plan and profile view, as indicated on figure 3-5; if they don't, it indicates that the same point on the hull was occupying two different locations in space, an obvious impossibility and one that drives boatbuilders mad.

One line not described in our cucumber experiment is the *fairbody line,* identified on figures 3-4 and 3-5. Actually, if we wanted to add a keel to our cucumber hull, then the profile line along its "keel" would become the fairbody line and the appendage would be drawn on separately. So the fairbody line is a simple device to allow drawing the hull, sometimes called the canoe hull, as one entity and the appendage as another; this is much simpler than endeavoring to draw the entire hull as a unit.

Displacement is perhaps the single most important physical characteristic of a vessel. It is defined as the weight of water that is displaced by the floating hull, which is precisely equal to the weight in air of the vessel. This is known as Archimedes' principle and can be demonstrated as follows:

Cut and trim a piece of two-by-four so that it weighs precisely a pound. Float it in a pan of water and put it in your freezer. When the water has completely frozen, take out the pan and remove the two-by-four from the ice. Accurately measure one pint of fresh water, which will weigh about a pound, and pour it into the cavity; it should just fill it to the brim (with a bit of runover because of the shrinkage of the ice as it freezes). This demonstrates that the one pound two-by-four displaced exactly one pound of water when it was floating free.

Displacement is stated in long tons of 2,240 pounds (about equal to metric tons of 2,204 pounds [1,000 kilograms]) or for small craft in pounds (kilograms), or in terms of volume, that is, cubic feet (cubic meters).

A vessel's displacement is constantly changing as fuel and water are loaded or consumed and cargo or passengers are taken aboard or discharged; therefore, a naval architect establishes for each design a design displacement, which is the vessel's displacement in a normal operating condition. Usually the architect also calculates other displacements, such as light ship displacement (the complete vessel but with no cargo, crew, fuel, or other consumables aboard), or loaded displacement (with all tanks full and with maximum cargo on board).

Another term to be used very carefully in describing a vessel is length, about which there are many misconceptions. When a professional uses the term *length overall* (LOA) he is referring to the length of the hull (see figure 3-6), that is, the width of a door through which the hull could be passed sideways. *Not* included in the LOA is the figurehead, bowsprit, main boom, etc. Even LOA has minor variations, but a good definition is from the face of the stem at its top to the aftermost part of the hull (taffrail, for instance).

Length, waterline, LWL, is the total length of the plane of flotation, exclusive of any rudder that might pierce the surface. *Beam* is the width of the narrowest door through which the upright vessel, exclusive of guards, will pass. *Depth* is the vertical distance from the edge of the deck at side to the rabbet or intersection of plating

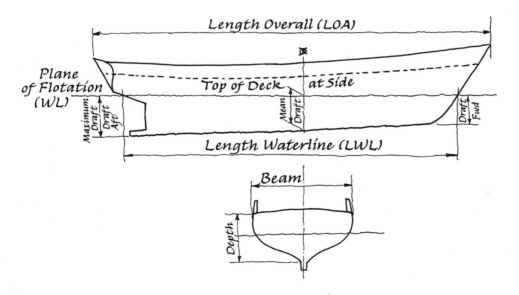

Fig. 3-6. Definitions of commonly used hull dimensions

with the keel, measured at the midsection. *Draft* is usually considered to be the maximum depth of the vessel below the LWL, but may if so specified refer to the depth below the LWL at the midstation or at the stem.

A very useful measure of hull size is the *cubic number* (CUBE), the product of length, beam, and depth, which is the size of the box in which the vessel will fit. The length used should be specified: it is properly LWL, but may be LOA, or for long-ended craft like a racing sailboat a mean of the two, (LOA + LWL)/2. CUBE is important because it is independent of the proportions of the hull. For instance, if two fishing vessels have the same CUBE but one is long and narrow, the other short and fat, they will have very nearly the same displacement, internal volume, and most importantly cost about the same. CUBE allows direct comparison of vessels of similar type but of different dimensions and proportions. For example, if cruise vessel A has dimensions (LWL × beam × depth) of 90′ × 26.5′ × 10.5′ for a CUBE of 25,000 ft^3 (27.4 m × 8.08 m × 3.20 m = CUBE of 708.5 m^3), 25% greater than that of cruise vessel B (100′ × 20′ × 10′ = 20,000 ft^3 [30.48 m × 6.10 m × 3.05 m = 567 m^3]), it will have very nearly 25% greater displacement, internal volume, and cost, regardless of differences in shape and proportion.

There are geometrical relationships among vessel dimensions that are helpful in the early stages of design in establishing the overall dimensions of the vessel. Experience and experiment have established suitable ranges of values of these relationships for vessels of various types and function. The most important relationships are defined and discussed below. For clarification of the dimension definitions, see figure 3-6.

Length-beam ratio, L/B: Usually for craft of moderate overhangs, L = LWL and beam = beam overall. For vessels with long overhangs such as some sailing craft it makes more sense if L = (LOA + LWL)/2 to more accurately reflect the actual operating length.

Beam-depth ratio, B/D: Beam overall and depth are measured at the widest point, or at the midsection, station 5. The B/D ratio, being independent of where the vessel is floating, that is, its loading state, is especially useful with reference to load-carrying craft whose draft is constantly changing with variations of load.

Beam-draft ratio, B/H: These dimensions are measured at station 5. This ratio has implications for initial stability and for hull resistance.

Displacement-length ratio, (displacement in long tons)/(LWL/100)^3: This ratio defines the burdensomeness of a vessel. A vessel with a high value of displacement-length ratio will for a given LWL have a greater displacement than one with a low value. When used with load-carrying vessels, the condition of loading must be clearly defined. A 100,000 deadweight ton tanker will displace about 120,000 tons when loaded, 20,000 tons with cargo discharged, and perhaps 40,000 tons when in ballast; since the LWL is nearly constant for all three conditions, there will obviously be a great variation in displacement-length ratio.

Length-displacement ratio, LWL/(displacement in cubic feet)$^{1/3}$: Preferred by some, this is another way of saying the same thing. It has the disadvantage that the lower the number the heavier the vessel, contrary to the displacement-length ratio. It is best to use this ratio when working with other than the English system of measurements.*

Accepted values of these relationships are given in following chapters. To be truthful, though, even for vessels in the same service there are differences of opinion as to the best values. Perhaps one of the most striking examples of this occurred in the Gloucester dragger fleet in the 1920s to 1960s. There were in the fleet quite a few World War I subchasers. Because of their comfortable motion and easy driving, these boats were very popular with fishermen, who kept them going long after their allotted life span had expired. In sharp contrast to the subchasers were the standard trawlers of the period which were designed and built to suit the wishes of their owners. Table 3-1 compares the pertinent dimensions and relationships of these two widely differing vessels, successfully used side by side in the same fishery.

There are several lessons to be learned from this comparison. One very obvious one is that there are few absolutes in vessel design. These two vessels were completely different in physical proportions yet in the same service satisfied their owners very well. So don't slavishly use so-called ideal proportions as though they were axioms; use them as starting points but if your instinct says to depart from them, go ahead. The difference between the average designer and the really good one is his ability to know when and how to depart from the accepted norms.

Table 3-1
Comparison: World War I Subchaser and Typical Gloucester Trawler

	Subchaser	Trawler
Length overall, LOA	110′ (33.53 m)	110′ (33.53 m)
LWL, estimated	100′ (30.5 m)	100′ (30.5 m)
Beam	14.75′ (4.5 m)	24′ (7.31 m)
Depth, estimated	8′ (2.44 m)	12.5′ (3.81 m)
Cubic number (CUBE)	11,800 (334 m³)	30,000 (849 m³)
Displacement, loaded, tons (metric tons)	90 (91.5)	300 (305)
Length-beam ratio	6.78	4.17
Beam-depth ratio	1.84	1.92
Displacement-length ratio*	90 (NA)	300 (NA)
Length-Displacement ratio*	6.82 (6.82)	4.57 (4.57)

*The displacement-length ratio remains the same when a vessel sails from salt water to fresh water since the vessel weighs the same in both instances even though the draft will be slightly deeper in fresh water. Length-displacement ratio is based on the volume of displacement, so must be adjusted for the density of the water it is floating in. Displacement-length ratio can only be used with the English measurement system; Length-displacement ratio is "dimensionless" and can be used with any consistent system of measurement, English, metric, or what have you.

In general in this book displacement-length ratio will be used. If calculated using displacement in metric tons and length in meters, divide by 35.9 to convert to English; multiply the English ratio by 35.9 to give the metric.

Since displacement varies closely with CUBE, and because the fishhold capacity is about in proportion to the displacement, the trawler can hold about three times as much catch as the subchaser before returning to port. To achieve this greater catch larger engines are installed in the trawler to tow larger nets, or she can stay at sea fishing longer, or a combination of both. We can also say that both construction cost and operating cost will be roughly proportional to CUBE or to displacement.

Describing these two vessels as being the same size on the basis of their equal lengths is a gross error. It is therefore clear that to merely describe a vessel by its length can give a very incomplete and inaccurate picture of the vessel's real size. For this reason it is best to use the invariant cubic number, CUBE, when describing the size of a vessel.

Given CUBE and values for L/B and B/D, it is possible to calculate quite quickly the overall dimensions of a vessel.

Given: $CUBE = L \times beam \times depth$

where: $L = beam \times L/B$

Depth = beam / (B/D)

therefore: $CUBE = beam \times L/B \times beam \times beam / (B/D)$

$= beam^3 \times L/B / (B/D)$

which gives: Beam = $(CUBE \times (B/D) / (L/B))^{1/3}$

$L = beam \times L/B$

Depth = beam / (B/D)

A less obvious but very important and useful relationship is the prismatic coefficient, C_p, sometimes called the coefficient of fineness. This is the proportion of the displaced volume of the hull to a prism whose section is the same as the hull's midsection and length is the LWL of the hull (see figure 3-7). The lower

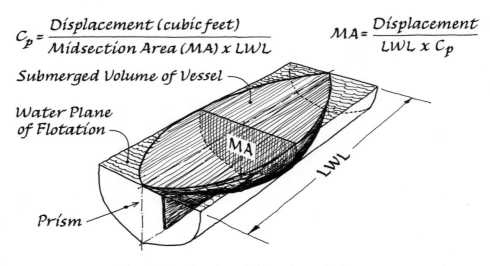

$$C_p = \frac{Displacement\ (cubic\ feet)}{Midsection\ Area\ (MA)\ x\ LWL}$$

$$MA = \frac{Displacement}{LWL\ x\ C_p}$$

Submerged Volume of Vessel

Water Plane of Flotation

MA

LWL

Prism

Fig. 3-7. Explanation of prismatic coefficient

the value of C_p, the finer is the hull; a destroyer would have a C_p of about .63, a barge a C_p of .95.

Because of its importance to hull resistance and vessel motions, the prismatic coefficient is one of the earliest values selected for a design. Representative values are given in table 3-2. With the displacement, LWL, and C_p known, it is easy to calculate the midsection area, MA, a great help in roughing out the design in the very early stages.

Learn to use these relationships, but thoughtfully not blindly; they will make the preparation of a preliminary design much easier.

Table 3-2
Representative Values of Prismatic Coefficient, C_p

Sailing yachts (exclusive of keel)	.55
Displacement-type powerboats	.55 - .58
Planing powerboats	.65 - .70
Destroyers	.63
Fast containerships	.65
Tankers	.85
$V/\sqrt{L}$ <1.0*	.60 - .80
$V/\sqrt{L}$ = 1.0 to 1.2	.53 - .58
$V/\sqrt{L}$ >1.2	.60 - .70

*$V/\sqrt{L}$ is the speed-length ratio (SLR), defined as the speed in knots divided by the square root of the LWL in feet. Two vessels traveling at the same SLR are going at similar speeds. For example, a 100′ vessel traveling at 10 knots (SLR=1) is going at the same relative speed as a 900′ vessel traveling at 30 knots (SLR=1). Both vessels will exhibit the same wave-making and wake characteristics. (The SLR used throughout this book is in English units, which appears to be generally customary. SLR is a dimensional coefficient so that it cannot be used directly in other systems of measurements. To convert from metric to English, SLR = V(knots)/$\sqrt{LWL(meters)}$ × 3.281.) In its original and proper engineering form, this very important relationship between LWL and speed is the dimensionless Froude number, Fn = v/$\sqrt{g \times LWL}$, where v = speed in feet per second, g = the acceleration of gravity = 32.2 feet per second per second, and LWL = the waterline length in feet. For being dimensionless, the English measurements of length can be replaced by any other measurement of length such as meters.

There is a class of vessel dimensions that can be very confusing; these are the register dimensions, which have evolved over the centuries to measure vessels for tax and regulatory purposes. Sometimes they don't seem to make a lot of sense, but you should be familiar with some of them.

The assorted lengths are shown on figure 3-8. The length that a responsible technician should *never* use is a length overall which includes all the overhanging spars, gallows, and broom handles at the bow and stern. This is a phony length used only by advertising people and the one-upmanship crowd, and has no place in describing a vessel; if for some reason it is important in a specific design, then it should be clearly defined so as not to confuse it with the *real*—stand up, please!—LOA.

Registered length: The length, measured parallel to the DWL (as all these are), from the after face of the rudderpost to the intersection of the main deck with the rabbet line on the stem.

Length between perpendiculars: The distance from the after face of the rudderpost to the intersection of the fore side of the stem with the DWL.

Length overall: The length measured over the extreme limits of the vessel's hull.

Length, waterline: The extreme length of the DWL water plane.

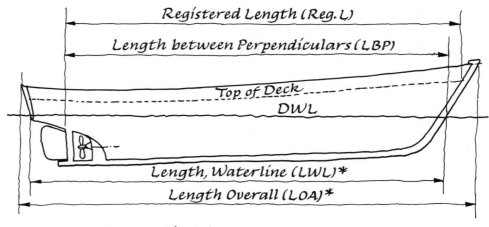

Fig. 3-8. Hull lengths for regulatory and tax purposes defined

As confusing as these lengths are, there are two "weights" that are not weights at all but measures of internal volume used for tax and regulatory purposes. Although frequently and mistakenly quoted when describing the weight or displacement of a vessel, these two tonnages have virtually nothing to do with actual displacement.

Gross tonnage: This is essentially the entire internal volume of the vessel's hull and of selected houses above the measurement deck, measured to the inside surfaces of the frames, ceiling, and beams.

Net tonnage: Gross tonnage less selected spaces including the propelling machinery space.

Gross tonnages and net tonnages are important in designing passenger vessels, and are tricky because there are many deductions and exceptions when calculating them. Since these enter into the regulations governing vessel safety, passenger capacity, crewing, etc., a careful study of the regulations is required to avoid a potentially expensive error.

A third tonnage is of considerable importance in cargo vessels, especially tankers, ore carriers, and other bulk carriers; that is, gross deadweight tonnage, abbreviated as DWT.

Gross deadweight tonnage (DWT): The actual weight of the variable loads of a vessel:

$$DWT = \text{full load displacement} - \text{light displacement}$$

in which full load displacement is the displacement of the vessel to its deepest flotation line, and light displacement is the weight of the structure, machinery, and outfit of the vessel before crew, supplies, stores, other consumables, and cargo have been added.

4. Calculations

SURPRISINGLY little mathematics skill is actually required in designing small craft. Nevertheless, one should have had at least a year of algebra, so that exponential concepts and calculations are not strange. Also an elementary knowledge of trigonometry is useful.

This is not to say that the serious student of naval architecture won't encounter much higher mathematics. Hydrodynamics is an extremely complex subject (just think of trying to define in fine mathematical detail the swirling turbulent flow in the wake of a vessel) and the pages of unintelligible notations and equations in papers on the subject will often be intimidating. When I study such a paper, there is little point in my trying to untangle the mathematics; instead, I read the text portions as carefully as I can to get the gist of what is going on. In any good paper, if one reads the abstract, introduction, and conclusions, the meaning and usefulness of the study for the engineer should become clear.

So the word is, "Don't let a fear of mathematics turn you away from the fun of preparing a preliminary design of your dream boat." What follows should provide all the mathematics you will need in the rest of the book.

First some basics. We start with the concept of a point, a unique spot in space. Although we draw a point as a dot, in the mathematical sense it has an infinitely small diameter so that it doesn't actually exist except as a concept. If we take a point and drag it along in a particular direction, we have a line; since the point has no dimension, then the line has no width although it does have length determined by the distance we moved the point. We can call the length L.

If we now slide the line sideways in a straight path, it covers an area that would lie flat on a table or drawing board and which we call a plane. We can make a square if we move a line of length L sideways a distance of L; the area of the square is $L \times L$, or L^2. Finally, moving the square upwards a distance L produces a solid, this one called a cube because it is L long on all sides. It has a volume of $L \times L \times L$, or L^3. Figure 4-1 illustrates the development of a cube from a point and suggests how the exponential values are developed. The "dimension" time has been added, providing us with a 4th dimension. (It has been reported that it is possible to envision as many

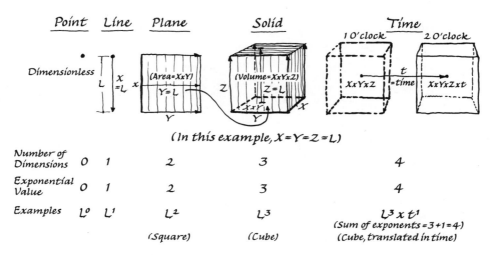

Fig. 4-1. Relationship of line, area, volume, and time

as 11 dimensions, even though in our mundane visual and tactile world we can cope with only 3 dimensions.)

Note that in our construction of the cube, we traveled in three different directions, or, to state it properly, along three axes. We can call the original line L, the X axis, the direction in which the L line was translated the Y axis, and the upward direction in which the square was translated the Z axis. Each axis has a positive direction and a negative direction, signified by + and –, respectively. This is normal three-dimensional notation, and you will frequently encounter it in technical literature. In naval architecture, conventionally the three axes and their signs are as indicated in figure 4-2.

There are some very useful relationships that can be culled from the above discussion. For instance, when comparing similar figures, defined as being larger or smaller than each other but having the same shape and proportions, the geometric characteristics of one can be expressed in terms of a linear dimension of the other. For a line this is obvious: if a line is twice as long as another it is $2 \times L$ long.

Similarly, if one square has sides twice as long as another its area will be $2L \times 2L = 4L^2$. If L=1, the proportion of the areas is 4/1, or 4, which is 2 (the scale of the second to the first) squared. Defining "scale" as the relationship of a side of one figure to the same side of a similar figure, we are able to say:

Areas of similar figures vary as scale^2

In the same way, if we make a cube out of a $2L \times 2L$ square we end up with a volume of $2L \times 2L \times 2L = 8L^3$. The proportion of the volumes is then 8/1, or 2^3. Hence:

Volumes of similar figures vary as scale^3

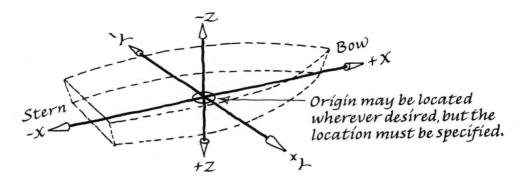

Fig. 4-2. Axis system used in describing vessel motions

These important relationships are the basis of relativity and similitude (R&S), a concept that allows us to know exactly what we are doing when we change any or all of the dimensions of a vessel. This often occurs when we are making a new design somewhat smaller or larger than an older one. A look at table 4-1 may suggest other ways in which R&S may be useful as a design tool.

Table 4-1
Relativity and Similitude
Relationships between two exactly similar craft of scale S
(S can be any number greater than zero)

Characteristics	Examples	Relationships
Length	Length overall, waterline length, beam, draft, depth	S
Area	Wetted surface, planking or plating area, deck space	S^2
Volume	Displacement, cost (approximately)	S^3
Stability	Righting moment (displacement $(S^3) \times$ righting arm (S))	S^4

Except for the poor point, which doesn't even exist, all figures have physical properties. Even the line, which also doesn't really exist (it has no width or depth), has a lineal dimension.

Area—sail area, wetted surface, material requirements, rudder size—is an important part of naval architecture. The area of any plane figure can be easily calculated.

Trapezoidal rule: For any number of equally spaced ordinates, the area equals the sum of one-half the end ordinates, plus the other ordinates, times the spacing.

Calculating the area of a two-dimensional (plane) figure can often be done using standard formulas but even the area of an irregularly shaped figure can be easily calculated using the trapezoidal rule, defined and illustrated in figure 4-3.

38 : Preliminary Design of Boats and Ships

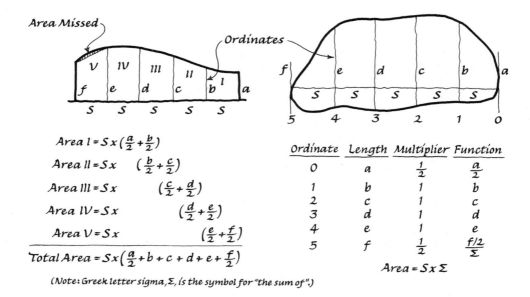

$$\text{Area I} = S \times \left(\frac{a}{2} + \frac{b}{2}\right)$$

$$\text{Area II} = S \times \left(\frac{b}{2} + \frac{c}{2}\right)$$

$$\text{Area III} = S \times \left(\frac{c}{2} + \frac{d}{2}\right)$$

$$\text{Area IV} = S \times \left(\frac{d}{2} + \frac{e}{2}\right)$$

$$\text{Area V} = S \times \left(\frac{e}{2} + \frac{f}{2}\right)$$

$$\text{Total Area} = S \times \left(\frac{a}{2} + b + c + d + e + \frac{f}{2}\right)$$

Ordinate	Length	Multiplier	Function
0	a	$\frac{1}{2}$	$\frac{a}{2}$
1	b	1	b
2	c	1	c
3	d	1	d
4	e	1	e
5	f	$\frac{1}{2}$	$\dfrac{f/2}{\Sigma}$

$$\text{Area} = S \times \Sigma$$

(Note: Greek letter sigma, Σ, is the symbol for "the sum of".)

Fig. 4-3. The trapezoidal rule, for measuring regular and irregular areas

It is frequently necessary to locate the center of a plane figure—a sail, for instance. The center of many regular shapes can be found by calculation, but for any shape, regular or not, the simple methods shown in figure 4-4 can be used. The hanging pattern method will find the point center of gravity, while if the location of the center is required in only one direction (such as the fore-and-aft center of a water plane) the folded pattern method is quick and doesn't leave holes in the living room wall.

Theoretically, planes have no thickness and hence no mass. But in practice we are dealing with a sheet of a material—plywood, metal, fabric. If the material is homogenous (the same density throughout), then the center of area is also the center of gravity, a term one sometimes sees used in this context.

Many of the objects a naval architect deals with are three-dimensional—boat hulls, keels, etc.—and finding the exact area (defined as the exposed surface) can be difficult. For our level of design, we can be satisfied with approximations, in effect squashing the surface of the object down flat and applying the trapezoidal rule, with an allowance to take care of the area lost or gained by the squashing.

Three-dimensional objects contain space, and we often wish to know the volume of this space. For regular objects (spheres, cubes, pyramids, etc.) there are simple formulas for finding the volume. For irregular objects, such as the submerged portion of a boat's hull, we can use the trapezoidal rule. As illustrated in figure 4-5, we measure the area of each section and, using some convenient scale such as $1'' = 10 \text{ ft}^2$ (or in metric it might be $1 \text{ cm} = 1 \text{ m}^2$), we measure the length of each ordinate

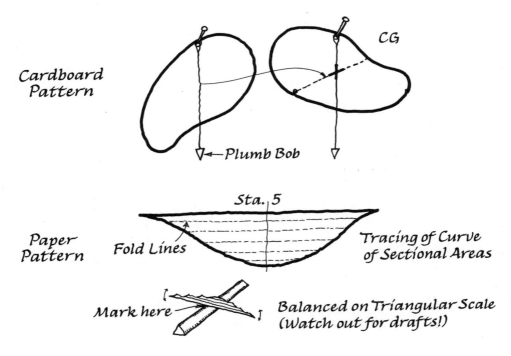

Cardboard
Pattern

CG

←— Plumb Bob

Paper
Pattern

Sta. 5

Fold Lines

Tracing of Curve
of Sectional Areas

Mark here —→

Balanced on Triangular Scale
(Watch out for drafts!)

Fig. 4-4. Finding the center of gravity of a plane. *Top,* hanging
pattern method; *bottom,* folded pattern method

to be proportional to the area of the corresponding section. By this means we have transformed the volume of the hull, a three-dimensional object, into the area of a plane figure. This figure is known as the curve of sectional areas; we can use the trapezoidal rule to find its area and hence the volume of the hull.

Center of gravity (CG) is defined as a point at which all the mass of an object can be assumed to be concentrated. (Physicists use mass instead of weight because the mass of an object is constant throughout space. A man who weighs 175 lb standing on the earth weighs nothing orbiting in a spaceship, but his mass is unchanged.) Thinking of the mass, or weight, of an object as concentrated at a point is very useful in working out problems of trim, stability, flotation, momentum, etc.

The material making up three-dimensional objects is sometimes homogenous (the water displaced by a vessel's hull, a ballast keel, or the fuel in a tank) or it may be of various materials and densities (a completed vessel or a piece of machinery). To find the fore-and-aft CG of the displaced water of a vessel, we can easily apply the pleated pattern method to the curve of sectional areas.

Usually, though, we are forced to cope with an object of many materials. Our boat, for instance, is made up of wood, metal, fiberglass, fabrics, liquids, and things such as the paint on the surfaces. The naval architect establishes the CG of the ves-

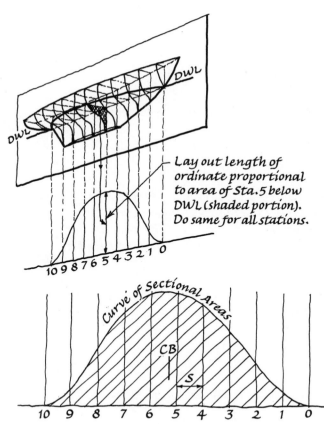

Lay out length of ordinate proportional to area of Sta.5 below DWL (shaded portion). Do same for all stations.

1. Lay out ordinate lengths proportional to section areas below DWL.
2. Calculate area under Curve of Sectional Areas (shaded) by the trapezoidal rule.
3. Adjusting for scale and expanding to full size gives displacement in cubic feet.
4. Displacement in lb is found by multiplying displacement in ft³ by 64 (salt water) or 62.4 (fresh water).
5. Cut out paper pattern of Curve of Sectional Areas, accordion-fold it, and balance it. The CG of the pattern is the same as the fore and aft Center of Buoyancy (CB) of the hull.

Fig. 4-5. Finding the displaced volume of a hull using the trapezoidal rule

sel (which is essential to know if she is to float level) by calculating the moment of every component making up the vessel and what it carries. The moment equals the weight of the component times its distance from a reference axis.

Figure 4-6 shows how this works. Dad (he could be any heavy weight, such as an engine) wants to find out where he must locate himself so that the seesaw (representing the boat) will sit level. It is clear that when the sum of the moments on one side of the pivot equals the sum of the moments on the other side, the seesaw will be level. Since the water in which the vessel floats is yielding, we must balance out all its moments in the same way if we want it to be level.

As for trigonometry, it is necessary to understand angles at least in the degree-minute-second notation, and helpful to have a familiarity with radians. Sometimes, although not frequently, the three basic trigonometric functions are used—sine, cosine, tangent.

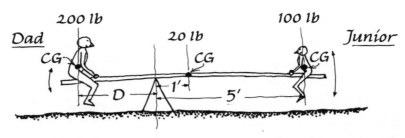

Problem: How far out from the pivot must Dad sit on the seesaw
to balance Junior?

Dad weighs 200 lb

Junior weighs 100 lb – CG located 5' from pivot (fulcrum)

Seesaw weighs 20 lb – CG located 1' from pivot

To balance, Dad must sit at some distance, D, from the pivot so that Dad's moment on one side of the pivot just equals the combined moments of Junior and the seesaw on the other side. Set up as an equation, therefore:

$$\text{Dad's weight} \times D = \text{seesaw weight} \times 1' + \text{Junior's weight} \times 5'$$
$$200 \times D = 20 \times 1 + 100 \times 5'$$
$$200 \times D = 520$$
$$D = 520/200$$
$$D = 2.6'$$

Fig. 4-6. Seesaw explanation of balancing moments

A knowledge of graphs, both making them and reading them, is almost an essential; you should be familiar with Cartesian (cross-section), semi-log, log-log, and polar graphs, and nomograms. It is often convenient, even necessary, to present in graphical form a series of numerical values in order to identify trends or determine intermediate values. Even the popular literature on naval architecture in publications and nontechnical books depends a great deal on graphical presentations. So if you are not familiar with graphs, it might be well to obtain a simple text on the subject.

It may be difficult to find a simple text on semi-log and log-log graphs so I will take a stab at it here. Log stands for the word logarithm; a logarithm is the exponent of 10 (to base 10), which gives the desired number. For instance, the logarithm of 10 is 1, since $10 = 10^1$, of 100 is 2 ($100 = 10^2$), of 1,000 is 3 ($1,000 = 10^3$). To find the logarithms of intermediate values, we use a table of logarithms, where we find that the log of 250 is 2.3979 ($250 = 10^{2.3979}$).

One must understand how logarithmic scales are laid out in order to read them properly. Figure 4-7 illustrates how logarithmic graphs are constructed. One immediately notices that the divisions are not even; on a logarithmic scale the point halfway between 10 and 100 is not 55 ([10 + 100]/2), but 31.6, the logarithm of which is 1.5 (halfway between the logarithm of 10, which equals 1, and the logarithm

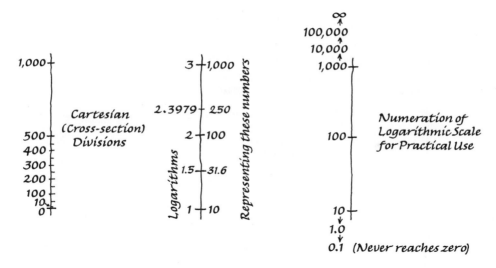

Fig. 4-7. Graph divisions. *Left,* Cartesian, or even, divisions (cross-section
graph paper); *center* and *right,* logarithmic divisions

of 100, which equals 2). So read logarithmic scales carefully. (If the bottom, X, scale
is evenly divided and the vertical, Y, scale is logarithmically divided, the graph is
called a "semi-logarithmic graph"; if both sides are logarithmic scales, the graph is
a "log-log graph").

Why the emphasis on logarithmic graphing? Logarithmic scales have two distinct advantages: geometric progressions (exponential equations) plot as straight
lines, and the values at the small end of the curve are expanded and at the large end
compressed. On the Cartesian graph in figure 4-8, curve A is the plot of a simple
arithmetic progression (10, 20, 30, 40 . . .). Curve B is the plot of a geometric
progression in which the value of Y increases 35% each year; as can be seen, it starts
with very small increments and steepens rapidly. However, if we plot curve B on a
semi-log graph, the "curve" becomes a straight line.

The ability to plot geometric progressions as straight lines has several advantages. Obviously, of course, it makes drawing the graph of such a function very
simple; the curve can be drawn if one point and the slope, or rate of change, are
given. If, for instance, one wanted to increase the values of curve B by 50%, using
the semi-log graph form it would only be necessary to find the value of 15 (which
equals 10 × 1.5) on the Y axis at X = 0, and draw a curve parallel to the present
curve. For any given value of X, the value of the new (upper) curve will be $1\frac{1}{2}$ times
the value of the lower curve.

A second advantage of logarithmic graphs is that the scale is opened up at the
lower end, so that the distance on the graph from 10 to 20 is the same as the distance
from 100 to 200. Trying to pick accurate values off the lower end of curve B on the

cross-section graph would be very difficult, but easy to do when plotted on a logarithmic scale.

Plotting rates of change on cross-section graph paper can be very misleading, yet one sees this all the time in the daily press and even in pretty esoteric professional publications. We tend to look at a graph with curve A (fig. 4-8) and say to ourselves that this represents a healthy, continuing, steady growth; when in actuality,

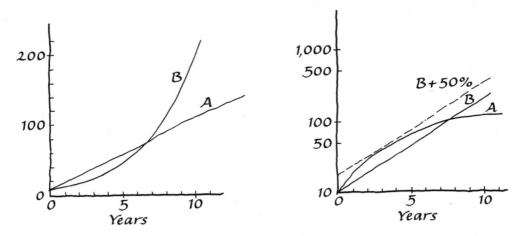

Fig. 4-8. The use of cross-section graph paper for arithmetic progressions, logarithmic or semi-logarithmic for geometric progressions

the percentage increase declines with advancing years. (The annual percentage change from 10 to 20 is 100%, but from 100 to 110 is only 10%.) Curve B on Cartesian coordinates shows better performance, but it is still difficult to say whether or not the annual percentage increase improves with increasing years. Plotted logarithmically, it is obvious that curve B represents the same percentage increase for all the years; if it curved up, the percentage rate would be increasing, if it curved down, decreasing. The next time you see a Cartesian graph purporting to show a constant rate of change (percentage improvement), try replotting it in your mind to a logarithmic scale and see what a difference it makes.

This emphasis on semi-log and log-log graphs may seem a bit extraneous. But you will be dealing quite a bit with graphs, and when doing so you should have a clear idea of their validity or lack of it.

Sometime you may find yourself faced with a confusing graph entitled "curves of form." The graph will consist of a number of curves, referenced to several scales along the bottom and left side. The curves of form is graphical shorthand by which the naval architect compresses onto a single piece of paper a great deal of information about the physical characteristics of a design. From it he can project the state of the vessel under a wide range of loading conditions, and predict the result of changes that might be made to the vessel. The curves of form is not ordinarily constructed for the preliminary design, but it is so packed with information that it is worth a brief explanation here.

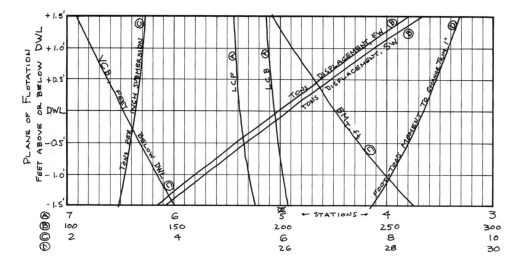

Fig. 4-9. A sample curves of form, concisely summarizing
the physical characteristics of a vessel

A sample curves of form is shown in figure 4-9, following which are the definitions and some of the uses of the various curves shown. Note that the reference, or datum, plane is the designed waterline. (The datum plane is the one from which all the design work is done; it may be other than the DWL, for instance a baseline located below the keel.) The vessel may never float right at the DWL, but it is necessary at some point in the design process to establish this datum plane.

In using the curves of form, one must be very careful to read the values from the correct scale. (Note: A curves of form in metric will have very much the same format.)

Descriptions of curves shown in figure 4-9:

Vertical CB (VCB): Vertical center of buoyancy of the hull, measured below the DWL or above the baseline.

Moment to change trim 1″ (MCT1″): The foot-pounds or foot-tons (it will say which) necessary to trim the boat 1″ by either the bow or the stern.

Tons per inch submersion: The weight which if added to the vessel will sink it an inch or if removed will allow the boat to float up an inch.

Tons, fresh water or salt water (curves of displacement): The displacement in pounds or tons (of 2,240 lb) to the waterline the curve crosses. It is well to have two curves of displacement, one for salt water at 64 lb per ft³ (1,025 kg/m³), and one for fresh water at 62.4 lb per ft³ (1,000 kg/m³).

LCF (longitudinal center of flotation): The longitudinal location of the center of flotation on the appropriate water plane, relative to the midstation, station 5.

LCB (longitudinal center of buoyancy): The location relative to the midstation.

BM$_T$, ft (transverse BM): Height of the transverse metacenter above the center of buoyancy. This, combined with the vertical center of gravity (established during the weight calculations), gives GM, the metacentric height, the fundamental measure of stability (see chapter 6).

So the mathematics part wasn't so bad after all, was it? You will find that these few skills will greatly enhance your ability to understand and think about the various factors involved in vessel design.

5. The Forces of Nature

ONE of the fascinations of the marine life for the sailor, whether male or female, whether sailing for fun or profit, is the constant presence and pressure of nature. Waves, wind, temperature, all the natural forces working for and against the sailor, make up an environment full of challenge and change. Unpleasant at times, occasionally dangerous, sometimes of surpassing beauty, always interesting, one can never escape the natural world at sea, be he in a skiff or the largest tanker.

Even a vessel at night resting in a quiet harbor, with not a whisper of air or the tiniest surge, is constantly being acted on by natural forces. A cooling temperature shrinks metal parts, water from dripping dew or a heavy shower works into small crevices, incipient decay lies in timbers waiting for the temperature and moisture conditions that will bring it to destructive life, barnacles and grass quietly grow on underwater surfaces, unseen electrical currents steal electrons from one part and deposit them on another, and seawater presses in from the outside, tortuously following the smallest crack, or molecule by molecule seeping through the fiberglass, to help fill the sailor's bilge pump the next morning.

The naval architect is the mediator between the forces of nature and the sailor and vessel owner. It is up to the naval architect to see that the negative effects of natural forces are minimized and the positive effects maximized. He must provide a platform for the sailor that is acceptably safe (although never forgetting that the sea can conquer even the largest vessel) and efficient (making the best of a myriad of difficult compromises), and that performs as well as possible the tasks for which it is designed.

By all odds the natural element most significant to the naval architect is water. It is 800 times the density of air and its interface with air—the surface we travel upon— is rarely still. Wind, tides, and the passage of hulls distorts the naturally flat surface of the sea into complex waves which in severe circumstances can overwhelm the strongest vessel, or turn the stoutest stomach. Much of the art of naval architecture is devoted to fashioning a vessel that is affected least by the waves; in this the designer of vessels has a much more difficult task than designers of airplanes, houses, or bridges. And water, when not aggressively attacking the vessel, is slyly using its friction to hold it back.

Yet water is a wonderful "pavement" for travel. It is the only medium capable of supporting the largest animal that ever lived (the blue whale), and its buoyancy and relatively low friction allow man to build and operate vessels carrying over half a million tons of oil and large enough to take aboard the Sears Tower and have 50 feet left over. The largest ships move easily; a small fraction of one horsepower will move each ton of oil in the tanker 16 nautical miles (about 18 statute miles [30 km]) in one hour. This energy efficiency, translated into automotive terms, would mean that a 2,240 lb compact car would get about 600 miles to the gallon at 18 MPH. The usefulness of this efficiency was recognized in the canals of the premachinery age; when four horses pulling a wagon could haul one ton 12 miles in a day, the same four horses could tow 100 tons in a canal boat 25 miles in a day.

Water has three qualities that are of major importance in vessel design: buoyancy, viscosity or stickiness, and surface waves.

Buoyancy: This is the quality Archimedes discovered in his bath with the cry, "Eureka!" The law he discovered states that a body in a liquid is buoyed up by the weight of the water it displaces. This applies to both floating and nonfloating bodies. A piece of wood displacing 1 ft³ of water is buoyed up by exactly 64 lb in salt water which weighs 64 lb per ft³, or 62.4 lb in fresh water which weighs 62.4 lb per ft³. In the same way, a submerged block of iron weighing 450 lb but still of 1 ft³ is buoyed up by 64 lb in salt water and 62.4 lb in fresh water. In metric terms, an object displacing 1 m³, whether floating or not, will be subjected to a buoyancy of 1.025 metric tons in salt water and 1 metric ton in fresh water (see figure 5-1).

To demonstrate Archimedes' principle, fill a beaker or pitcher with water until it runs out the spout. When the overflow ceases, carefully lower a wooden block of known weight into the water until it floats. Catch all the new overflow and weigh it; you will find that the weight of this overflow water exactly equals that of the wooden block.

How about an object that doesn't float, like a block of steel? Set up the beaker in the same way, filled with water. Hang the block of steel from a scale, and record the weight. Slowly lower the block into the water, again catching the overflow, and record the new scale weight. You will find that the difference between the weight of the block in air and the weight in water exactly equals the weight of the overflow water. In other words, the submerged block of steel was buoyed up by a force equal to the weight of the water it displaced. (This experiment can be used to see if that statue picked up for a song at the flea market is gold or "gold.")

Viscosity: This is the name for "stickiness" of a fluid. Molasses has high viscosity; watch oil has very low viscosity. The motion of any object through a liquid such as water is resisted by the viscosity of the liquid; this is known as "frictional resistance," and is important because it typically constitutes about half the total resistance of a moderate speed boat or ship.

To get a quantitative feeling for frictional resistance, try dragging a well-shaped oar blade edgewise through the water. At low speed the resistance is hardly noticeable, but as you increase the speed the resistance increases dramatically, to a point where you can no longer hold the blade against it. The resistance you feel is almost entirely frictional in nature, resulting from the viscosity of the water.

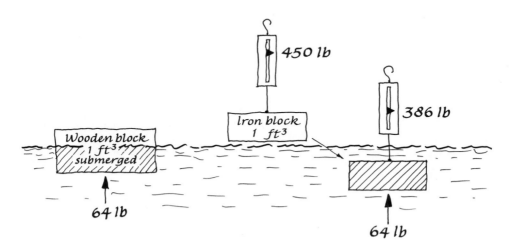

Fig. 5-1. Archimedes' principle demonstrated

If you were able to measure the resistance of the oar at various speeds, you would discover an interesting and very important fact about frictional resistance, (symbolized by R_f):

> R_f increases as the square of the speed. If you double the speed, the frictional resistance will increase by a factor of four.

Look over the side of your boat and you can "see" frictional resistance. Traveling at 4 or 5 knots in smooth water, you will observe that the water closest to the hull is being dragged along at nearly the speed of the hull, while a foot or two out from the hull the water is not moving at all. The water close to the hull is being dragged along due to the viscosity, or attraction of the water to the hull. In fact the molecules of water touching the hull are moving exactly with the hull. The water between the hull and the line of no movement is known as entrained water; the entrained water is swirling around in confusion, a condition known as turbulence.

But what happens when the water is moving by the hull really slowly, at half a knot or less? Now the water appears to move smoothly by the hull, and the degree to which the water is dragged along by the hull—the thickness of the entrained water—is much less. This condition, where the molecules of water are flowing past an object one behind the other in single file instead of in the chaos of turbulence, is known as laminar flow (see figure 5-2).

As one might expect, the resistance offered by laminar flow is much less than that offered by turbulent flow; after all, in turbulent flow there is a lot of power consumed in stirring the water into turbulence and in hauling along the larger mass of entrained water. Since laminar flow is only possible at very low speeds, however,

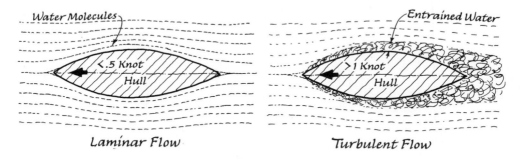

Fig. 5-2. Laminar and turbulent flow about a hull

and with a very smooth bottom, and only for a short distance aft of the leading edge of the hull or keel, its importance is restricted to high performance sailboat racing in light airs. So practically speaking turbulent flow may be assumed to exist at all times.

Waves: Open water waves can have several different sources. There are the tsunamis, caused by earthquakes; tidal waves, caused by the gravitational pull of the sun and the moon; wind waves, built up by the wind blowing over the water; wake waves, created by the passage of a boat or ship through the water. The naval architect is interested only in the last two: wind waves and wake waves.

The internal structure of a wave is interesting and quite complex. Obviously the entire wave doesn't advance as a unit; if this were the case, an eight-foot wave advancing at 12 knots would demolish anything it encountered, and it would be impossible to steam against such seas at a ship speed of anything less than 12 knots. We are saved from this awful prospect by the fact that water particles in a wave travel in a circle, as shown in figure 5-3. In deep water, the diameter of this circle is equal to the height of the wave. The water particles at the crest are moving in the direction of the wave system, at the trough in the opposite direction, and halfway between they are moving vertically.

One of the intriguing characteristics of waves is that a plumb bob suspended on a life ring as shown in figure 5-3 will always hang perpendicular to the wave surface at that point, assuming the wave is large relative to the plumb line length. This may be the reason why waves are often grossly overestimated as to height, as suggested by the sketch showing the sailor looking at what his senses tell him is straight ahead, and then "up" at the top of the wave, enough to give anyone a fright. The bottom sketch shows how to estimate wave height with pretty good accuracy.

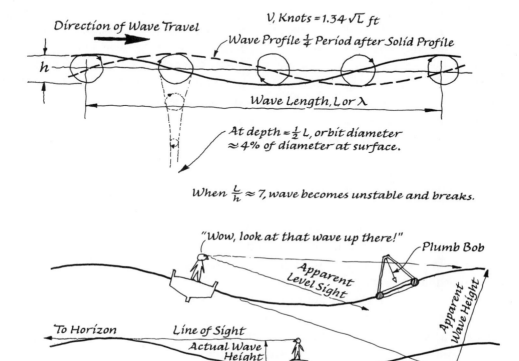

Fig. 5-3. Physics of waves at sea

All deepwater ocean waves conform to these laws, regardless of what generates them. The reason a tsunami is not sensed in deep water, even though it may devastate coastal areas, is that if it is traveling at 200 knots it will have a length of over 3.67 nautical miles (5.9 km)—the reason for this is made clear below. Even if it is 20' (6.1 m) in height it would not be noticed until it began to slow down and hump up due to the friction of a shoaling bottom. Nevertheless this inconspicuous wave has a total energy of about 68 million ft lb per foot of crest length (31 million kg-m per meter of length); although some is lost to friction on the sea bottom, it is easy to understand why these waves cause such havoc on land.

Wind waves are created by the frictional drag of air blowing across the surface of the water because air, too, has viscosity, and it is that viscosity which pushes the water up into waves. These sometimes reach staggering heights; the highest recorded wave was in the North Pacific and was accurately measured to be at least 112′ (34.14 m) high! By contrast, the average U.S. coastal yachtsman rarely sees a wave over 10′ or 12′ (3 to 3.7 m) high north of about 30° north latitude or 6′ to 8′ (1.8 to 2.4 m) south of that line.

The naval architect is interested in wind waves because they can slow his vessel down, give it motions that can be not only uncomfortable but unsafe, and in extreme cases cause the loss of vessels such as the large ore carrier *Edmund Fitzgerald* on the Great Lakes and the decimation of the Fastnet fleet in 1979. It is my belief, and I think generally accepted, that there is an ultimate sea condition that is mortal for every vessel no matter how well designed, built, and manned. This deadly sea can be defined as one that has an excellent chance of overwhelming the vessel regardless of what the crew does.

Figure 5-3 illustrates a typical wave; normally the length-to-height ratio is about 30, and a fairly steep wave about 20. At 7 a wave becomes unstable and breaks. Table 5-1 gives information on wind wave characteristics and the conditions for their formation. Wave conditions are normally reported as the height range for the highest third of the waves; for example: "Wave height will be 3′ (.9 m) to 5′ (1.5 m)" means that the highest 33 of 100 waves will be in that range. Adlard Coles, in his excellent *Heavy Weather Sailing* suggests that the highest wave encountered will have a height about equaling the sum of the reported range, 8′ (2.4 m) in the example given.

An equally important class of waves is created by the passage of the vessel through the water. There are two sets of wake waves (see figure 5-4): the bow train coming off each bow at an angle of about 20° to the course; and the stern waves whose crests are about 90° to the course. These waves not only require a good deal of power to manufacture—most of the half of the horsepower not used to overcome frictional resistance at moderate speeds is absorbed in wave-making resistance, R_w—but they limit the top speed attainable by nonplaning craft.

The speed of advance of a wave in knots is directly proportional to the square root of the wave length from crest to crest. Stated mathematically,

$$\text{Wave velocity, } V_w, \text{ knots} = 1.34 \times \sqrt{\text{wave length (ft)}}$$
$$= 2.42 \times \sqrt{\text{wave length (m)}}$$

This relationship is immutable for all deepwater waves in salt water. If you know the wave length, you can with very close precision calculate the speed of advance of the waves. The reverse is also true; if you know the speed, you know the wave length. This very important factor in vessel design will be covered in detail in the next chapter.

Table 5-1
Deep Ocean Wind Wave Data

Wind, velocity knots	Fully developed height, feet [a]		Average developed length, feet [a]	Observed [b]		
	Theoretical [c,d] Significant [e]	Observed Maximum	Theoretical [c] Length	Length	Speed, knots	Period, seconds
5	0.3	1.5	8	23	6.4	2.1
10	1.4	3.5	27	45	9.0	3.0
15	4.0	7.5	61	80	12.0	4.0
20	8.0	12	117	124	14.9	4.9
30	27	23	250	260	21.6	7.1
40	45	37	444	450	28.4	9.4
50	68	(49) [b]	700	690	35.2	11.6
60	94	(63) [f]	990	930	40.9	13.5

a. To convert feet to meters, multiply feet × 0.3048.

b. *Wind Waves at Sea, Breakers and Surf*

c. *Handbook of Ocean and Underwater Engineering*

d. The disparity between observed and theoretical heights at wind speeds of 30 knots and over is due to the infrequency with which storm winds blow at constant velocity and direction over the long fetches required for waves commensurate with those winds to develop to their full heights. Wave heights are commonly overestimated; there are few reliable reports of maximum wave heights in excess of 40′.

e. "Significant" wave height is the average of the highest one-third of the waves observed.

f. Extrapolated.

Note: Providing useful and reliable wind wave data is difficult for two reasons: (1) waves constantly change in size and proportion as they build up (increasing in both height and length), reach maturity (length continuing to increase after maximum height has been reached), and decay (removal of the generating wind causing the height to decrease rather rapidly, the length to decrease much more slowly); and (2) even in a steady wind, wave heights may vary among themselves by a factor of 3 or 4 or more.

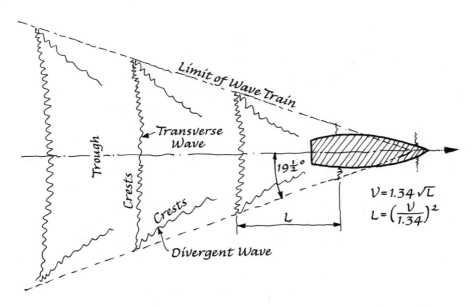

$$V = 1.34 \sqrt{L}$$
$$L = \left(\frac{V}{1.34}\right)^2$$

Fig. 5-4. Divergent and transverse wake waves created by
the passage of a vessel's hull

The power in waves is tremendous. Robert Louis Stevenson's father measured forces of 6,000 lb per ft² (2.9 kg/cm²) in breakers on the west coast of Scotland. At the entrance to Amsterdam Harbor, a 20-ton concrete block was lifted 12' (3.7 m), landing 5' (1.52 m) above high water mark. These are extremes, of course, but suggest why open water waves are so seriously considered by the naval architect from the safety standpoint, and why wake waves affect a vessel's forward progress so profoundly.

Air is the other fluid of importance to the naval architect. Fluid mechanics treats all fluids, including air and water, in a similar fashion, even though water is about 800 times as heavy as air. Therefore, even though air is a gas and thus compressible and liquids like water are essentially incompressible, all fluids can be treated similarly.

Obviously the designer of sailing craft and his clients are consumed with interest in the forces resulting from the flow of air about sails and rigging. But all vessels are affected to some degree by wind force; not only does it introduce considerable resistance to forward travel (a 25-knot vessel steaming into a 25-knot wind can experience a resistance of approximately 13 lb per ft² [63.5 kg/m²] of frontal area) but unusually heavy winds such as in a tornado or heavy thunderstorm can capsize an otherwise safe power craft.

As with water, air pressure, against the side of a house for instance, increases as the square of the wind velocity. The empirical equation for frontal air pressure is

$$\text{Pressure, P, lb ft}^2 = .0053 \times V^2$$
$$\text{Where V = knots}$$
$$(\text{Pressure, P, kg/m}^2 = .0259 \times V^2)$$

Flow of fluids around an object: As anyone knows who has observed the flow of water about a hull or in a stream, or air flow manifested by smoke, the flow patterns of fluids can be, and usually are, extremely complex. But there are certain simplifying approaches to help us think in realistic terms of flow about a foil shape, such as a keel or a sail. Figure 5-5 shows a foil such as an airplane wing, a boat's keel or rudder, or a wing sail. Indicated are the pattern of flow of the fluid (air or water) about it, and the direction of the forces that the flow imparts to the foil.

Thanks to a man named Bernoulli, we know that where the streamlines are closer together, the local velocity of flow is increased and the pressure is reduced. Where the streamlines are farther apart the flow is slower and the pressure increases. From the flow lines, representing the paths of particles of air, sketched in figure 5-5, it can be seen that the lines over the top of the foil must travel farther than those along the bottom and hence will travel faster; with Bernoulli's help, we realize that this means lower pressure over the top of the foil. By the same token the more widely spaced flow lines over the bottom of the foil represent slower flow and higher pressure. With high pressure below and low pressure above, it is obvious the foil must provide a net lifting force.

The foil is also subject to resistance forces, which are collected under the term drag. These stem from the friction of air over the surfaces, from the form (bulk) of the foil, and from the loss of energy in bending the flow lines.

These two effects, lift and drag, combine into the resultant force vector, which is the summed direction of all the forces acting on the foil; the origin of the vector line as shown is approximately at the center of pressure. This resultant force vector

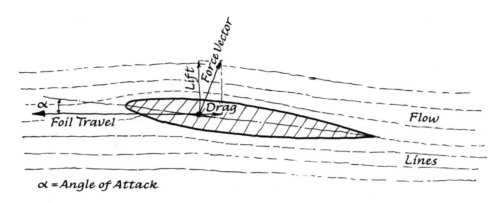

Fig. 5-5. Flow lines of air or water about foils such as
keels, rudders, or wing sails

can be divided into two (or more) component vectors; these vectors can be in any direction, but when added together must combine to equal the resultant force vector.

The lift vector represents the force doing constructive work, such as holding up the airplane, or preventing leeway of a sailboat through the action of the keel foil; the system of vectors for a wing sail would be laid out differently to be useful, but the component vectors must always equal the force vector. The drag vector is the negative force, the force holding the plane or boat back, that must be overcome by the driving power of engine or sails. Obviously the aim of the designer is to maximize lift and minimize drag, that is, achieve the highest possible value of the fraction lift/drag.

It is obvious that the designers of foils, whether airplane wings, boat keels and rudders, propeller blades, or sails, are totally preoccupied with developing a shape that gives streamlines which will produce the highest lift-drag ratio. Some comments on the more desirable shapes will be made as the various vessel types are discussed. Sails and hang-glider wings, by the way, make up a special class of "soft" foils, with no thickness.

There is another consideration in dealing with foils, something called aspect ratio. Aspect ratio is simply defined as the area of a foil divided into the span squared or, for simple shapes, L/C; this is illustrated in figure 5-6. Notice that if the foil ends on a hull or fuselage the effective aspect ratio is twice L/C. (C stands for chord, the average front-to-back dimension of the foil.) The lower part of the figure shows how aspect ratio affects the efficiency of the foil; the shorter the foil (the lower the aspect ratio) the more high pressure air leaks around the tip from the underside of the foil, thus reducing the vacuum on the top of the wing. In selecting an optimum aspect

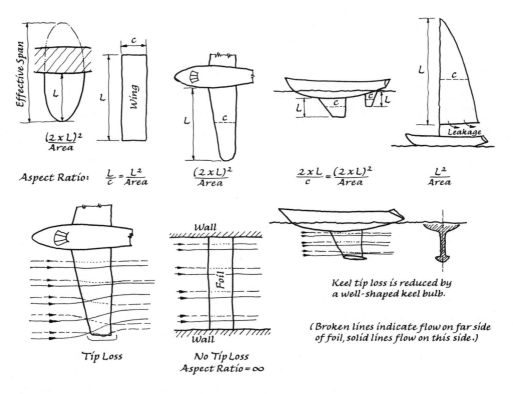

Fig. 5-6. Effect on efficiency of foils in air or water
of aspect ratio and tip loss

ratio plane designers carefully balance the loss of lift of a low aspect ratio against the structural strength and weight requirements of a high aspect ratio; high performance aircraft like sailplanes and the world-girdling *Challenger* have extremely high aspect ratios to reduce tip loss to practically nothing. In much the same way, designers of high performance sailing craft must balance the better performance of a high aspect ratio rig against its greater heeling moment, higher weight, and various boat handling complications.

Wind currents, created by the heat of the sun and shaped by the rotation of the earth, are what drive sailing craft. These currents are highly variable in both direction and velocity, constantly testing the skill of the sailor especially since moving air is largely invisible. Two factors that can help him make decisions about sail carrying and sheeting are (1) wind pressure increases as the square of the velocity, and (2) the velocity is subject to a wind gradient, or a decrease in wind velocity from an altitude of about 60′ (18 m) down to ground level. A typical curve of this wind gradient is shown in figure 5-7.

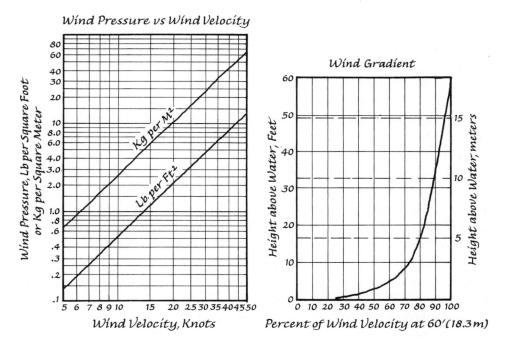

Fig. 5-7. Graphs of wind pressure against velocity and wind velocity against height above the water surface

There are other natural factors to be considered in vessel design and construction. Gravity, of course, is omnipresent in everything we gravity-bound earthlings do. There are also such factors as the molecular composition of various materials, the interactions of chemistry, and the characteristics of light. But it is not necessary to consider most of these in detail at this preliminary stage of design; it will be the task of the naval architect to ensure that they are properly considered in the final design.

It will help to have a passing acquaintance, however, with the phenomenon of acceleration. We all are familiar with acceleration in an elevator; when the elevator starts upwards, that is, accelerates upwards, we momentarily feel heavier; if we were standing on a set of spring (not balance) scales, they might briefly indicate a 5% or so increase in our weight. At the other end of the ride, when the elevator is slowing down, the scales would show a temporary reduction in our weight of maybe 5%.

Acceleration is defined as any change from a steady state of motion. Standing in the elevator waiting for the doors to close is a steady state. The instant it starts to move, it is accelerating. This upward acceleration seems to increase the force of gravity, the mysterious attraction between the earth and our bodies, which presses a 200 lb (91 kg) person down on the scales with a force of 200 lb (91 kg) when the elevator is stopped, but shows perhaps 210 lb (95.3 kg) when the elevator starts upwards. (To be accurate, we are attracting the earth to us at the same time that it is attracting us to it. Our weight, or mass, is so small relative to that of the earth that we think in terms only of the attraction of ourselves to the earth.) During the middle part of the ride, when the speed is constant, we are again in a steady state and there is no acceleration. Then as the elevator slows down, no longer in the steady state, we are again subject to acceleration (which we sometimes call "deceleration").

In the example above, our feet press on the elevator floor because of the earth's gravitational attraction of our bodies. But acceleration also works apart from gravity. In the classic case, astronauts at "zero gravity" condition, in which they are free of all influence of the earth's gravitational field and hence weightless, experience acceleration any time they change direction, start or stop, or move an object. Acceleration is also felt when we are thrown against the side of an automobile in a sudden turn, when we are pressed against the airplane seat back during takeoff and pressed forward against the seat belt when the reverse thrusters are turned on after landing. In fact, any change from a static, steady-state, equilibrium condition of motion brings acceleration into play.

Acceleration is measured in terms of g's. One g is the acceleration of gravity on the surface of the earth which equals 32.2 ft per second per second (9.81 meters per second per second), the rate at which the speed of a falling body increases due to the force of gravity acting on it. At 1 g a 200 lb (91 kg) man will show 200 lb (91 kg) on the scales. The weightless astronaut has zero g. The man in the elevator starting upwards experiences a g of 1.05, and would show 210 lb (95.6 kg) on the scales; when slowing down his g would be .95 which would show as 190 lb (86.2 kg) on the scales.

Forces of 2 g are not unknown on vessels, especially smaller ones, in which case the 200 lb (91 kg) man's weight on a scale would increase to 400 lb (181.4 kg). Such values of g suggest that heavy fittings high aloft must be well anchored to prevent being literally thrown off a deeply rolling vessel, and explain why heavy chain well forward in a decrepit vessel pitching in a head sea can act like a hammer pounding the forebody to pieces.

Even the most insulated urban dweller cannot escape the powerful forces of nature; they are of vastly greater importance to mankind when he ventures out to sea, on small vessels or large. In the next chapter we explore some of this cautious relationship between nature and man afloat.

6. Vessels in Nature

VESSELS are unique among transportation devices in that they operate at the interface between two fluids, air and water. Even though water is 800 times as dense as air, air moves at much greater velocities, which causes it to have important effects upon the water, especially at the surface, the air/water interface. As a result, the continual and rambunctious conflict between these two fluids affects surface vessels in ways that profoundly influence naval architecture. By contrast to the environmental problems faced by marine surface craft, airplanes (and fully submerged submarines) function in a relatively simple and stable one-fluid environment, and land transportation operates *on* a hard surface that is not materially affected by the elements.

Water molecules are always in constant motion, jiggling around at any temperature above absolute zero, −459.4°F (−273°C). The higher the temperature, the greater the molecular motion, and the less dense is the water. Water in a pan, even if it appears absolutely still, is in motion because of the currents of convection; warmer, lighter water rising; cooler, denser water descending. It was thought that the deepest water in the seas, in the Marianas trench off the Philippine Islands, which is a mile deeper than Mt. Everest is tall, would be totally still and lifeless, but a submarine descent to the floor of the trench found organisms viable only in the presence of oxygen, which had to be brought there by currents. (This finding blasted hopes that such deeps would provide a completely safe dumping place for nuclear wastes.)

The nautician traveling over the seas is concerned with the more obvious motions of water—most importantly waves, but also the complex and forceful currents and tides resulting from the interplay of the gravitational pull of the sun and moon, the rotation of the earth, and the heat of the sun. This chapter will cover the major aspects of the relationship of a vessel with the sea and the air and the interface between them.

We have already learned about Archimedes' principle, stating the most fundamental fluid concept in naval architecture—buoyancy—the support of the weight of a craft by the volume of water it displaces. Remembering Archimedes, we can understand that if we floated a vessel weighing 134.67 tons, then froze the water around the hull and removed the vessel, the water required to fill the cavity would weigh precisely 134.67 tons. In other words:

The weight of the water displaced by a floating vessel
exactly equals the weight of the vessel.

Displacement is defined as the weight of a vessel described in terms of the weight of the water it displaces. The task of the naval architect is to design a hole in the water of just the right size and shape to support the weight of the vessel and to give it good operating characteristics.

Displacement is the primary size descriptor of a vessel; it is stated in pounds (kilograms) for smaller craft, and long tons (or metric tons, usually used interchangeably) for larger vessels; the displacement is often stated in cubic units such as ft³ (m³). Don't be confused by a number of other tonnages used to describe a vessel's size, including gross and net tonnage (indicators of internal volume of the entire vessel) and deadweight tonnage, DWT (the weight of cargo a vessel can carry); the one of fundamental interest to the naval architect is displacement tonnage, the actual weight of the vessel and everything aboard it as measured on scales. Figure 6-1 illustrates how water pressure works on a boat shape to provide the buoyancy to support the weight of the boat.

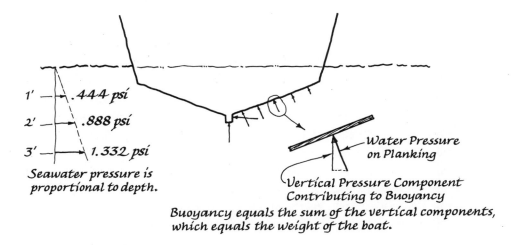

Fig. 6-1. How water pressure provides buoyancy to support the weight of a boat

Displacement comes in various sizes, known as conditions of loading; three are commonly used in describing vessels. *Light displacement* is the basic weight of the completed vessel, with no consumables (fuel, water, food), crew, passengers, or cargo on board. *Loaded displacement* is the light displacement plus full tanks and supplies, complete crew, full complement of passengers, and maximum cargo deadweight. *Designed displacement*, the displacement calculated to the waterline shown on the plans, is usually somewhere between light and loaded, for example, light displacement plus tanks two-thirds full, full crew, average complement of passengers, average cargo deadweight. Figure 6-2 shows typical waterlines for a trawler in these three conditions.

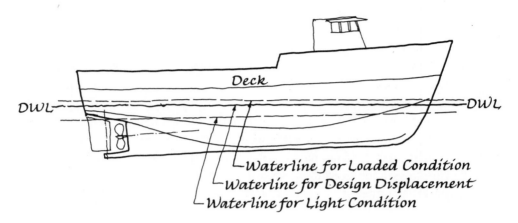

Fig. 6-2. Waterlines on a fishing vessel for various conditions of loading

Because it reflects very publicly on his professional skill, an architect's nightmare is to see a vessel of his creation sink well below her designed waterline when launched. He may be observed absenting himself while mentally kicking his behind and *swearing* that he will be *extremely* meticulous and conservative in calculating the weight of his next design. To avoid such a nontriumph, it is much better to overestimate the weight so that the boat floats a bit too high than to underestimate weight so it floats too deep. Ballast can always be added to bring the light vessel down to her lines, but it is uncommonly difficult to remove enough weight to allow an overweight vessel to rise appreciably.

So one of the first tasks of the architect, after determining the approximate dimensions of the new design, is to estimate the boat's displacement, which is the actual weight of the structure of the craft, ready for use. As the design progresses he keeps refining and improving the weight estimate and finishes by doing a complete weight calculation, that is, a summation of the weight of every item in the vessel from the keel to the paint. Fortunately, for a sketch design you will only need to go as far as a weight estimate (although it should be as precise as you can make it), leaving the full weight calculation to the architect.

In addition to a vessel rising or sinking bodily as weight is subtracted or added, it can sink by the bow or stern (at the same time, of course, rising by the stern or bow, respectively); this is called trim. For instance, if you are sitting on the center thwart of a skiff and move to the stern, the stern will sink and the bow rise. This is known as trimming by the stern. Similarly a move to the bow will trim the skiff by the bow. It is important to note that since no weight will have been added to or subtracted from the skiff the mean level will remain the same. The point that neither rises nor sinks is at the center of flotation of the water plane.

Your moving in the boat created a "moment to trim" (the product of your weight times the distance you moved). This trimming moment can be divided by the "moment to trim 1″ " of the boat to give the amount of trim in inches (see figure 6-3).

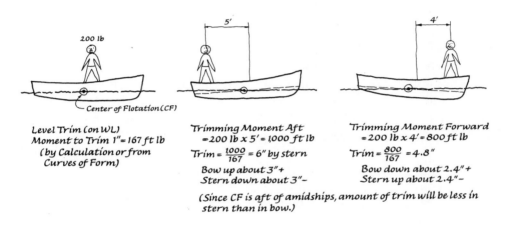

Fig. 6-3. Calculating trimming moment and the amount of trim

This matter of trim is not trivial. There are instances of small outboard boats being lost in choppy weather because the operator had to go aft to work on the motor. His trimming moment added to the "at rest" trim caused by the weight of motor and fuel at the stern would give enough trim by the stern for the sea to flood over the transom. To achieve optimum performance the operating trim should be close to the designed trim; one fishing vessel in my experience steamed faster when loaded than when light, even though she displaced about 50% more; this appeared to be because the loaded trim was level whereas the light trim was quite a bit by the stern.

In working with trim and flotation problems in which weights are added or subtracted, several factors are important. These include center of gravity (CG) of the vessel and of any weights added or subtracted; center of buoyancy (CB) of the hull; center of flotation (CF)—same as water plane center of gravity (WPCG); pounds or tons per inch (kg or metric tons per cm) of submersion; moment to change trim (MCT) 1″ or 1 cm. The values for a particular craft are found on its curves of form;

they are defined and explained in chapter 4, and their use is illustrated in figure 6-4 and described in the accompanying text.

The top sketch in figure 6-4 shows the vessel at rest and in equilibrium, when the CG and the CB are lined up vertically. (The CG and CB will always be lined up in a floating object.) As is typically the case, the CF is a little aft of the CG/CB axis. Now we are about to lower a heavy winch, w, on board for installation at the stern. (The positions and changes have been exaggerated to clarify the illustration.)

In the middle sketch the winch has been set on deck directly over the CF. Accordingly, the vessel, while still level, has sunk down to an interim waterline by an amount calculated as follows:

> Submersion (amount of sinkage [or rise]), inches = weight of
> winch divided by pounds per inch submersion

The CG and CB remain in essentially the same positions, still lined up vertically, and displacement is increased by the weight of the winch, w.

The bottom sketch shows the final waterline of the vessel after the winch has been moved aft a distance, d. The stern sinks and the bow rises by a combined distance equal to the trim (be sure to remember that trim equals the sum of the rise of one end of the boat and the drop of the other):

$$\text{Trim, inches (cm) by the stern} = \frac{(w \times d)}{\text{moment to trim } 1'' \ (1 \text{ cm})}$$

> where: (w × d) = trimming moment caused by moving winch

While the displacement hasn't changed from the middle sketch, the CG has moved aft as the weight was moved, and the CB had to chase along after it in order to remain aligned with it. Note that the CG/CB axis is always vertical to the plane of flotation (waterline). In removing the winch, the same calculation would be done in reverse.

Calculating trim caused by the moving of weights is often very confusing and can lead to mistakes, so the reader is urged to make sketches like these when he has a trim problem to solve.

The calculations carried out above to determine flotation and trim of an existing boat are well worth the modest effort involved. Guesswork is not good enough—even experienced boat people sometimes make mistakes, often ending up with a mess that can be very expensive to fix.

We have discussed so far a vessel at rest in still water, which is actually an unnatural condition. Our real interest lies in the functioning vessel, which is normally moving through a disturbed environment. The chief disturbance is waves; as the seasick traveler will testify, wave action can have a profound effect on vessel motion. To understand these complex motions, naval architects recognize six ways in which

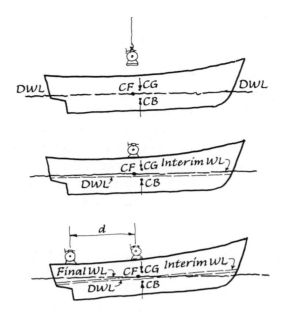

Fig. 6-4. Trimming effect of adding a winch to a fishing vessel

vessels move, or six degrees of motion. These are illustrated in figure 6-5 and described below:

Roll: the tipping of the boat from side to side as a result of waves coming at it from the side. *Heel* is when a boat tips more or less steadily to one side under the influence of external forces such as the wind. *List* is the tipping of a vessel as a result of internal forces, such as a shifted cargo.

Pitch: analogous to roll, but in a fore-and-aft direction, the bow and stern alternately rising up over a wave and dropping down the other side.

(Rolling and pitching may combine into a corkscrew motion when the waves are striking the vessel in a quartering direction.)

Heave: the bodily rising and falling of a vessel. When the waves are fairly large relative to the size of the vessel, it is clear that the center of gravity will rise above its normal level and fall below it due to wave action, regardless of what other motions are occurring; this is heaving. Heaving may occur with waves coming from any bearing.

Yaw: change of direction whether a vessel is moving or not. This can happen when a quartering sea twists the vessel momentarily, or due to rudder action turning the vessel. *Leeway,* in which the centerline of a sailing craft maintains a steady angle with the actual course made good due to the side pressure of the wind on the sails, may be considered a special case of yaw.

Surge: the gain or loss of a vessel's speed from the average, due to wave effect. A vessel running before a sea will exceed its average speed when sliding down the face of a wave, and will go slower than average when climbing the back. This results from both the orbital motion of the water particles and the gravitational effect as the vessel climbs up or coasts down the wave slope.

Sway: the sideways motion of a vessel from its mean position. Sway is usually due to wave action, but the Massachusetts merchant marine schoolship *Nantucket* was said to sway appreciably when alongside a dock due to the inertial effect of its transversely aligned, heavy, slow speed, steam engine.

Of these six degrees of motion, only the first four are of interest to us. Since heave is usually included by inference in roll and pitch, we will take a closer look at only roll, pitch, and yaw.

Rolling is the most noticeable motion of a boat and, including list and heel, probably the most conducive to accidents. We are mostly aware of rolling because it makes moving around on deck difficult, and is perhaps the major cause of seasickness. But it also is mortally important to the sailing dinghy which fills when held overlong to a puff, the fishing vessel overturning as the result of trying to bring too large a catch over the side, the cargo vessel whose deck load comes adrift due to the accelerations of rolling.

The *quality* of the rolling of a vessel not only affects our work and comfort on a boat but also is a measure of the stability of the vessel and can hence be an indicator of how safe the vessel is. A vessel that doesn't seem to roll to high angles but has a quick motion is very safe from the standpoint of stability but is uncomfortable and difficult to work aboard; the deck seems to be continually moving out from under us. Hard rolling can be tough on gear; I know of a radar antenna carried away by the violent rolling of a lobster boat.

At the other extreme is the vessel with the slow, easy roll, often to rather high angles of heel, but without the "snap" at the end of each roll characteristic of the stiff vessel. The easy roller is often very comfortable, but may be quite unsafe. In the last days of passenger liners, U.S. vessels had a reputation for being uncomfortable, while most foreign-flag vessels had an easy motion that endeared them to little old ladies. The fact was that U.S. Coast Guard regulations required a certain level of stability to make them safe, whereas the comfortable vessels were frequently quite deficient in stability, a fact which might have unsettled the little old ladies had they known about it.

Two factors influence the rolling characteristics of a vessel—the hull form and the vertical position of the CG. This relationship can be understood by examining figure 6-6. Sketch *a* shows a barge of normal proportions at rest, with the vectors through the centers of gravity and buoyancy being equal and opposite. If we forcibly heel the barge (with a sail, for instance) as shown in *b,* the CB will shift off to the side to the position shown, although the CG remains fixed in its original position.

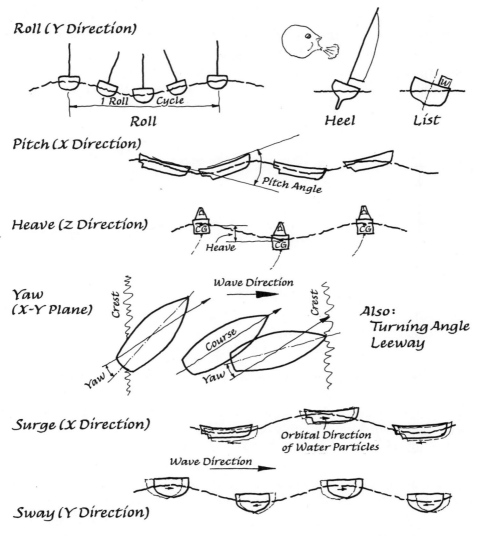

Roll (Y Direction)

1 Roll Cycle

Roll   Heel   List

Pitch (X Direction)

Pitch Angle

Heave (Z Direction)

Heave

Yaw
(X-Y Plane)

Wave Direction

Crest   Course   Crest

Yaw   Yaw

Also:
Turning Angle
Leeway

Surge (X Direction)

Orbital Direction
of Water Particles

Wave Direction

Sway (Y Direction)

Surge and sway are the horizontal motions resulting from
the orbital motion of water particles in waves, and represent
the change of position from the vessel at rest in smooth water.

Angular	Linear
Roll	Heave
Pitch	Surge
Yaw	Sway

Fig. 6-5. The six degrees of motion (roll, pitch, heave, yaw, surge, and sway)
to which a hull is subject in waves

Now the CB vector is still equal to the CG vector, but not lined up with it. The horizontal distance from the CB vector to the CG is the "righting arm," and the buoyancy (or displacement, since they are equal) times the righting arm is a moment, the righting moment. Because the moment in the sketch tends to right the vessel in the direction of the arrow, this barge is inherently stable.

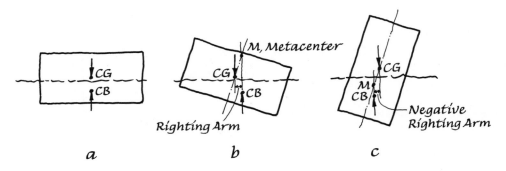

Fig. 6-6. Inherently stable (a and b) and inherently unstable (c) floating bodies

However, if the barge was narrow and deep as in *c*, we would have quite a different picture. The CB doesn't move as much to the low side as does the CG, so it is obvious that the arm is negative and this shape will be unstable, capsizing in the direction of the arrows.

This relationship among CG, CB, and hull shape is extremely important, influencing as it does the comfort of people aboard the vessel because of the quality of the motion, the safety of the vessel due to the rolling stability (including list and heel), and the ability of a sailing craft to stand up to a breeze.

The naval architect has found it convenient to use as a general measure of stability, GM, the distance from the center of gravity to the metacenter. The metacenter (M) is the intersection of the buoyancy vector with the centerline of the vessel, as indicated in figure 6-6. It is obvious from the diagram that when M is above G (CG) the vessel is stable; this GM is considered positive. When M is below G, GM is negative and the vessel is unstable. Since GM remains essentially constant for the first few degrees of heel, it can be calculated with the vessel upright.

The center of rolling, the axis about which the vessel oscillates back and forth, which is the axis of least or no motion, can be assumed to be about halfway between the vertical center of buoyancy (VCB) and the vertical center of gravity (VCG). This is the place to put delicate equipment or people suffering from motion sickness; figure 6-7 indicates how one's position on the vessel relative to this rolling axis can affect what he feels.

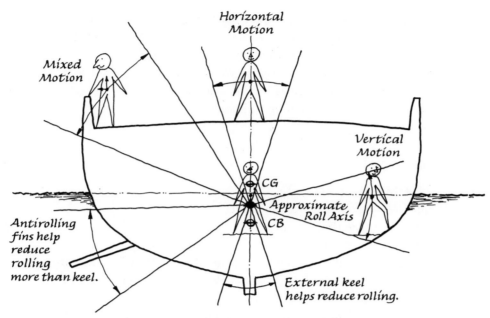

Note: All angles are the same. The length of the arrow indicates distance traveled in equal time.

Fig. 6-7. The effect of distance from the rolling axis on personal comfort and on effectiveness of antirolling devices

The vertical center of gravity is established by the weight calculations. The vertical center of buoyancy can be found by calculation or by balancing patterns of the underwater portion of the sections; in the preliminary design stage, its position can be estimated to lie about one-third the distance from the DWL to the rabbet line at station 5. BM, the distance from the center of buoyancy to the metacenter, is calculated as follows:

$$BM = I_T/V$$

where: BM = the distance in ft (m) from the CB to the metacenter, the vessel in the upright position,

I_T = the transverse moment of inertia of the water plane; see figure 6-8 for estimating

V = Displacement, ft^3 = tons × 35, or lb/64 (salt water) (m^3 = metric tons/1.025 for salt water)

There is a rather neat and easy way to estimate the GM of an existing boat. Every boat has what is called a "natural rolling period." For a given condition of loading and VCG, the vessel will roll at a certain rate, or period. (The rolling period is measured in seconds from all the way over on one side, to all the way over to the other side, and back to the original position.) When the period is being measured, the boat can be on a mooring, or loosely tied to a dock or another boat so the lines do not restrict its rolling. Heel it to one side by a line or lowering a weight onto one rail; then release the line or pick up the weight and let the vessel roll through several cycles, timing the series with a stopwatch. Dividing the number of cycles into the seconds will give the natural period. The equation relating the period to stability is simple:

$$\text{Natural period, } T = K_r \times \text{beam}/\sqrt{GM}$$

Solving for GM gives:

$$GM = (K_r \times \text{Beam}/T)^2$$

where: GM = metacentric height, feet
       Beam = waterline beam, feet
         T = measured rolling period, seconds
         K_r = a constant, preferably derived precisely when the vertical position of the CG is known through calculation or experiment, otherwise use .42 for fine water planes, .44 for average, and .46 for full. (When meters are used instead of feet, K_r would be .76, .80, .83, respectively)

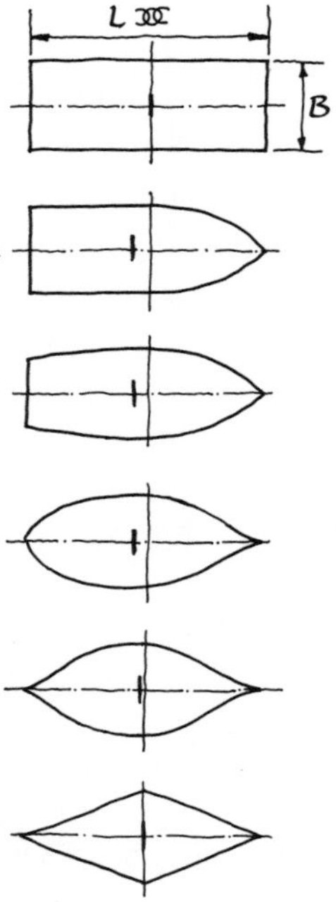

	Water Plane Area $=K_A \times L \times B$	CG, % Aft of Sta.0	Transverse Moment of Inertia $I_T = K_T \times L \times B^3$	Longitudinal Moment of Inertia $I_L = K_L \times L^3 \times B$
1	$K_A = 1.00$	50	$K_T = 0.083$	$K_L = 0.085$
2	0.83	58	0.060	0.053
3	0.78	56	0.050	0.048
4	0.67	55	0.040	0.033
5	0.61	52	0.035	0.026
6	0.50	50	0.022	0.020

Fig. 6-8. Approximations of water plane characteristics
for various shapes of hull

70 : Preliminary Design of Boats and Ships

An interesting inference can be drawn from this equation: If a vessel is lying in beam seas with a period of encounter (seconds between each crest reaching the hull) equal to its natural period of roll, it will go into a state called rhythmic rolling, analogous to pushing a swing. By applying to the swing a small force at the proper moment of each swing, the angle of swing gets higher and higher until with rigid swing chains the swing will go through 360°. By the same token, when lying abeam in regular swells with a period matching its own natural rolling period, a vessel will roll to increasingly high angles until it theoretically can roll right over. I don't know that this has ever happened, but a couple of centuries ago a British fleet lying at anchor in roads on the south coast of England was struck by large seas from a Bay of Biscay gale of just the right period for the line of battleships. It must have been an awesome sight as these huge vessels with their tall rigs rolled yardarms under on both sides every 10 or 12 seconds. So far as I recall, all the vessels survived this grueling test.

A handy use of this relationship between GM and the rolling period was told to me by Jan-Olof Traung, for many years Chief of the Fishing Vessel Section of the Food and Agriculture Organization of the United Nations. We were in Indonesia discussing some of the perilously loaded small craft one sees in developing countries. In order to evaluate the safety of these craft quickly and on site, he used the criterion that if the rolling period of a boat was greater than the beam of the boat in yards (or meters), then the GM, and hence its stability, was questionable. For instance, if you time the rolling period of a boat with a beam of 18' (6 m) as more than 6 seconds, it would be best to stay off it.

There is no consensus among the naval architectural community on the best value of GM—that is, one that provides ample stability for safety under all conceivable conditions (requiring a high value) and at the same time gives the vessel a comfortable motion for living and working. K. C. Barnaby in *Basic Naval Architecture* suggests a range of 1.5' to 2.5' (.46 to .76 m) for powered craft. The use of some function of the beam has considerable merit—I was very comfortable on a large tanker in ballast that had a GM of about 26' (8 m)—but for the size of vessels most readers will be interested in, probably Barnaby's recommendation is a good one to follow.

The transverse stability of sailing craft has a more important function than providing a comfortable, safe ride—to withstand the overturning moment of the wind in the sails. Here GM is maximized by adding ballast, as much as 80% of the displacement of a 12-meter racing yacht, as low down as possible. While the large GM helps the sailing characteristics, it turns the average sailboat under power and with no sail set into a veritable bucking bronco with its violent rolling. Sailboat stability will be dealt with in greater detail in chapter 15.

Pitching is like rolling—oscillating back and forth due to wave action—but because it takes place in the longitudinal dimension of the vessel its effect is quite different.

Vessels have a natural pitching period, although not as dramatic in its effect as the natural rolling period. There is also a "pitching angle" (the angle between the extremes of a pitch cycle), but this is more usefully expressed as pitching "amplitude," the amount the bow rises and falls during a pitching cycle, which can be considerable. Coming back from the Philippines after World War II on a 600′ (184 m) transport in large following seas, I estimated the bow to be rising and falling through a distance of 50′ (15.4 m). Had we been steaming into these swells, the ship would have to be slowed down to prevent "slamming" and boarding seas.

The natural pitching period can be estimated :

$$T, \text{natural pitching period, approximately} = .35 \times \sqrt{\text{LWL}}$$
$$(\text{metric}, .63 \times \sqrt{\text{LWL}})$$

But the natural period is very much subject to the fore-and-aft distribution of the water plane area and of the weights in the vessel. Everything else being equal, the finer the ends of a vessel's hull, the longer will be its pitching period; the fuller the ends, the shorter the period. But distributing the weights toward the ends will increase the pitching period, placing them amidships will decrease it. We can, for example, cause a fine-lined launch to pitch more rapidly, that is, respond more promptly to oncoming waves, like a full-bodied launch, by concentrating all machinery, tanks, people, and gear amidships. If these weights are relocated in the ends, the pitching will slow down appreciably. Here is a prime opportunity for the naval architect's skill at compromise. If the vessel is too quick, the boat will be very dry, but a rider in the bow will experience high accelerations. If the pitching response is slow, the motion will be comfortable but the boat will be wet, and may even present the bow-rider with a lapful of water occasionally.

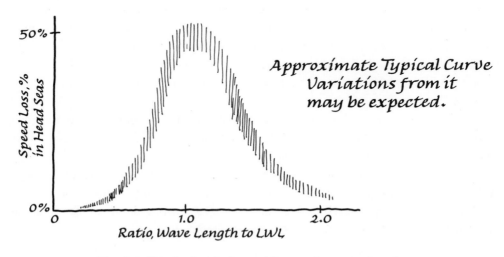

Fig. 6-9. Graph of typical speed loss against wave length
when steaming into a head sea

This matter of pitching is very important to sailing craft. A boat that is too quick will create such vacillating wind currents aloft as to impair the efficiency of the sails. At the other extreme, quieting the sails by having hull weights distributed toward the ends will increase the driving force but, because the vessel will be more out of phase with the waves, it will likely experience greater resistance from the waves.

It has been found that there is a dramatic increase in pitching amplitude coupled with speed loss when steaming into a sea the wave length of which is close to the LWL (see figure 6-9). If the period of encounter with the waves also equals the vessel's natural pitching period, a rough ride can be expected. The tactic here is to either slow down, which shifts the period of encounter away from the natural period, or to steam across the seas at a slight angle which does the same thing by making the apparent wave length longer than the LWL.

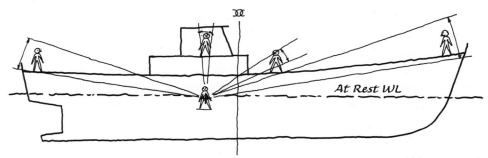

Approximate relative travel is shown by arrows at various positions on a vessel pitching 10° total angle. The effect of heave is not shown.

Fig. 6-10. Variation of personal comfort along the length
of a vessel pitching in head seas

The pitching axis when steaming, or for that matter rowing or sailing, into a head sea may be assumed to be located approximately 4/7 of LWL aft of the bow, about 30′ on a 50′ waterline length, and vertically located about on the rolling axis, which may be taken to be halfway between the VCG and the VCB. Since the typical pitching period is generally somewhat less than the typical rolling period, the fore part of a vessel can be pretty active in a head sea. In figure 6-10 it is obvious that the fellow on the bow is going to have a more exciting (and perhaps wetter) ride than the figure farther aft, the one on the stern, or the lucky one at the axis. This suggests that the arrangement of a boat should be laid out so that the day-to-day working areas (galley, mess, bridge) are as close to the axis as the function of the vessel will allow, putting the least used or least sensitive spaces (such as storage) in the bow.

In view of the physics of pitching, it is a mystery to me why the southern shrimp vessels still have the bridge way up in the bow at the forward end of the deckhouse. The motion at that position is maximum; no view of the working deck aft is possible, and it is the wettest spot. By contrast, in a boatyard in Nicaragua a number of shrimp vessels had their houses rebuilt with the bridge at the after end instead of the forward end of the deckhouse; this was a fine arrangement in every way. There must be *something* good about the bridge forward because almost all southern shrimp vessels are still built that way, but I haven't been able to find out what it is.

Pitching is another one of those areas of compromise with which the architect is constantly struggling—how to achieve a satisfactory mean in a vessel between a comfortable pitching motion and dry decks.

The last motion we are concerned with is yaw, course changing. This can be involuntary yaw, as when a following or quartering sea pushes the hull in the direction of broaching, or voluntary yaw, as in steering and course-keeping.

All watercraft will exhibit a tendency to yaw under certain conditions, most severely in a breaking quartering sea. In extreme cases broaching occurs; the vessel is completely out of control and swings around to lie abeam to the seas.

The severity of involuntary yaw is, given equal wave conditions, a function of hull form and the shape of the lateral plane, that is, the underwater profile. Most conducive to yaw is the combination of a sharp, deep forefoot with a large square transom. Even rapid reaction to give corrective rudder angle is often not sufficient to halt the broaching action. Most every year a Maine lobster boat is lost in bad weather, very likely because the typical wide stern and fine forebody caused it to broach and roll over in a quartering sea. It can therefore be stated with some assurance that for best resistance to broaching a vessel should have approximately symmetrical ends both above and below the waterline, and should have ample skeg area and a good-size and quickly trainable rudder.

My father recounted spending an afternoon on the breakwater at Manasquan Inlet in New Jersey. There was a powerful ebb tide and strong onshore wind, making for a treacherous sea at the entrance. The Coast Guard tried to halt boats from entering until the tide had changed, but without success. Most boats had a tough time getting through, and several ended up broaching and slewing onto the breakwater. Then in came a small open double-ended whaleboat, low powered and with one man aft at the tiller. This nicely balanced hull, presumably with a good profile below, came through the messy conditions without the least problem.

Whatever the design of the vessel, involuntary yawing in following seas can be minimized by selecting a boat speed that is well above or below the ambient wave speed. If traveling at wave speed or close to it, the craft may bury its bow in the back of a wave for an appreciable period of time while the stern is on the next crest. Because of orbital motion, the water particles at the crest are moving with the rudder, thus reducing its effectiveness, so the hull becomes uncontrollably locked into the wave system. The result is often a broach, flooded decks, or, as with the Great Lakes ore vessel *Edmund Fitzgerald,* being driven under the sea.

How a vessel steers, its voluntary yaw characteristics, is of prime importance to a good vessel. The ideal craft will have a small turning radius as a result of quick response to rudder action, but will also hold course well with minimum rudder action. The vessel that best holds course—has good "directional stability"—is often one which responds slowly when agile maneuvering is required. Yet the responsive craft in tight quarters may leave a wandering wake on a passage between point A and point B, no matter how capable the helmsman. Here is where the designing skill and the art of compromise of the naval architect can be displayed.

Let's take a look at how a rudder works. Suppose, for instance, we are steaming straight ahead and push the tiller to port 15° so that the rudder swings to starboard. We can feel through the tiller the force being exerted on the rudder by the water flowing against it, a force that causes the stern to swing to port in the direction of the force vector. If we hold the tiller in that position, the boat will eventually settle down into a circular path with the bow angling in toward the center of the circle and the stern angling out (see figure 6-11).

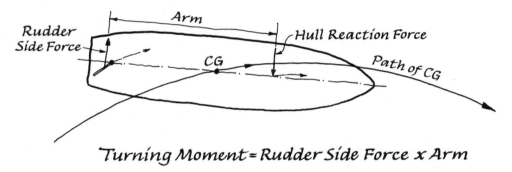

Fig. 6-11. Rudder and reaction forces working on a turning hull

The rudder force is thus easy enough to visualize, and to measure and establish the point of application; this can all be calculated before the vessel is built. But we also know that every force has an equal and opposite reaction, and the question about the rudder-hull system is where this opposite force is applied. The distance, or arm, between these two force vectors—between the centers of pressure of the rudder force and of the equal and opposite force—is a measure of the steering moment available for turning the vessel or keeping it on course.

Look at the two profiles in figure 6-12, one a sailboat with rudder attached to the after edge of a short keel, the other a fishing vessel with the rudder well aft. The center of pressure on the rudders will be about 35% aft of the leading edge, which is approximately true of all foil-shaped lifting surfaces like wings, rudders, and keels. We can make an educated guess at the location of the reaction pressure against which the rudder force will work since the vessels' profiles also constitute foils. From the sketch we can see that the arm for the sailboat turning couple is only about 35% of her LWL, of the dragger about 65%. So it is obvious why most trawlers are well behaved under way, while a sailboat of this configuration can be very difficult to steer and hold on course.

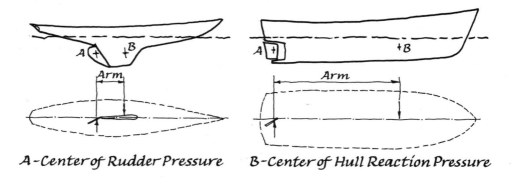

A-Center of Rudder Pressure   B-Center of Hull Reaction Pressure

Fig. 6-12. How underwater shape influences turning moment

A rudder is often seen attached to a narrow skeg, especially on sailing craft. A skeg, which without loss of efficiency can be up to 17% of the total area of the skeg and rudder, has the effect of making for better course-keeping, but it interferes with maneuvering, not only slowing the turns down but slowing the boat itself down by adding resistance. For cruising and ocean racing, use a skeg; for around-the-buoy racing omit the skeg.

The moral of this section on yawing is that, while it may be fun to draw pretty underwater profiles, which *look* neat and fast, think of *function* not looks, because no one will see them once they are in the water. So in the design of your underbodies, incorporate the ability to steer well even if they aren't beautiful.

We met transverse stability in our section on rolling, but it is of vastly greater importance as a matter of safety than as a matter of comfort. Very obviously, sailing craft rely on stability to carry sufficient sail for their purpose. But stability is a quality vital to the safety of *all* watercraft, from the smallest to the largest. The 1987 capsizing of a modern cross-channel ferry in less than a minute and in calm water, with 200 passengers drowned, reminds us of the paramount importance of stability. (Through a lapse in precise communication between crew members, the bow loading doors were left open. The unbelievable rapidity of the capsizing resulted from tons of water pouring rapidly in and piling up on the low side of the vehicle deck. The capsizing moment of this water, aggravated by the listing due to the vessel's turning, caused this large and presumably seaworthy vessel to flop over on its side almost instantly.)

It may help to divide stability into two conceptual levels: operational and ultimate. Operational stability meets the day-to-day needs of the vessel as it carries out its work or play. A sailboat heeling a bit as it beats into a sunny breeze, a heavy-lift vessel heeling 7° as it lowers a 300-ton component onto a drilling platform, or a fishing vessel lifting 3 tons of fish over the rail are all exhibiting operational stability. Ultimate stability can be illustrated by the rolling over of many of the sailboats in the 1979 Fastnet Race, by the capsizing of an Alaska crab vessel icing up with too many traps on deck, or in the small outboard motor boat found upside down with its occupants "missing and presumed drowned."

These two levels of stability are shown in figure 6-13. In *a*, the sloop is heeled a nice 22°, but the skipper (or designer!) is wondering whether she is too tender or too stiff; what are the best values of stability and sail area to give desired perfor-

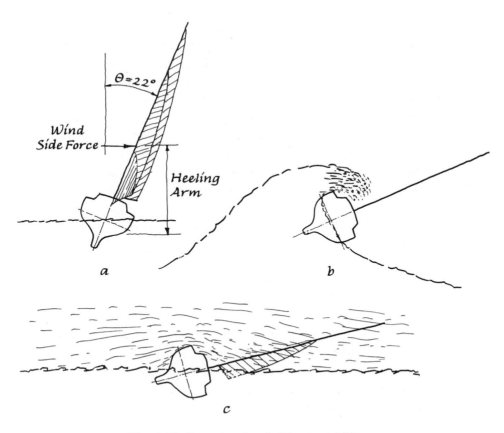

Fig. 6-13. Operational and ultimate stability

mance? In *b*, the sloop is in the middle of being rolled down by a 30' or 40' (9 to 12 m) breaking sea, and the skipper's thoughts are much more fundamental; will she go all the way over, and if she does will she right herself? These are euphemisms for "Will I get out of this alive?" The situation in *c* is midway between the other two, being a "reductio ad absurdum" of *a* in which the boat is struck by a scud-raising squall, but it should not attain the terror of *b*, if the boat has been well designed.

These three situations find their analogs in powered craft. A mackerel seiner provides a good illustration. When hauling in (drying out) the seine net, using its power block high on a boom, the vessel will normally heel somewhat. But schooling pelagic fish have been known to sound simultaneously, producing enough momentum to capsize the fishing vessel by a sudden heeling force similar to that in *c*. As for ultimate stability, the designer and operator should never lose sight of the fact that a vessel of virtually any size can be subject to the overwhelming sea of *b*.

Operating stability can be thought of as a static quality; changes tend to be rather slow and small, and there are periods where the heeling and righting forces are in steady equilibrium. This static quality lends itself to mathematical and graphical solutions, making easy work for the designer. Matching up the righting moment to the heeling moment can be done with reasonable confidence, especially if the stability has been measured on the actual vessel.

Figure 6-14 illustrates a vessel with a weight hanging over the side. If the heeling moment (W × HA) = righting moment (displacement × GZ*), then the vessel will be in equilibrium and will hold the position shown. A sailing craft would have about the same forces working on it except that the heeling moment would equal the wind side force × heeling arm, as shown in figure 6-13 *a*.

The relatively straightforward calculations for static stability provide a good first indication of the overall stability characteristics of the vessel.

By contrast, ultimate stability involves a great many dynamic forces and inter-relationships between them. For instance, a sailing vessel struck by a squall will initially heel deeply then straighten up a bit. This over-heeling uses up the momentum energy of the squall which is imparted to the vessel by the sails and rigging. Once the excess energy has been dissipated, the vessel rights to an equilibrium state. This over-heeling phenomenon is present in all instances of rapid heeling, whether from the wind, wave action, or a suddenly applied load.

Waves do funny things to stability, too. As a vessel is lifted to the top of a wave and starts back down again, it loses weight, just as you do when the elevator slows at the top of its run. The righting moment of the vessel is reduced by that loss of weight (remember that righting moment = displacement × righting arm), and we cannot even say for certain that the righting arm is not also momentarily reduced. The orbital path of water particles in waves also has an effect on a vessel, reaching an exaggerated level in a breaking sea as shown in figure 6-13 *b*; note that the break-

*Also abbreviated RA.

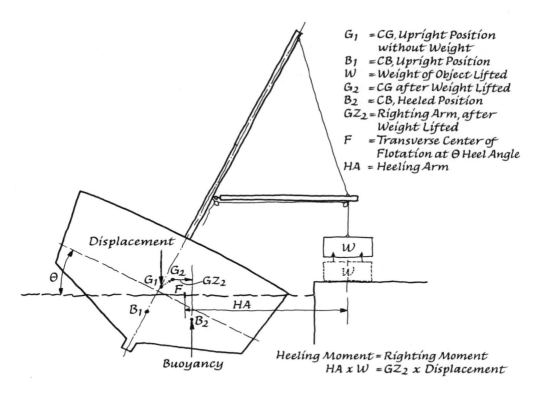

G₁ = G_1 = CG, Upright Position without Weight
B₁ = B_1 = CB, Upright Position
W = Weight of Object Lifted
G₂ = G_2 = CG after Weight Lifted
B₂ = B_2 = CB, Heeled Position
GZ₂ = GZ_2 = Righting Arm, after Weight Lifted
F = Transverse Center of Flotation at Θ Heel Angle
HA = Heeling Arm

Displacement

Buoyancy

Heeling Moment = Righting Moment
HA x W = GZ₂ x Displacement

Fig. 6-14. Stability considerations for a workboat
lifting a weight over the side

ing head of the wave will sluice down the face of the wave much faster than the water it is riding on, further tending to trip up the boat.

Increasingly, efforts are being made to quantify and qualify the factors involved in ultimate stability and safety in rational and reproducible terms; these are already increasing our understanding of these frightening conditions. My own opinion is that, even though the survivability of watercraft is being materially improved, for the immediate future instinct, experience, and common sense will continue to be the best aids for survival in ultimate conditions. Severe ocean conditions are so variable from place to place and from second to second, that no matter what conditions the naval architect designs for, there is bound to be an Achilles' heel in the vessel's abilities that nature can find under the right conditions. This does not diminish the value of the investigations being done, but does suggest that reliance on the results should be only part of the process of designing for ultimate safety.

In chapter 5 we saw that a wave at sea, generated by whatever force, has a speed in knots equal to 1.34 √wave length in feet (2.42 × √wave length in meters). This relationship has fundamental importance in vessel design, as a look at figure 6-15 will illustrate. This shows two displacement-type sailboats traveling at a speed of 9.38 knots with a corresponding wave length of 49′ (14.9 m). The 49′ (14.9 m) LWL sailboat is nicely nestled between the bow wave and stern wave crests of its wake. The 25′ (7.62 m) LWL sailboat at 9.38 knots, though, is trying to climb the back of its own bow wave with its stern sunk into the trough; obviously this boat is struggling and it is doubtful that a true displacement boat could ever reach this speed.

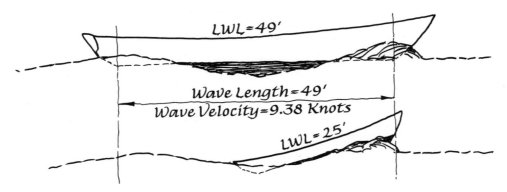

Fig. 6-15. Effect of speed-length ratio on performance of displacement hulls.
Both vessels are traveling at 9.38 knots, creating a 49′ wake wave.
Upper boat, at SLR of 1.34, is moving easily; lower boat, at SLR
of 1.88 is wasting energy climbing the back of its bow wave.

Because of the importance of wake wave length with respect to a vessel's speed, naval architects frequently refer to, and use in describing the speed of a boat, the relationship of waterline length to boat speed in a coefficient known as the speed-length ratio, SLR.

$$\text{SLR} = V \text{ in knots} / \sqrt{\text{waterline length in feet (meters)}}$$

For the two boats in the example, the SLR of the 49′ boat = $9.38/\sqrt{49'}$ = 1.34 ($9.38/\sqrt{15m}$ = 2.42), and for the smaller boat SLR = $9.38/\sqrt{25'}$ = 1.88 ($9.38/\sqrt{7.62m}$ = 3.40).

From this example, it can be seen that the length of the wake waves from crest to crest will have a powerful limiting effect on the maximum speed attainable by heavy displacement power or sailing craft. There is thus no point in trying to power a fishing trawler or a cruising sailboat for speeds in excess of a $V/\sqrt{L}$ = 1.3 (2.35). (Actually, higher SLRs have been recorded by displacement sailboats, but this is usually attributed to conditions in which the boat is able to surf for appreciable periods of time down the face of waves traveling at well over the boat's maximum SLR.)

In naval architecture, vessels sailing at the same SLR are considered to be traveling at the same relative speed because the wake wave patterns are the same for both craft. This is important in estimating wave-making resistance; for two similar but different-size hulls traveling at the same SLR, wave-making resistance is proportional to the displacements.

The relationship of SLR to waterline length was graphically demonstrated to me one cold December afternoon off Southwest Harbor on Mt. Desert Island. Southwest Boat Corporation had built two small patrol boats for the Coast Guard. Sent up from Boston to pick one up was *Duane,* then a fairly new Coast Guard vessel of 327' (100 m) LOA. Towing the patrol boat out for the pickup was a local 75' (22.9 m) Coast Guard cutter, and I was aboard a 25' (7.62 m) lobster boat from the boatyard. When *Duane* was under way towing the patrol boat at 10 knots, there was no discernible wake (see figure 6-16). The 75-footer was steaming alongside at about normal cruising speed with a nice bow wave and moderate wake. The little 25-footer seemed to be screaming along, throwing a large bow wave on each side and trembling with the effort. Yet we were all going 10 knots. The difference was that *Duane*'s SLR was .55 (1), the 75-footer's was 1.15 (2.09), and ours was 2 (3.6), or in relative terms about four times *Duane*'s speed. For *Duane* to travel at our SLR (2 [3.6]), her speed would need to be 36 knots; for us to travel at her SLR (.55 [1]), we would have to slow down to 2.75 knots.

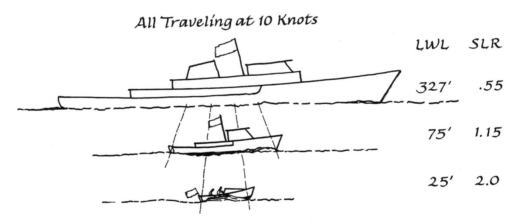

All Traveling at 10 Knots

	LWL	SLR
	327'	.55
	75'	1.15
	25'	2.0

Fig. 6-16. Visual effect of various LWLs and speed-length ratios

The shape of a boat is obviously very dependent on speed-length ratio and the maximum SLR can be very dependent upon the hull shape, so this is a coefficient that should be set very early in the design process.

There is a way to beat some of the wave-making resistance—by the addition of a bulb reaching forward from the stem below the waterline, as shown in figure

6-17. The bulb if properly designed has the effect of increasing the wave length in which the vessel can efficiently operate, and of reducing the size of the wake waves and hence the wave-making horsepower required. An unlooked-for benefit of the bulb is a reduction in the amplitude and violence of pitching. The bulb is not of benefit to vessels operating at SLR greater than 1.3 or so, nor even below that level is it always effective. The manager of a large fleet of tankers told me that their investigations showed that bulbs were beneficial only when the tankers were in ballast or about half the time. Nevertheless the gain in fuel consumption was sufficient to warrant the retrofitting of bulbs to the tankers that didn't have them. Very likely the determination of whether or not bulbs should be used can only be made positively through towing tank tests.

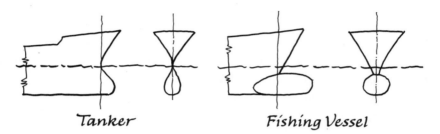

Tanker   Fishing Vessel

Fig. 6-17. The bulbous bow, for reducing resistance

A small boat or a large vessel, once at sea, becomes a part of the environment; it is no longer a device man uses to conquer nature (nature is continually laying traps for us to show how foolish we are to use the word conquer). So the designer must continually have in mind how compatible his design is with nature, and how the natural environment affects the people aboard the vessel and the job it is intended to do. The next chapter explores how man fits into this partnership with nature.

7. People Afloat

THE day of the unmanned vessel has not yet arrived (even though technically it appears to be quite feasible); so watercraft have people aboard at all times they are functioning. The purpose of boats and vessels is to provide a place for men, women, and children to live and do things such as catch fish, transport people and cargo, fight wars, enjoy themselves, or do any of the many activities for which people leave dry land. In carrying out these activities people are vitally affected by the constraints placed upon them by being afloat. During a sailing cruise around the world, half a dozen people might live cooped up for weeks at a time in a tossing home with about the total volume of an average living room. That small amount of enclosed space must contain all the life-support systems necessary to maintain the crew, such as water supply, food storage, sewage treatment, electricity, heating/cooling equipment, and the many pounds of personal impedimenta, plus propulsion machinery and fuel, and repair parts and tools. On top of all that, this capsule world must be shaped and built so as to be able to navigate the often stormy oceans of the world efficiently, safely, and reasonably comfortably.

At the other end of the scale is the huge 1,300' (396 m) supertanker with as few as 20 in the crew. Spending months at sea, with turnaround times measured in hours, the stress here is not from the crowding together of bodies but from their separation. Because of relatively infrequent encounters between crew members, there is a tendency toward antisocial attitudes. Here the naval architect must also practice sociology and psychology in designing the accommodations.

The design and construction of a fishing vessel is even more demanding. It must provide a platform on which the crew can work with acceptable safety (this is still to be achieved; statistically, fishing is one of the most hazardous occupations in the U.S.) and efficiency among dangerous machinery and gear, and then retire below to sufficient amenities to enable them to rest and recharge their vital batteries before being called on deck for another 12-hour watch. In addition, the fisherman is not able to choose his weather; the fish do that for him, and it can sometimes be unpleasant. Even during frequent and strong gales and subfreezing temperatures, the economics of fishing require him to work through it if at all possible.

Whatever the type of watercraft, it is the responsibility of the vessel designer (including the reader) to provide his client (himself?) with the best possible mix of safety, comfort, functional efficiency, and operational performance. This responsibility causes much anxiety to the designer because he knows he cannot fulfill these requirements 100%; perhaps the best he can do is 70% or 80%. What are the thoughts of the naval architect when even large modern freighters of his design are lost at sea without word or trace, possibly the result of an encounter with an ultimate sea?

Regardless of the type of vessel, comfort and safety are tied closely together and will be treated in general terms in this chapter. Functional efficiency and operational performance, having different meanings for vessels of different types, will be dealt with in the chapters dealing with each type of vessel.

The effect of vessel motion on humans can be physiological and/or neurological and/or psychological. The psychological effect, via the power of suggestion, is usually manifested as seasickness and is obviously of consuming interest to many people (sometimes including myself), but is beyond the scope of this discussion. The only useful suggestion I can offer is to not allow any talk of seasickness on board, especially of a teasing nature.

A very real psychological effect of noise, motion, darkness, cold, and exhaustion, is fear. Everyone who has been afloat very much has felt fear and has coped with it; having known this fear inculcates a sense of caution that helps a person become a good seaman. But some people are so overwhelmed by fear that they are completely incapacitated, and become a hazard to themselves, their shipmates, and even the vessel. Unfortunately there is not much the boat designer can do to alleviate psychological seasickness or unreasoning fear.

I am by no stretch of the imagination an expert on motion sickness and the effect of motion on motor functions. Nevertheless there are some things the naval architect can do to alleviate the rigors of life afloat. To that end some of my empirical observations may be of interest.

From the standpoint of overall design, it can be said that maximum comfort and safety will be achieved in the region of the rolling and pitching axes, discussed in chapter 6. With this in mind, some general rules follow; but keep in mind that the larger the vessel, the less important these rules are:

Living quarters: Whatever the purpose of the vessel—pleasure, fishing, passenger-carrying, freighter—the preferential distribution of living quarters is, starting closest to the pivot axis: galley and mess/leisure, sleeping, toilet and bathing facilities. While some hard-bitten cases do not mind roughing it afloat, the general trend over the past several generations has been to improve living conditions on vessels, whether yachts or commercial craft. The total time, or percentage of time, spent at sea can be a good measure of the level of accommodations to be sought; the longer the period, the more habitable the accommodations should be.

Vessel operational spaces: The bridge should be as close to the pitching axis as possible, and only as high above the WL as required to allow good visibility over the bow, to both sides, and aft onto the stern. Engines don't seem to mind motion much, but if the engine room is to be partially or fully manned, it is best to locate it so that the control area is close to the motion axis. Because of other space and motion demands, vessels often have the engine room well forward, which makes the previous stricture quite important. Locate the control center at the aft end of a forward engine room and use the forepeak for storage or other infrequently accessed uses. Fuel and water tanks don't care where they are, but in locating them one must keep in mind the effect of variable loads on trim and on the pitching motion.

Functional (working) space: The fishholds of most small and moderate size fishing vessels are located fairly near amidships to minimize the trimming effect as the hold is filled and emptied, and this location could hardly be improved upon from the standpoint of working in them. Fishing gear on deck, and processing facilities on deck and below, should (unless they are unmanned) be located well aft of the bow; most of this equipment is massive, rotating, and/or sharp, so minimum motion is important from a safety standpoint.

For the research vessel, it is undoubtedly best to have the wet laboratory amidships on the main deck directly over the motion axis, with the dry laboratory preferably directly below it, or just forward or aft of it if on the same level. Gear cranes could be located port and starboard abreast the motion axis, and a gantry for heavy lifts over the stern. For some functions it may be desirable to cut a "moonpool" down through the hull close to the motion axis to minimize motion when launching or retrieving tricky or heavy objects such as minisubs.

On passenger craft that are apt to operate in a seaway, locate dining facilities as close to the motion axis as possible, and the galley adjacent to it.

Every vessel designed must have adequate accommodations for the people who will man it. This has not always been a major concern of shipbuilders; the word "accommodation" could hardly apply to the living conditions on Viking longboats, early sailing warships, U.S. whaling vessels. Those days are not completely gone. Not long ago a mutiny was reported on a Japanese fishing vessel. As I recall the vessel was 130′ (40 m) long and had a crew of 90 people. They rebelled at being kept at sea for months at a time, and were finally flown back to Japan for a vacation and assured they would be kept at sea no longer than six months in the future. An acquaintance of mine boarded a similar Japanese vessel and remarked on the number of bookshelves in the wheelhouse. He was informed that those were bunks for the crew.

One of the reasons for improving living conditions afloat is that "brute strength and ignorance" are no longer enough to qualify someone for crewing on a vessel. In addition to the ageless demands for seamanship skills which the old-timers had in vast measure, the modern seaman must have a reasonable facility with written and spoken language and a smattering of math and science; ability to operate and maintain a number of esoteric electronic devices and to assimilate and synthesize their output; a good knowledge of often highly specialized mechanical, electrical, and hydraulic machinery; and a working understanding of subjects such as meteorology, oceanography, marine biology, and pollution. The seaman with these capabilities will use his skills to better advantage when he is provided good conditions aboard ship for both work and nonwork activities.

So, instead of designing berths the size of bookshelves into our modern craft, we must provide a working and living ambience that is as pleasing as possible. In doing so, it would be well to take a look at how a day is divided in order to place some kind of priority on the importance of the spaces used for the various activities. Table 7-1 is an effort to break down a day's activities by time; wide variations can be expected in this breakdown because of climate, vessel function, and personal preferences, so the list should be revised as necessary to suit each application.

Overall conditions are as important as are the gadgets we surround ourselves with, even though we tend to treat them perfunctorily. Excessive noise, glaring and misdirected light, too little or too much heat, lack of colors or colors that are too stimulating, and overcrowding are some of the factors that can lead to unhappiness, poor performance, and an increased injury rate. All these factors are carefully considered even in small shops ashore but are only now beginning to receive the attention afloat they deserve.

Table 7-1
Hours Per Activity Per Day Per Person

Activity/service	Yacht Crew	Yacht Pass.	Fishing vessel	Tow boat	Excursion/ party fishing Crew	Excursion/ party fishing Pass.	Cruise (overnights) Crew	Cruise (overnights) Pass.
Sleeping	8	7-9+1*	8	8	0	0	8	9+1*
Eating	$1\frac{1}{2}$	2	$1\frac{1}{2}$	2	$\frac{1}{2}$	$\frac{1}{2}$	$1\frac{1}{2}$	$2\frac{1}{2}$
Head (personal rooms)	1	$1\frac{1}{2}$	$\frac{1}{2}$	$\frac{1}{2}$	$\frac{1}{2}$	$\frac{1}{2}$	1	$1\frac{1}{2}$
Working	10	2	10	6	6	—	10	—
Lounging/relaxation	$3\frac{1}{2}$	10-8	4	$7\frac{1}{2}$	2	7	$3\frac{1}{2}$	11-10
Galley	4	—	8	8	6	—	12	—

*Sleeping plus 1 hour of napping.

Noise/sound: Most vessels are loaded with sources of high level noise, enclosed in what might be described as a huge noise generator. People must live and work in that sound box for hours, days, weeks, even months at a time. There are well-established maximum sound level standards for all kinds of activity spaces, and these should be met if at all possible. Several measures can be taken to achieve these levels:

1. Place the sources of sound vibration away from areas requiring low sound levels. For instance, if the crew's quarters are forward try to locate the engine room in the stern.

2. Mount the generators of sound vibrations so that they transmit minimum vibrations to the hull. This can be done in two ways: by rigidly fastening the vibration generators (prime movers, compressors, etc.) to massive foundations which are in turn rigidly fastened to the hull (this works because the natural vibration of the hull is usually not in harmony with the machinery vibration); or floating the machinery on flexible mounts, with flexible shaft couplings and pipe connections to further minimize vibration transmission. Sometimes panels of the hull, particularly with fiberglass construction, will be found to vibrate just like drum heads; when found, these should be stiffened to change their natural frequency.

3. Insulate decks and bulkheads, separating low sound areas from noise generating areas to prevent the *transmission* of sound vibrations through the surfaces. This can be done by massive insulation, such as lead sheets, but there are effective systems combining less massive insulation with flexible mounting that perform very well. Also becoming available are sound barrier housings for individual items of machinery; these are lighter in weight than full compartment treatment, and reduce the sound level in the engine room or compartment, which the engineer will appreciate. Since this type of insulation is usually in an engine room or compartment, it should be fireproof, and preferably designed specifically for marine use.

4. Install sound deadening coverings such as carpeting, curtains, and acoustical panels to reduce the *reflection* of sound waves which do get into the low sound areas.

Illumination: There are also standards for acceptable light levels for various activities, and these should be adhered to if possible. While avoiding glare coming directly into the eyes, having the light sources visible without glare is often a help in maintaining the crew's orientation in space. If alternating current is used, avoid the use of fluorescent lighting where machinery is powered by electric motors. All spaces apt to be entered should have some illumination at all times, even at threshold level. Have red lighting available in areas such as the bridge where intermittent illumination may be required in an area that is otherwise kept dark for functional reasons.

Temperature control: Environmental control needs are very much a function of where the vessel will be operating. In cold climates, there should be an area, presumably the lounging area, where the crew can enjoy a comfortable "shirt sleeve" ambient temperature. Similarly, in warm climates the lounging and/or sleeping area should be cooled to an acceptable level, perhaps 70°F (21°C). Shelter the crew as much as possible from the direct rays of the sun and from cold winds and rain. Make sure each crew member is dressed suitably for the temperature conditions prevailing.

Ventilation: All compartments must be ventilated as required by the use of the compartment and based upon the number of people and the time they spend there. Clean air must be introduced and foul air, together with any toxic or explosive fumes, discharged. To reduce the sound level of forced ventilation in living spaces, locate the blowers away from the spaces; a further reduction can be achieved by lining the ducts with fireproof sound insulation. In addition to normal ventilation, the engine room should be fitted with aspiration ventilation for all the prime movers, with intakes of $\frac{1}{2}$ square inch (3.3 square cm) of opening per installed horsepower and located so as not to backflood from boarding seas.

Color: In the work area, color can be used to indicate safe and unsafe locations and to improve the light conditions. For instance, painting the inside of the bulwarks white helps greatly in working around a deck at night, as does a light-colored deck itself.

In accommodations there is a great opportunity for increasing attractiveness by the use of color, which need not include painting cherubs or Squirrel Nutkin on the bulkheads. Pleasing, muted colors can be used to lighten or darken the interior, for northern or southern waters respectively, and for delineating areas of different functions.

Security: Every vessel, no matter its size or type, will occasionally take a heavy roll, or come up hard when pitching. To avoid a mess, make everything twice as secure as you think necessary, with drop or latching drawers, secure stowage for all loose items, and substantial risers, fiddles, handles, etc.

Inside/outside separation: The outside elements are constantly trying to get into the peace and security of the inside, and every effort should be made to thwart them. Wherever possible incorporate a "weather lock" where crewmen can change from their oilskins and dirty clothes; if possible have a toilet room which is accessible only from the lock or the deck.

With these general comments in mind, we can design the specifics of the various spaces on our vessel. If you don't find a needed dimension below, or want to test for your own needs some that are given here, set up dummy full-size models and experiment with them.

Personal room: The terms toilet room, bathroom, and head are all euphemistic and incomplete in describing these very personal spaces. They might more precisely and appropriately be termed "personal rooms." Daily usage of personal rooms varies—$\frac{1}{2}$ to $1\frac{1}{2}$ hours per person depending on the facilities provided and the type of "clientele." As might be imagined, ventilation is very important; recommended is a water-trapped or waterproof ventilator intake, plus an exhaust blower tied into the light switch.

See figure 7-1 for small boat toilet installation suggestions; if overboard intake and discharge are used, locate discharge some distance aft of intake.

The wash basin can be higher than house-style, about 34"-36" (85-90 cm). Allow space over it to duck one's head for face-washing without denting skull or woodwork. The basin drain can empty into a sump, directly overboard, or into the toilet bowl. Don't tie it into the toilet discharge seacock (if there is one) without a check valve, because if the toilet is pumped when the seacock is shut off what someone put into the toilet will come spraying out of the basin. Not good!

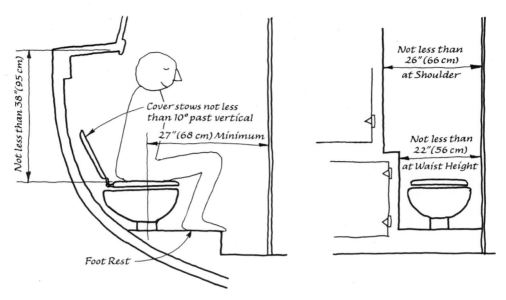

Fig. 7-1. Some useful biometrics to ensure that a small craft
personal room has enough space for a person to function

Galley: Daily usage of the galley varies from 4 to 12 hours. Ranges are probably better located close to the vessel's side and facing inwards so that they are subject to vertical rather than horizontal accelerations. Sinks on small boats draining overboard must be high enough above the waterline to avoid back flooding. A U-shaped layout seems to combine best use of space with maximum convenience; there must be enough space between the legs to have easy access to under-counter lockers. A location near a door or companionway, plus an exhaust blower, will help remove galley odors and fumes.

Mess/lounging/relaxation: Daily usage is 2½ to 13½ hours. Except on the largest vessels the mess space is also the space for lounging, playing cards, watching television, etc., accounting for the high number of hours spent in eating and in lounging/relaxation. For this reason the comfort level should be greater than is necessary for simple cafeteria use. Figure 7-2 gives some guidance for comfortable chair/table dimensions.

There should also be ample lounging space on deck as required by the function of the vessel—lavish for the cruise passenger, minimal for the hardworking fisherman. Provide good weather and bad weather on-deck areas for paying passengers; being on deck in the fog or rain is not joyful but after a day in a fuggy saloon with everyone else it can be a pretty nice change. Many yachts with berths for six (used approximately 8 hours) have a cockpit (occupied about 10-16 hours) that will barely hold them all squeezed up together; this is to be avoided.

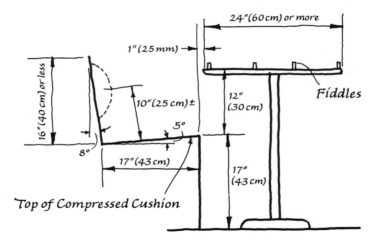

Fig. 7-2. Dimensions for comfortable sitting at table

Sleeping: Daily usage of the sleeping area is 7 to 10 hours. Berths should run fore and aft. Single berth width of 30″ (76 cm) is best, 36″ (90 cm) maximum, 21″ (53 cm) minimum; a double berth should be 42″ to 48″ (107-122 cm) wide. Minimum roll-over clearance between the upper and lower berth is 21″ (53 cm). Each person should have at a minimum 3′ (90 cm) of shelf space, 1½ to 2 ft³ (.04-.06 m³) of drawer space, 4″ (10 cm) of rod space in hanging locker with 38″ (96 cm) minimum space under (48″ [122 cm] desirable).

Working Area: Daily usage is 2 to 10 hours per person. Provide as much clear and unhindered deck space as possible. Keep trawl warps up in the air if possible. Have guards on everything that might entrap a hand or leg, a hank of hair, or a tattered sleeve. The best surface can become slippery under certain conditions, so provide handholds and rails along the sides and dividing up large clear areas. By careful layout of the gear (winches, bollards, cutting tables, etc.) minimize the amount of moving around necessary to carry out the work of the vessel.

When it comes to going to sea, there is little doubt that man would be better off if he were a dolphin. It is the duty of the vessel designer to make man's return to the sea as painless, pleasurable, and productive as possible.

PART II

THE ACTUAL DESIGN

8. The Design Process

A VESSEL design begins as an idea, a mental picture. This picture may appear involuntarily as if by magic, or it may be the result of conscious ratiocination when the brain is presented with a specific problem ("What is the optimum passenger boat for the Kennebunk River?"). The mental picture doesn't spring to life full-blown; it is built up from personal experience, from reading the literature, from observing similar craft in action, and from visiting docks and shipyards. The more input from these sources that goes into the picture, the better the output is apt to be.

The architect, given this concept out of his own head or by his client, then embarks on a course of action that can be plotted as a design spiral, shown in figure 8-1. Starting at the top with the overall concept, which has by now been transcribed from the brain to the back of an envelope, a shingle, or a drawing pad, the designer follows the spiral around as many cycles as necessary. He stops at each node to examine that particular aspect of the design and to see if, during his last circuit of the spiral, he has introduced details that require changes in that aspect. Having made the appropriate adjustments at that node, he moves on to the next and repeats the

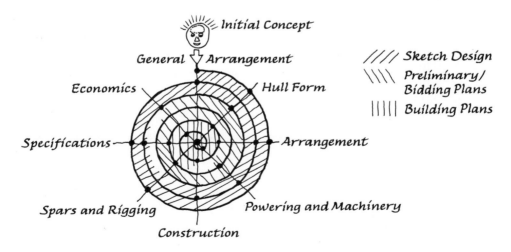

Fig. 8-1. The design spiral—a naval architect's road map

process. He considers the design completed when he can go all around without finding any unanswered questions.

The design spiral is a conceptual guide for the designer. If he follows it he will have to do a minimum of backtracking and discarding work already completed, no mean achievement in such a complicated and indeterminate process as designing even a small vessel. During the process, of course, he must always keep in the forefront of his mind the overall goals and constraints established for the particular design. There are no rules for using the design spiral. You can go around it as many times as you wish or find necessary, and you can back up or go forward. The point is to keep working it over until there are no more changes to make.

You have perhaps noticed that there is not a sector for calculations. Each sector has its own set of calculations, and at each stopping place the specific calculations are carried out to whatever level of refinement is needed.

By following the design spiral the neophyte designer will avoid a common mistake—completing one plan, all pretty and inked, before all the necessary decisions and determinations have been made. I have seen a beautifully finished lines plan that had to be discarded because when the final weight calculations were made, there wasn't enough displacement to support the weight. To add insult to injury, the desired arrangement plan would not fit into the original hull. This kind of error is devastating and can significantly diminish one's enthusiasm for the profession.

Tape a design spiral on the wall over your table and gaze at it thoughtfully once in a while. And remember that no line, no specification, no number is sacred in the early stages of design. Any of them can be changed, and should be changed if the design requires it.

The examples used in this chapter are pleasure craft. However, the same process is applicable to gunboats, skiffs, and supertankers. Once the initial requirements have been clearly determined, which is the *essential* first step, use the procedure described here. From the initial, very rough sketch to establish the overall dimensions all the way to the completed sketch given to your naval architect, you should continually refine your sketches as you track around the design spiral until you are satisfied.

Probably every naval architect has developed his own procedure for preparing a design, refined over the years so that he can accomplish the most work in the briefest time, and can produce the best possible designs. My practice, developed over 50 years, is to break the design process down into phases. Each phase has a separate and distinct function, and at the end of each phase the entire project can be reviewed to evaluate the correctness of what has been done previously, to lay out the work to be done in the next phase, and in special cases to evaluate whether or not the entire project should even be completed.

"Envelope" sketches: Rough sketches made as inspiration strikes on any available surface. With these are developed the basic concept, dimensions, and arrangement of the proposed craft.

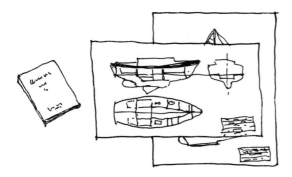

Sketch design: The phase described in this book. The ideas developed in the envelope sketches are further refined and expanded in a series of simple sketches to scale, with some initial calculations carried out, and a set of brief specifications drawn up.

The rest is done by your naval architect.

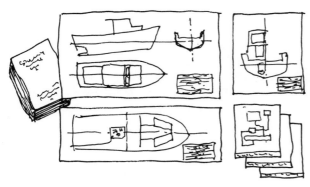

Preliminary/bidding/contract plans: During this phase, all the major design decisions are made by the architect and his client, and the final version is submitted to builders for quotations. These plans and specifications as amended can become a useful part of the building contract.

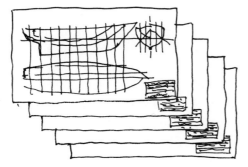

Construction plans: These are all the plans which, together with the contract specifications and plans, are required by the builder to construct the vessel in the manner desired by the owner. Measured in tons for naval craft and in sheets for simple fishing craft, all important details must be illustrated.

Fig. 8-2. The design process—major steps

There are four phases in my design procedure: "envelope" sketches, sketch design, preliminary/bidding/contract plans, and construction plans, as shown in figure 8-2. Each phase has a distinct function, and each prepares for and leads into the next phase and except for the first is a progression and refinement of the one before.

Another type of guide or road map for the sketch designer is the flow chart, shown in figure 8-3. This more precisely suggests the steps to be taken to complete a sketch design with minimum redoing and maximum quality of results. There is no need to follow slavishly the course it illustrates, but it would be a good idea to do so at least the first time.

"Envelope" sketch (Could be called a "shingle" or "napkin" sketch): This is a rough freehand sketch to no scale, in which the basic form and arrangement of the boat is developed. It typically is done sitting in an airplane or waiting for your turn in the barber's chair. It is the first appearance in open air of the concept that has been bubbling and boiling in your head. Because these sketches can be done in a few moments, it is possible to be very free and flexible in your thinking and sketch up gross changes quickly and easily. Using this sketch and information from magazines, books, and your files, the important characteristics of the design (LOA, LWL, beam, draft, displacement, sail area, horsepower) are tentatively established. Keep in mind that, while it is expensive to make a vessel larger than it need be—increasing all the dimensions by 10% increases the displacement and cost by 33%—it is much worse to make a vessel too small, a debility for which very little corrective action can be taken. So when in doubt, make the vessel larger rather than smaller.

Sketch design: This phase is made up of freehand scale sketches based on the dimensions and arrangement evolved in the envelope sketch. Generally it includes at a minimum an outboard profile or sail plan, interior arrangement, and a midsection, plus brief specifications. It may also include an inboard profile and deck plan, and may show some construction details. Preliminary calculations will be carried out before and during this phase to more precisely set the displacement, main engine horsepower, sail area, midsection area, tank capacities, etc. One may assume that the sketch design will go through at least one redrawing to incorporate such major changes as different dimensions or a complete arrangement revision.

(This is where the reader should stop, and he or she may well be glad to do so. All the major decisions will have been made before and during this sketch design phase, and the sketches will be sufficiently detailed and accurate to permit the naval architect to complete the design without important problems arising. These first two phases will be described in greater detail below.)

Preliminary/bidding/contract design: This phase has three functions important to owner, designer, and builder: it is the last opportunity for making decisions that might affect the final design; it contains all the information upon which a builder can make a firm, complete, and accurate (sharp-pencil) quotation for construction; and it will constitute an important part of the construction contract. Typically, this phase will consist of a full and complete set of specifications, plus at a minimum the following plans properly and carefully drawn to scale: outboard profile, arrangement layout for each deck, and construction section (large-scale). Included also may

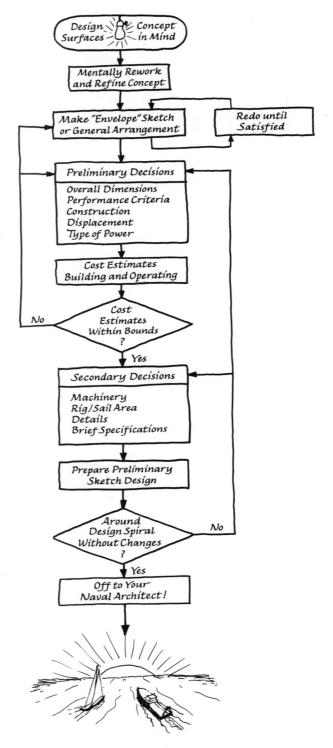

Fig. 8-3. Flow chart for carrying out the sketch design

be some or all of these: inboard profile, useful for showing construction and arrangement details; arrangement sections; preliminary lines; sketches or schematics of electrical, hydraulic, plumbing, steering, and machinery systems. A large-scale set of lines will have been started, and all calculations carried out to ensure that the vessel and its systems will operate satisfactorily; hydrostatic calculations will be incorporated in a curves of form. Preliminary approval required of U.S. Coast Guard, Lloyd's, American Bureau of Shipping, or other regulatory agencies will also have been obtained wherever possible.

Construction plans: These are the balance of the plans necessary to build the vessel, including complete large-scale drawings of the small-scale preliminary plans; finished lines and offsets; construction profile, plan, and sections; arrangement profiles, plan, and sections; schematic and installation plans of all systems; sail and spar plans; details of special features of construction, gear, or furnishings.

This, in very brief terms, is the anatomy of the complete design of a boat or vessel. The part you will play, through the sketch design phase, is described in greater detail below and in the following chapters.

Reader, you *are* lucky. In your two phases of the design process, the "envelope" design, and the sketch design, you have all the fun and excitement of creating the design, and none of the drudgery and responsibility (waking up at three A.M. wondering if the weight calculation is done correctly!) of making it work. Actually, to the dedicated professional naval architect, none of it is real drudgery. There is even an excitement about the hours of tedious weight and trim calculations, wondering how closely they will agree with the estimates. And the three A.M. crises of responsibility are amply compensated for when the vessel is launched and floats and performs as expected or, mirabile dictu, better than that!

To start, you have a vessel concept fairly well worked out in your mind. As an example, let's say it is a motor sailer (combining a powerboat hull with a sailing rig and sailing performance), which will perform reasonably well in both modes, has accommodations for two couples for multiweek cruises, and space for another couple for short periods. Space will be provided for scuba gear storage and use, and for the processing and storage of a small amount of collected marine biological and archeological artifacts. Construction will be timber, carvel planking on bent frames. Diesel power will be used for a maximum speed-length ratio of 1.2, and cruising speed SLR of 1.05.

Figure 8-4 shows the envelope sketch that I worked up; yours would probably be quite different. I start with a rough sketch of the arrangement because that is usually the most size-restrictive aspect of any boat or vessel design. Having laid out the various components as I wish them to be, I can assign an estimated length to each compartment and, by adding all these lengths up, arrive at a pretty good estimate of the LOA. Sketching in the profile is not always necessary, but often helps to validate the plan view, and is another expression of the design in your mind.

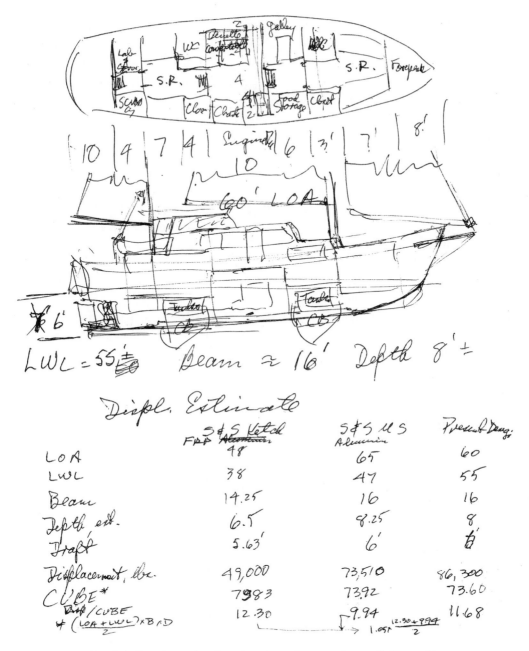

Fig. 8-4. Envelope sketch and early estimates of overall dimensions

This sketch might be one of several for the boat as objections or improvements become apparent. It is the purpose of the "envelope" sketches to help identify and correct those problems. For instance, returning to my sketch, if an overall length limit of 55′ (16.7 m) had been imposed for some reason, the layout would need to be reworked to save 4 or 5 feet. Or it might have turned out that bulkheads weren't located so that the masts could be stepped on them, and masts extending through the deck would shut off passages, which would require a reworking of the layout. But let's suppose we were lucky, and that it looks as though everything will go together well and meet the requirements.

Before starting the next phase, the sketch design, we must ascertain the dimensions of our vessel. See how approximate lengths of the compartments are noted below the plan view. These are probably generous but will allow a sense of spaciousness in the accommodations so, if we can afford it, let's stay with them. (If LOA is greater than permitted, we can reduce the forepeak a foot or two, each bunk space by 6″ (15 cm), the deckhouse by 6″ (15 cm), the lab/scuba gear space by 6″ (15 cm), and the after deck by 1′ (.3 m); this adds up to 4 or 5 feet (1.2 to 1.5 m), to give us an LOA of 55′ or 56′ (16.7 m to 17.0 m). There are other reductions that could be made to shorten the vessel even further if need be.) Subtracting approximate overhangs of 4′ (1.2 m) forward and 1′ (.3 m) aft from the LOA gives an LWL of 55′ (16.7 m).

We can also use the same means of estimating the beam as for the LOA. If we stipulate 2′ (.6 m) side decks, 4′ (1.2 m) dinette width, 4′ (1.2 m) center space, and 3′ (.92 m) pilothouse steering position, it adds up to a beam of of 15′ (4.57 m). This may be a bit narrow for the LWL, so we can widen the steering position (3′ [.92 m] is probably too restrictive anyway) for a tentative beam of 16′ (4.9 m). Probably a good L/B ratio is 3.44; it puts more of the cubic number (because this is a sailing craft, we use CUBE = (LOA + LWL)/2 × B × D to account for long overhangs) into length on the theory that a longer boat has a higher limiting speed and that a reduced beam will probably be a bit more comfortable in a seaway.

It is also possible, and necessary, to make a first estimate of the displacement. This fundamental property of a vessel can vary over a wide range, even for vessels that don't have the cargo variable to complicate the picture. The best method of estimating displacement is to find out the displacements of vessels of similar type and construction, and roughly similar size. The displacement will vary directly as LWL^3 for exactly similar craft, or as CUBE for vessels of different proportions. (The displacement length [or length displacement] ratio can be used if the value for a similar craft is known, but adjustment must be made if the proportions of the base vessel differ from the proposed vessel.) It's not a bad idea to increase the estimated displacement by 5% or so on the basis that it's better to err high rather than low; final adjustment will be made by the architect.

We have decided that our vessel will be fairly heavily built by the conventional carvel plank on bent frames. In a search through the magazines, we find a 48′ (14.6 m) fiberglass ketch with a displacement of 12.30 lb per CUBE (197 kg per MCUBE), and a 65′ (19.8 m) aluminum motor sailer with a value of 9.94 lb per CUBE (159 kg per MCUBE). Since our vessel will not have as high a ballast ratio as the ketch, and the construction will be heavier than the motor sailer, we will take a mean of these two values and add 5% to obtain an approximate displacement, giving a value of 11.68 lb per CUBE (187 kg per MCUBE).

What we now have is a clear idea of the arrangement on deck and below of our vessel, its outboard appearance, and its approximate dimensions:

Length Overall	60′	(18.29 m)
Length, Waterline	55′	(16.76 m)
Beam	16′	(4.88 m)
Depth	8′	(2.44 m)
Draft, maximum	6′	(1.83 m)
CUBE (MCUBE)	7,360 ft³	(208.7 m³)
Displacement	86,000 lb	(39.02 metric tons)

At this point we have all the information we need to start a sketch design, the final version of which we will be putting in the naval architect's hands for completion. As with all complex projects, it pays to take time at the beginning in preparing to do the job. Among the preliminary decisions are: choosing the scale of your plans, choosing the size of paper, and "designing" the layout of the views on the paper (nothing looks so amateurish as a plan with everything squeezed to one side and large open spaces on the other side).

Selecting the scales: In selecting the scales to use, there are a few things to keep in mind. One of these is convenience; you want the plans to fit on standard sizes of paper and not be so large that they are difficult to work with (a 200-footer [61 m] drawn to 1″ = 1′ (1:12) scale is awesome to think about!). Secondly, the scale should not be so small that essential information can't be shown; you won't be able to show much if you sketch a 25′ sloop on a scale of 1/8″ = 1′ (1:96). Thirdly, you are apt to use more than one scale in your design; keep them all of the same family, such as 1/8″, 1/4″, 1/2″, 1″, 3″, full size, or 3/16″, 3/8″, 3/4″, 11/2″, 3″, full size (1:25, 1:50, 1:100). Don't mix the scale families up because if one plan is drawn to 1″ (1:12) scale and the other to 3/8″ (1:40) scale, it is very easy to use 1/2″ (1:50) scale rule on the plan drawn to 3/8″ (1:40) scale; a bunk 5′(1.5 m) long will not be very popular!

Paper: It is often very convenient to make your sketches on cross-section (graph) paper, with the inches divided into eighths or tenths. Use graph paper with light blue lines; the blue does not copy well, and is much less intrusive visually when making the sketch than is a darker color. This paper comes in a variety of cut sizes. If a larger size is needed, tape or glue several pieces together. If graph paper with suitable divisions is unavailable, use a scale rule to measure the distances and dimensions—it isn't that much more effort.

Drawing the grid: The matrix within which your design will be created is the "grid," the construction lines providing the framework for the design (figure 8-5a). Note how the dimensions of the vessel are used to locate the views neatly on the paper, with clearance between the views, and with space at the lower right for a descriptive title block and the particulars of the craft. Once this grid (the dark lines) is drawn you may wish to make a few photocopies if you can find a copier that doesn't distort or change size; you will then have a supply for other versions and other views.

Sketching plan and profile: On the grid, and using the dimensions derived from the envelope sketch, lightly sketch in the plan and profile, as shown in figure 8-5*b*. All of this sketching should be *freehand* to avoid stiffness and the limitations of using drawing tools! Erase and redraw, erase and redraw, until the two views satisfy you, at least for today. Don't try to sketch in the interior or any other fine detail—the midsection must be drawn first.

Drawing the midsection: The midsection is about the most important view you will be drawing because, much more positively than the plan and profile, the midsection determines the shape and size of the final vessel and has a great influence on her performance. Start by establishing the location of the bottom of the keel and the top of deck at side (see figure 8-5*c*[1]), picking off their coordinates from the two views already sketched using a "tick strip" (simply any piece or strip of paper on the edge of which you can mark dimensions for transferring from one plan to another). Now, from the envelope sketch you have determined that your vessel is to displace 86,000 lb (39 metric tons) which equals 86,000/64 = 1,344 ft³ (39/1.026 = 38 m³). (Sea water weighs 64 lb per ft³ [1.026 kg per m³].) From table 3-2 you have selected a prismatic coefficient, C_p, of .55, so with the LWL, 55′ (16.7 m), and the displacement in ft³ (m³), you can calculate the required midsection area, MA, as follows:

$$C_p = \text{displacement, ft}^3/(\text{MA} \times \text{DWL}) \quad (= \text{displacement, m}^3/[\text{MA} \times \text{DWL}])$$
$$\text{or, MA} = \text{displacement, ft}^3/(C_p \times \text{DWL}) \quad (= \text{displacement, m}^3/C_p \times \text{DWL})$$

Therefore, for your vessel:

$$\text{MA} = 1,344/(.55 \times 55) \qquad\qquad (= 38/[.55 \times 16.7])$$
$$= 44.4 \text{ ft}^2 \qquad\qquad\qquad (= 4.14 \text{ m}^2)$$

Draw the midsection as shown on 8-5*c* (2) and (3) by lightly laying out a rectangle with a length somewhat less than the expected waterline beam and the desired submerged area of 44.4 ft² (4.14 m²). Then sketch a midsection so that the area taken out of the rectangle equals the area added beyond the rectangle; the area of the section should then equal the area of the rectangle. (For a hull with considerable deadrise, a triangle may be more satisfactory than a rectangle.)

Completing the vessel hull form sketch: After the midsection has been drawn and redrawn until you are satisfied—sometimes requiring revisions to the plan and profile—sketch in the DWL on the plan view (dotted on 8-5*b*). With a tick strip, pick off the waterline half-breadth on the midsection and transfer it to station 5 on the plan. Using the three DWL points you have, at stations 0, 5, and 10, you can sketch in the water plane, keeping in mind that the

102 : Preliminary Design of Boats and Ships

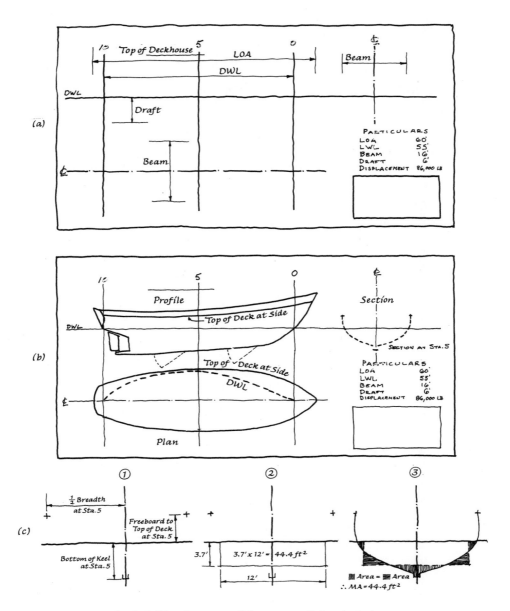

Fig. 8-5. Plan format and first steps of sketch design

center of flotation will be aft of station 5. Draw the DWL lightly in the plan view because it is a reference line only and if it is dark it will interfere with the perception of the interior layout.

Finishing the first draft arrangement: The sketch is completed by transferring to it the arrangement developed on the envelope sketch. It is generally a good idea to locate the bulkheads first, keeping in mind the uses and dimensional requirements of the areas they enclose (for example, don't put bulkheads enclosing berths 5'6" [1.7 m] apart). Show the bulkheads on both plan and profile plans.

After locating the bulkheads, before investing more time in this sketch you may wish to rough in a sail plan to make sure that bulkheads are compatible with the spars and rigging (see the section below on *sketching the sail plan*).

One of the crucial limits in interior arrangement in a small or medium-size yacht is the intersection of the top of the cabin floor, or sole, with the inside of the hull structure. If the sole is too low in the hull, it will be narrow and greatly restrict the placement of furnishings and the movement of people. If the sole is too high, there is ample width but the center of gravity of everything is higher than it needs to be, and the headroom under the deck is reduced (see figure 8-6).

To establish the edge of the sole, you must locate the inside of the hull structure; for this kind of construction one can assume a total thickness of about 2½% of the overall beam, or about 5" (13 cm), for the sides, and somewhat more for the deck structure (see table 8-1 for approximate thickness of other constructions). The inside boundary of the structure should be drawn now.

Table 8-1
Approximate Hull Structure Thicknesses
(Given as percentage of maximum beam)

	Percentage
FRP*, solid, exclusive of framing, including ceiling	1
FRP, cored, exclusive of framing, including ceiling	1.5
Wood, strip construction	1
Wood, bent frame, including frames and ceiling	2.5
Wood, sawn frame, including frames and ceiling	4
Ferro-cement, exclusive of framing, including ceiling	1.5
Steel, including frames and ceiling	2
Aluminum, including frames and ceiling	2

*FRP—Fiberglass-reinforced plastic

In this example, the critical areas in regard to the sole width are the forward cabin and the after cabin; the galley sole is raised up anyway, and the pilothouse sole is at or close to the main deck level. So, allowing a total of 7' (2.14 m), including 6'9" (2.06 m) headroom and 3" (8 cm) structure, from the top of the sole to the top of the deck or trunk, revise the three views until a sole width is achieved that permits the desired arrangement, yet doesn't result in inordinately high cabin trunks.

Figure 8-6 illustrates the importance of this space factor on a powerboat hull. The intersection of sole top with the inside of the hull is transferred to station 5 on the plan view and the intersection carried forward and aft, following more or less the path of the DWL. This same process is used for establishing the outboard edges of bunks, galley counters, tanks, etc. If greater precision is required in fitting in the arrangement than this method allows, additional sections can be drawn at, say, stations 3 and 7, using the keel, water plane, and top of deck points and sketching a section that is compatible with the midsection.

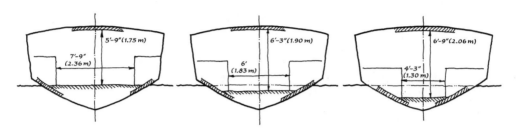

Fig. 8-6. The importance of floor width to the interior
arrangement of a small craft

Once the bulkheads and sole lines have been established, it is merely a matter of sketching the interior furnishings, engines, tanks, etc., to complete this part of the sketch design.

Specifications: (See chapter 18 for a full discussion.) The plans cannot provide all the information the architect should have in order to satisfactorily design your craft. What isn't on the plans can be included in a set of brief specifications. Preparing these specifications as the design progresses will help to remind you of some of the decisions you, not the naval architect, must make. Here is a list of material you will want to include in the specifications:

1. General comments on the use the craft will be put to, what you have in mind for quality (rough, first-class commercial, standard yacht grade, superior, etc.), who will be operating the craft, and perhaps some idea of the amount you can afford to spend *in toto.*

2. General hull construction—materials, building method, final finishing, fastening material, who will do the building (you or a professional).

3. Joinery on deck and below—materials, finish, any general desires or requirements you might have.

4. Propulsion and auxiliary machinery—type and manufacture of engine(s), cooling system, controls, sound and heat insulation, accessibility, auxiliary capacities, propeller and shaft and bearings, fire-extinguishing equipment.

5. Other vessel systems—electrical, steering, plumbing, hydraulic, fishing gear, etc. It will be very helpful to both you and the architect if you make up a schematic of each system as part of the specifications; figure 8-7 suggests what an electrical schematic might look like.

6. Rig—comments on spar materials and manufacturer (if you have one in mind), type of reefing, desired winches, provision for storm sails, list of racing sails, any features you especially want. For a fishing vessel, specifications for winches, trawls, expected loads, etc., should be incorporated.

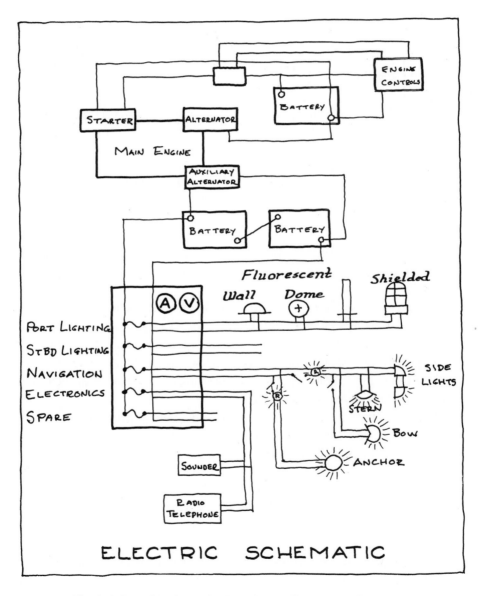

Fig. 8-7. Sample schematic plan of a small boat electrical system

7. Outfit—life raft, galley furnishings, air conditioning and heating, refrigeration, types of toilets, instruments and electronics, in other words anything of moment not covered elsewhere. One should figure on at least three to four single-spaced pages of specifications as a minimum, with no upper limit (but skip the flowery prose!).

Sail plan: May be at the same scale as the profile, which will require a larger piece of paper, or half that scale on the same size paper. This can be a pretty sketch, with decorative and clarifying shading to give the impression of a picture of the boat. Show all spars, rigging, and sails. It's a good idea to show the underwater profile, dotted if you wish to de-emphasize it for appearance sake, and put small ticks on the waterline at each station. There is a temptation to use straight edges for drawing rigging, spars, etc.; if you succumb to this urge, draw the lines in very lightly, then darken them freehand and your sketch will be much more attractive.

Testing a model of your design: You may want to find out how your hull will perform. With lots of money ($10,000 or so) you can have a model built and tested in a "towing tank." This is a laboratory facility where accurately made models of proposed boats (both sail and power) are towed down a tank of water. All the forces and changes of attitude are carefully measured and often photographs are taken; it is also possible to have waves generated in the tank to observe action in a seaway. From these tests, one can obtain a clear idea (with an accuracy of 2% to 3%) of how much horsepower will be required to drive the finished vessel over a range of operating speeds.

If you want merely to observe your creation in action, without all the precise measurements, it is possible to tow the model in a harbor or lake and get a good idea of wave formation, trim, how she acts in waves from various directions, and whether she looks attractive. Good lengths for models are 24" to 36" (.6 m to 1 m). As we learned in similitude (chapter 4), the weight of the model must vary as the scale cubed, and the speed as the square root of the scale. For a 36" model of a 30' boat (table 8-2), the scale, lambda = 3'/30' = 1/10, the model displacement will be $1/10^3$ = 1/1,000 of full size, and the speed will be $1/\sqrt{10}$ = 1/3.16, of the full-size speed.

The model can be built of pine, hollowed out to weigh somewhat less than the scale weight. Mark the position of the plane of flotation on it, and ballast it to float on that line. Tow it with rudders but with no other appendages.

Table 8-2
Model versus Full-size Vessel Characteristics

	Full-size	*Model*
Scale, lambda	1	1/10
Length, waterline	30' (9.2 m)	3' (.92 m)
Displacement, lb	10,500 (4,750 kg)	10.5 (4.75 kg)
Speed, knots, $V/\sqrt{L} = 2$	12	3.80

As shown in figure 8-8, the model may be towed with a pole from a long dock, with a tower and an observer. Or better yet, because it allows photos and movies or tapes to be taken, towing may be done from a skiff. Have a bucket along to use as a drag to get the skiff speed down to the model speed, and be sure the model is clear of the towboat's bow wave. Tow in smooth water initially, to obtain an uncomplicated picture of how she looks, then tow over a range of speeds in waves of various sizes and from various bearings to the model.

Fig. 8-8. Pole-towing a model

Things to observe in this kind of testing are: wake waves in smooth water (these should be smooth and regular, without auxiliary parasite waves); bow wave (is it smooth and regular? does it climb up the hull excessively?); separation (the water should leave the hull crisply and smoothly); pitching action heading into seas; directional stability (course-keeping) traveling with the seas. A test for directional stability is to give the free-floating model a straight shove ahead; if it coasts to a stop with little or no change in direction it may be presumed to be directionally stable.

Sailing craft can also be towed this way, but the towline must be along the line of the resultant wind force (see figure 8-9). Towing is done by a bridle hooked to a frame on the model. By adjusting the positions of the hooks and the lengths of the arms of the bridle, it is possible to tow the model on all points of sailing.

The results of this type of testing are entirely qualitative, and even in that mode the validity is somewhat problematical. Although the usefulness of these crude tests should not be overestimated, in towing a trawler model we were able to ascertain with good conviction that the stern had too much "hook" in the buttocks, causing the model to trim by the head and have a hard pitching motion at cruising speed.

The inventive reader may wish to have quantitative test results. This can be done by towing two models from a yoke. The model with the greatest resistance will pull its side of the yoke back. I have towed two powerboat models this way, revealing very clearly the relative characteristics of the two which were later confirmed by the full-size performance. With more complex gear, this comparative testing should also be possible with sailing craft.

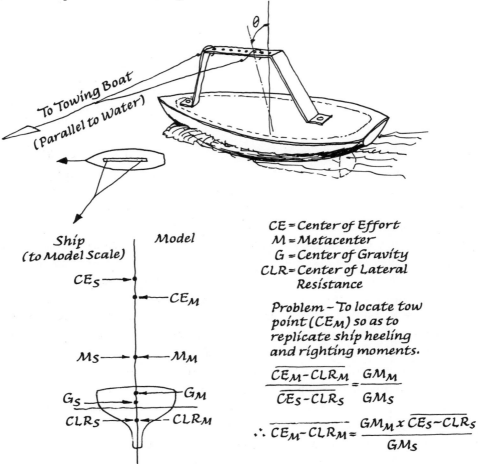

CE = Center of Effort
M = Metacenter
G = Center of Gravity
CLR = Center of Lateral
      Resistance

Problem – To locate tow
point (CE_M) so as to
replicate ship heeling
and righting moments.

$$\frac{\overline{CE_M - CLR_M}}{\overline{CE_S - CLR_S}} = \frac{GM_M}{GM_S}$$

$$\therefore \overline{CE_M - CLR_M} \approx \frac{GM_M \times \overline{CE_S - CLR_S}}{GM_S}$$

Fig. 8-9. Towing a sailing craft model along the line of resultant wind force,
and method of adjusting for model stability in setting towing point

This chapter is intended to acquaint you with the entire design process so that you can see where you fit into it. It also gives some general hints on what should be included in your part of the design; additional aids will be given in succeeding chapters.

9. A Vessel's Function

> Plan for reality, not dreams.
> —JBH

EVERY boat or vessel is designed and built to fulfill a function. The function may be satisfying a yacht owner's desire for beauty, catching a certain species of fish in a profitable manner, or responding to an industrial need for dredging up sand. Since a vessel, once built, is extremely difficult and costly to revise it is important that the prospective owner have a very clear and well-defined vision of precisely what the vessel is to do for him. Therefore, the first and most important task in vessel design is for the owner to concisely define that function. In doing so he must be tough and critical in analyzing and verbalizing his motives:

1. Am I really going to sail around the world, including a beat around Cape Horn? Or in reality won't my sailing be restricted pretty much to coastal runs and gunkholing? If the latter, I surely will be unhappy with a short ketch rig, heavy dogged hatches, all chain ground tackle, and the other appurtenances of the hard case ocean cruiser. And my wife will be even more unhappy.

2. Will my routes support a container vessel, or should it be a roll-on/roll-off vessel, or even a break-bulk? Can I rebuild one of my other vessels, or should it be new-built?

3. Do I really want to give my kidneys real problems pounding around the ocean at 50 knots? Or won't most of my boating actually consist of taking crowds of kids and parents deep-sea fishing plus an occasional cruise? Wouldn't I really be better off with a good sea boat capable of a top speed of 15 to 20 knots and a very comfortable cruising speed of 10 knots?

4. Just because Joe got himself a 70′ (21.5 m) dragger, is that any reason for me to upstage him with a 75-footer (23 m)? Perhaps a rigorous analysis of my fishing strategy and finances will reveal I could do better with a 65-footer (20 m) or an 85-footer (26 m).

A good way to begin analyzing your vessel needs is to write down what the proposed vessel is supposed to do. Bringing the mental image of the vessel at work out into the open in this fashion allows you to refine your views in a simple but concise way. The effort to be precise in drawing up this statement of intention often reveals considerations that had not been adequately dealt with in the mental image.

The statement should at least include: (1) a clear definition of how and where the vessel is to be used; (2) physical and functional measures of the vessel's accommodations (how many passengers and crew?), speed and power capability, cargo/fishhold capacity, and other needs that will affect the size of the vessel; (3) the amount of money available to spend on the vessel, including a 15% to 20% cushion for contingencies.

Whether the vessel is for pleasure, commercial, or institutional use, it is possible to learn a great deal by making an informal model of its operations. (The computer aficionado can program such a model for his computer but this is by no means necessary.) Such an evaluation process for fishing vessels was described in *National Fisherman Yearbook 1983* and is reprinted here in appendix IV. The same approach can be tailored to any other type of vessel. The modeling process described here is a rational one. But do not discard your subjective internal feelings about the vessel. These are often more accurately aimed at a satisfactory result than is coldly analytical reasoning. So add your instincts in sensibly balanced proportions into this mix.

Completion of the statement of intentions is a good time for introducing the concept to the others who will be involved in its use. The wife and children of the yacht owner, the captain and crew of the commercial vessel, the managers and financial sources of all types, can often provide valuable input and their early inclusion forestalls backtracking later on.

These initial planning steps can be fascinating in their own right, and will lead very logically to the envelope sketch phase of your sketch design.

Following are general comments that may help in answering the question, "What do I *really* want in my vessel?"

Pleasure craft: The function of this type of craft is to give pleasure to those who use it. For one person "pleasure" can be a frigid thrash to windward in a half gale, for another to be sprawled in the tropic sun surrounded by a bevy of compliant scantily clad beauties. Unless you are a loner, whatever your taste, be sure you are not alone in it or you will *be* alone.

It is not difficult to determine major requirements such as the number of berths required, other details of interior arrangement, type of rig or power plant. But there are less obvious aspects which, if not properly considered, can diminish the pleasure one takes in the boat.

Access, for instance, should be a major concern in terms of both convenience and safety. It is highly desirable to have two access routes to the deck from each major compartment. From the pilothouse there should be doors directly out to the deck on both sides. In smaller craft the engine compartment should be accessible when the boat is under way without the need for shifting heavy hatches or furniture about the boat; hatches should be in small easily handled sections and hinged to avoid the hazards of moving a heavy awkward object around on a rolling vessel.

A cardinal rule for any boat is that every spot in the boat should be readily inspectable and at least marginally accessible. "Murphy's Marine Law" states that if anything goes wrong it will happen in the only place in the boat you can neither see into nor reach with tools, so don't allow such a place. Be sure that any large items (tanks, machinery, ice box) can be removed for maintenance or repair without destroying thousands of dollars worth of joinery or structure. And everything that needs to be worked on for maintenance or repair should be within 24″ (.6 m) of the reacher's shoulder; better yet would be 18″ (.45 m) or more of body space surrounding any piece of machinery or equipment that might require servicing.

Ventilation—It is much better to have too much air flowing in and out than not enough; it's easier to close off excess openings than it is to chop a hole through the cabin side to increase air flow. Ventilation should be all-weather, able to function in all but boarding seas. The fact that it is surprisingly difficult to locate adequate ventilating intakes and discharges where they are needed without interfering with people, rigging, or gear, must not deter you from having them. Locate all openings close to a sailing yacht's centerline so they won't contribute to the filling of the vessel in a knockdown.

Ventilating the engine room is a special case. The engine room ventilators should be isolated from the rest of the hull to minimize the possibility of carbon monoxide poisoning, the spread of fire, and the transmission of noise into the living quarters. In *addition* to ventilating the engine compartment itself, there *must* be enough intake air volume to support engine aspiration, perhaps $1/2$ square inch (3.2 square centimeters) of clear opening per total installed horsepower. If not carefully designed, engine room ventilation can be especially vulnerable to flooding.

You won't be concerned with microventilation on your sketches, but when your boat is built be sure that every space, compartment, nook, and cranny on your boat has at least two openings so that there will be a small but constant and important flow of air; you will bless the results—a low-humidity, mildew-free interior. On my 27′ (8.3 m) sloop, well ventilated summer and winter, I kept inexpensive steel tools under the berths for years without a sign of rust.

Safety—Most aspects of safety dealing with fire, foundering, and the safety of those on board are covered by regulations and recommendations from the U.S. Coast Guard, American Boat and Yacht Council, Underwriters Laboratory, National Fire Protection Association, American Bureau of Shipping, and individual insurance companies. The work of these agencies and organizations will be given full consideration by your architect, and need not be covered at this stage of the design. Nevertheless, for the reader's information, some of the publications of these bodies are listed in the Bibliography.

Lifelines should be clearly shown on your sketch design. They should be of adequate height (lifelines less than 22″-24″ [55-60 cm] high will come below the

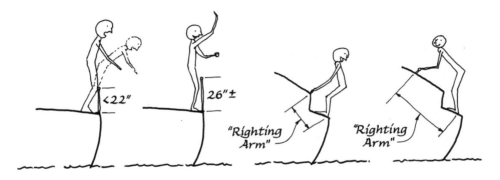

Fig. 9-1. Staying on board—lifelines and handrails

Fig. 9-2. Handrails for going forward

knee and tend to tip a person overboard—see figure 9-1), the higher the better. For ocean sailing, intermediate lines not over 12"-16" (30-40 cm) apart are highly desirable. Bulwarks on working vessels should if possible be 36" (90 cm) high.

Getting forward on many powerboats with deckhouses can be a hazardous occupation even under good conditions, let alone when in the trough of a rolling sea. To facilitate passage forward and aft avoid narrow varnished covering boards. Instead, have a deck of adequate width fitted with a toe rail and a handrail located on the house to give positive support against the frequently severe angular momentum when rolling (see figure 9-2). If the deck is wide enough (it's even worth adding a bit of flare or flam amidships to get adequate width), run lifelines abreast of the deckhouse; as an alternative, sometimes the pulpit can be extended aft at least to the side doors. On a small boat sliding pilothouse doors save space and are more weatherproof, but if a hinged door is used on the side, hinge it on the forward edge or you may find yourself catapulted over the side by the force of the wind catching the door as you open it from the inside.

Commercial craft: The function of commercial craft is to be commercially successful, to make a profit. While any owner or skipper likes to be proud of his vessel as it steams into harbor, esthetic considerations trail far behind the need to be financially successful. Among commercial vessel owners, "Handsome is as handsome does."

Criterion of success—A vessel may be deemed a commercial success when its annual revenue exceeds the annual costs of ownership and operation. With the help of the information given in chapter 13, one can develop a pretty good idea of which vessel characteristics will give the highest profit.

Working vessels are defined as commercial craft used for the performance of work tasks at sea. Included would be fishing vessels, party fishing boats, dredges, lighters, and offshore drilling vessels. Typically the work will require adequate open and enclosed deck space, and task-related machinery and gear. The vessel itself must provide a suitable platform, meeting requirements of size, stability, motion, protection for the crew, powering, trim change, and strength.

A unique requirement of most working vessels is that the crew must be able to carry on their daily life and work on deck and below in extreme weather and sea conditions, because only when the vessel is working is it earning. Therefore, while the first aim of the designer is to satisfy the work-related mechanical requirements, a close second for functional success requires that there must be adequate living conditions for the crew when off watch.

Service vessels include cargo vessels, ferries, cruise vessels, dinner/excursion vessels, crew boats (servicing offshore oil rigs), tugs, and push boats. The aim of these vessels, once they have left port, is to survive until reaching port again. Where passengers are carried, personal safety is a primary concern and a review of U.S. Coast Guard regulations covering passenger craft will have a significant effect on the vessel design. Speed is an important characteristic, efficient speed in the case of cargo carriers and tug/push boats, often high speed for passenger service.

Institutional craft: This category includes government craft (military, patrol, icebreaking, buoy tending, etc.), and semi-publicly owned vessels like research or pilot boats, in fact any vessel not included in the pleasure craft and commercial categories. While these are all working or service craft, their success cannot be measured entirely in economic terms. Nevertheless, to varying degrees the costs of building and operating vessels are important and cannot be ignored.

Because the functions of institutional vessels are so varied, it is difficult to formulate useful guidelines to their design. Think carefully of what the function of the vessel requires for success and incorporate those requirements into the design.

Through all these cogitations and decision making, one must be prepared to compromise, to give a little here in order to gain something there. The success of even the single-minded 12-meter sloops designed for the America's Cup depends upon optimum compromises being made among sail area, stability, displacement, and length. More than perhaps any engineering discipline, naval architecture is in large measure the art of compromising, of synthesizing a vast number of competing design elements into a whole that does the best possible job.

10. Esthetics and Delight

ESTHETICS is defined as "of or pertaining to the beautiful as distinguished from . . . the useful," suggesting that beauty is useless. Yet if it were useless would our civilizations place such value on it? We are learning that beauty does indeed have a positive effect upon what we do and the enthusiasm with which we do it. A completely functional and cold workroom can be improved by taking into account light, color, sound, juxtaposition of equipment, etc., in its design, resulting in greater productivity by its inhabitants. A uniform does no more for keeping the body modest and protected from the environment than simple one-color clothing, but the wearer of the uniform (military outfit, doctor's coat, headwaiter's jacket) approaches his tasks with a different attitude than does the drably or haphazardly dressed person.

The effect on us of an esthetically appealing sensory experience is delight, whether it be in a picture, a piece of music, a scene, or a boat. Of course, tastes differ—beauty lies in the eye of the beholder; what delights one will not delight all. So one should approach the esthetics of a boat as a subjective quality, intended first of all to please you, the owner. For some our own pleasure is enough, but for most of us the delight of others is an important ingredient in our pleasure.

Part of the design process is to analyze your own feelings in this context. Do you want a conventional but beautifully executed boat? Do you want a different but attractive craft? Or is function everything to you, so that if it performs, it looks good and hang the viewers? Let the cold light of day in on your innermost feelings in this regard because these feelings will be exposed to the test of public view the first time you sail into your home port.

This chapter will discuss some of the fundamental esthetic considerations that can cause your craft, whether pleasure or commercial, to be a more pleasing and effective vessel. We will start with the exterior.

"Reverse sheer! The middle higher than the ends! On a sailboat? Yecccccch!" This was the reaction after a design of mine for a 30' (9.14 m) light displacement, glued strip sloop was, at the suggestion of Farnham Butler (Mt. Desert Yacht Yard, Mt. Desert, Maine), revised to have a reverse sheer. This boat, *Controversy,* was the first of the Controversy family of sailing craft, the designs of which Farnham and I collaborated on. We were subjected to plenty of abuse for the reverse sheer, good natured but nevertheless heartfelt, from the yachting community which felt we were flying in the face of the gods of sailing.

The very reasonable and practical rule, "form follows function," is too often these days corrupted into "form follows fad." The Controversies (boats of this generic type were designed in lengths from 21' to 41' [6.4 m to 12.5 m]) followed the original version of the dictum, being designed specifically to achieve more space on deck and below. Figure 10-1 shows how the reverse sheer accomplishes this, in

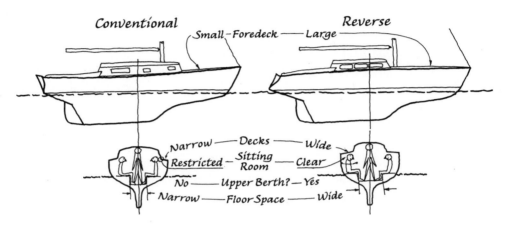

Fig. 10-1. Conventional and reverse sheers

comparison with a conventional hull having the same freeboard at stem and stern as the reverse sheer boat. The *function* part of "form follows function" was working out just fine; but what about the *form* part of it? Although the reverse sheer on sailing yachts was not new—George Owens of Massachusetts Institute of Technology had used it many years before, and it was enjoying some popularity in the United Kingdom—it was obvious that the sheer should have an intrinsic flow and grace even if, in this land of the Friendship sloop, the curves were perceived as going the wrong way.

Charles G. Davis, in *The ABC of Yacht Design,* stressed that the sheer curves in both plan and profile should be similar, as in figure 10-2. If this is carried to its logical extreme, then each curve is a direct function of the other. Pictured another way, if a half-model is made of a boat with a sheer laid out according to this principle and laid upside down on a flat surface, then the deck line from stem to transom should everywhere touch the surface.

Ted Earl, of the Mt. Desert Yacht Yard, translated this principle into a drawing procedure by establishing a plane (the flat surface on which the model was laid) in which all points of the sheer lay. When this plane intersection method of sheer layout was applied to the Controversy design, it resulted in a sheer line which, once its upside-downness had been accepted, was attractive from every point of view—from above or below, from abeam or from a quarter.

The proof of the "form/function reverse sheer" pudding came when a prominent young yachtsman of the day sailed one of the Controversies for a week. He said later that as he rowed out to the boat, he really wondered whether he wanted to be seen in such a thing. Rowing ashore a week later, after he and his family had tasted the benefits of the reverse sheer, he didn't think it looked too bad! So here was an instance where esthetic concerns were satisfied because the form followed a very practical function, even though traditional esthetic instincts led to an initial opinion

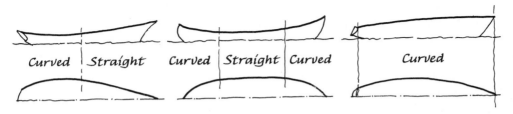

Fig. 10-2. Compatibility of sheer curve in profile and plan views

that the design was objectionable. Speaking of the Controversies, it is of interest that a slightly forward-raking transom, which is the only type that seems to fit the reverse sheer, has some practical uses. A couple of wide guards on it provide steps for convenient access to the boat from a dinghy. These guards have handholes cut in them which can be used by someone who is overboard for getting back aboard; it is amazing how difficult it is to board a boat from the water without such an assist even if there is only a foot or so of freeboard. Also with the forward-raking transom, we discovered that when towing a dinghy, the way to make it a perfect lady if a rolling following sea causes it to behave badly is to bring its forefoot up on the lower guard so that only the stern is in the water; this has been discovered by fishing motherships towing a brood, and by tuna seiners and their net boats.

The case of the controversial reverse sheer is reported here to illustrate that virtually anything is possible, but that there can be a good way of doing something different and a bad way. Let us remember that the traditional sheer lines we grew up to admire were conceived not for their beauty, but for their function. Early fishing vessels were low amidships to ease the work of hoisting dories and gear aboard by hand, while the ends were high to keep off boarding seas. On the other hand, Horatio Hornblower's frigates and ships of the line were built with nearly straight sheers so that the lower tiers of guns amidships were as high as possible out of the sea. So when you see a containership, supertanker, car carrier, or fishing factory ship, think of why they are flat-sheered and boxy and observe them from that point of view. You will be missing much of interest and pleasure if you ignore something that floats merely because it doesn't look like a Friendship sloop. Conversely, of course, don't waste your time running after that insubstantial "form follows fad" will o' the wisp.

The title of this chapter is "Esthetics and Delight," but you have no doubt noticed that it follows the chapter on "Function." This order is for a good reason—one should design a craft to perform a function and then make it esthetically appealing, rather than the other way around. But if, after function has been taken care of, it is possible to maximize the appearance, the following suggestions may help:

1. When sketching a boat or vessel, keep in mind that the shape of the sheer line in profile is by far the most important visual determinant of appearance. It should be a smooth even curve, avoiding bumps and straight places.

2. When sketching the sheer in profile, relate it to the plan view as illustrated in figure 10-2. If, for instance, the latter is straight amidships and curved at the ends, like a Dutch botter, the profile should be fairly straight amidships, curving up boldly at the ends. A Friendship sloop in plan view is nearly straight for the forward quarter or so then sweeps around in almost an arc to the transom; the sheer in profile should do the same thing.

3. Before you give up a design as having too much freeboard for esthetic satisfaction, try adding to it a fairly wide boot topping and a contrasting sheer stripe. A guardrail defining the lower edge of the latter is a great functional help if you lie alongside pilings or large vessels.

4. If the house or trunk seems too high, try accentuating the windows with shading as they would appear in life. Care in picking color and density of deckhouses and cabin trunks can also improve appearance. Using a light-colored paint on cabin tops will help reduce the apparent height of cabin trunks.

5. After the sketch is the way you want it, get a new look by hanging it on the wall and looking at it from several feet away. If possible have a print of it made backwards; it's surprising how different a boat looks heading to the left when you are accustomed to seeing it heading right.

6. Above all don't be afraid to experiment. Try a number of variations and select the one that pleases you most. See how other designers have handled similar instances.

7. As a last and best step, I encourage you to build a half-model of the boat you have sketched (see figure 10-3). It doesn't need to be a large model or a complex one. Some people enjoy tinkering with a full model, complete with deck structures, rig, steering wheel, etc. Others, including myself, prefer to use the model as a design tool, in which case a half-model will give a very good idea of the appearance of the vessel from all angles. The half-model can become a full model if mounted on a reflective surface. A model has the additional use of helping you visualize the flow

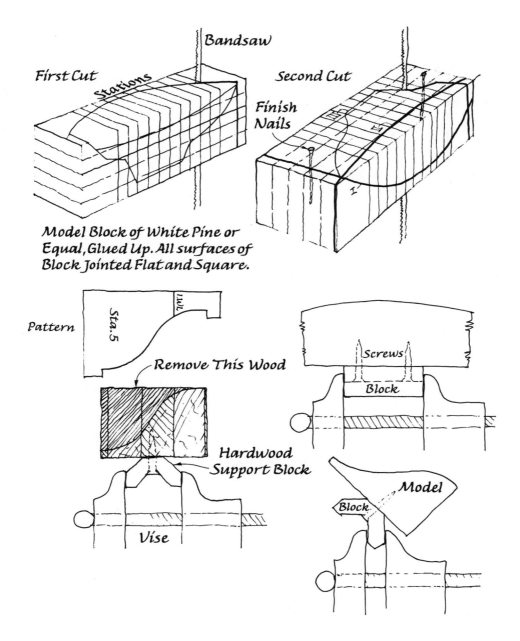

Fig. 10-3. Building a half-model

of water around the hull. Most models are built of wood glued up in lifts, but an attractive and useful model can be made of cardboard.

Painting schemes can do much to improve the appearance of a vessel, and at small cost. Look at a boat which you admire and try to picture it all one color; I cannot imagine any instance in which the appearance of a boat or ship would be improved by being a single color. So use contrasting colors (and don't forget the effectiveness of shadow lines caused by rub rails, etc.) to accentuate the sheer line and to reduce apparent freeboard and height of cabin trunks. Do this with restraint, though, to avoid a World War I camouflage vessel appearance.

Esthetics is at least as important inside as outside. After a hard day's work—whether sailing a brisk race or manhandling heavy otter trawls—the accommodations to which the crew retires should be pleasing and restful as well as utilitarian. In addition to the selection of textures, patterns, and colors, the layout itself should not be claustrophobic or cluttered.

Lighting on deck and below often seems to be an afterthought, or the fixtures are located where they will fit, not where they are needed. *All* lighting should be nonglare; a light source shining directly into a worker's eyes should never be accepted. Lighting can be classed as regional, by which areas are illuminated for passing through or for simple tasks, and directed, when the illumination is concentrated directly on the work area but without shadow or glare.

Another esthetic no-no is noise, defined as unproductive and unattractive sound. The difference between working all day with an unmuffled dry exhaust banging away a couple of feet from your ears and working all day with a well-muffled exhaust separated from you by several feet is improved efficiency and satisfaction with the work. Noise can be *reflected* from surfaces and *transmitted* through structures; each mode must be coped with by different means. Reflected sound generated within the space you are occupying is carried by oscillating waves in the air, and is easily coped with by covering the reflecting surfaces—bulkheads, floors, overheads—with an absorbent material such as acoustical tile, carpeting, or wall hangings. Transmitted sound is generated outside your compartment, and is transmitted through the air or through vibrations of the surrounding structure itself. Generally the best way to halt its passage through a surface is to add mass to the vibrating surface, that is, make it heavier and thus less subject to the sound waves that set up the vibrations. Once transmitted sound escapes into a compartment, it becomes reflected sound and can be coped with as above.

The old saw that "beauty is in the eye of the beholder" is very true. I see many boats that I don't find pleasing, and very few to which I would give high marks on appearance. But virtually every one of these vessels is the apple of someone's eye. It is going to be your vessel and it is your eye of which it is going to be the apple, so let your naval architect know quite clearly what your views on esthetics are. Don't hesitate to let him know if his sketches and conceptions miss the esthetic mark.

11. Construction

FIFTY years ago in the 1930s, when I started being a naval architect, there was really only one building material to consider for small craft—wood. There was a choice in the framing (to steam bend the frames or saw them to shape) and a choice between galvanized and bronze fastenings. Planking invariably was either carvel or lapstrake, and, because there was no suitable marine plywood, decks were laid and covered with canvas if of light scantlings, otherwise caulked, and bulkheads and other flat surfaces were generally built up of tongue and groove stock. In fact, I remember being very depressed at one time at the thought that there would be no need for yacht designers in the future; there would be nothing new since everything had already been invented and perfected.

Well, little did I know! In the past 40 years there has been a veritable explosion of basic building materials, each with its own subtle variations. The exploitation of the properties of these materials has brought naval architecture to a state of high technology and has permitted mass production of small boats in the hundreds of units. (In the thirties a run of 20 identical boats was a major event.) A myriad of design decisions and selections must be made in wending through this bramble patch of building materials and methods.

Fortunately the sketch designer does not need to get into the bewildering complexities of detail designing for a specific material. Your naval architect will handle that aspect of things. But it will be up to you to select the basic construction material of which your boat is to be built, and this decision should be made early in the design process.

Following are several charts and comparisons of the various materials available for your craft. But there are some general comments that should come first.

1. As a general rule, it can be assumed there is not a great difference in building cost among the various materials for boats of the same quality and function. Picking the material you favor most strongly for your boat should not affect the total building cost more than about 15%, other things being equal. By and large, selection of the building material can be made independent of the cost factor, remembering that in comparing materials it is not fair to compare a high performance racing craft full of exotic construction and design features with a comfortable cruising boat.

2. Virtually all basic materials and methods can, if properly used, build strong, good boats. But any of them can fail if poorly engineered or built.

3. A one-off boat is not necessarily more expensive than an equivalent stock boat. Although the production cost of a stock boat will be less, overhead and profit tend to be higher in production yards, and there must also be a sales commission built into the selling price of the product. So before giving up the idea of sketch-designing your own unique boat, inquire about costs of comparable custom-built craft; you might be pleasantly surprised.

4. Keep in mind that stock boat designs are nonspecific, aimed at having the maximum appeal for the maximum number of people; therefore, a discriminating person's personal preferences are often not adequately addressed. This can be especially so in commercial craft. If you are seriously reading this book you have probably already found this out from practical experience.

There is an intermediate step you may choose if you particularly want a stock building material; buy a stock hull and finish it out to suit your own wishes. Most of this book is applicable to sketching the completion of a "store-boughten" hull, and should help you select the right one for your purposes. Sketch your ideal boat, *then* go looking for the hull that fits.

5. Two construction materials will likely be used regardless of the basic material: plywood and aluminum (read also carbon fiber) spars. Where exposed to the weather, plywood should be marine grade, otherwise *good* exterior grade is generally satisfactory. The imported plywood seems to be of a much better quality than the run-of-the-mill domestic varieties. As for aluminum spars, despite the fairly recent advent of laminated spars, aluminum remains far and away the material of choice. Unless you have a truly fanatical yearning for wood masts, stick with aluminum spars on sailboats. In commercial craft, the traditional steel spars, booms, and gallows would often, in my experience, be much better made out of aluminum. Welded aluminum rigs weigh about half as much as the equivalent steel spars, and will last as long as the vessel without loss of strength from rusting, yet require no maintenance.

6. In selecting the basic material, bear in mind the probable need for maintenance and repair in the future. Accordingly, select a material that is compatible with the area in which the boat will be used. This is generally not a problem in the United States, but could be anywhere else. On a world cruise, for instance, wood or steel would be indicated; these materials, and the skills to use them, are found nearly everywhere. If a more exotic material is selected for the world-girdler, the skipper should plan on taking along a supply of repair materials and tools.

7. The building material should be selected early because displacement, and frequently stability, of the vessel are tied directly to the choice of material. If a light displacement boat is desired, use aluminum, glued strip, molded plywood, or cored fiberglass; other materials will generally result in normal or heavy displacement craft. This relationship of material to displacement is especially important in multi-

hulls; the large area of plating exposed to wind, weather, and waves calls for a strong material with a low weight per square foot.

8. The choice of material can also influence the internal volume of the hull. A sawn-frame wooden vessel should have a cubic number 10% to 15% greater than a wood bent frame, aluminum, or steel vessel to give the same internal volume, and a glued strip, molded plywood, fiberglass, or ferro-cement vessel perhaps an 8% to 10% smaller cubic number.

9. Steel, aluminum, plywood, and other sheet materials share the drawback of being easily bendable in only one dimension, simple curvature. To understand this, take an index card and bend it in various directions. It does this very easily. Now try to fold it into a boat shape—it can't be done. In other words a flat sheet can't be bent into a compound curvature without softening it by heating, stretching, and/or shrinking portions of it (draw a grid on the card, soak it and form it over a three-dimensional figure like a lamp base, and see how the grid is distorted), or by cutting triangular gores around the edges.

10. Don't be afraid to mix materials if they are compatible. Joel White (a fine boatbuilder whose Brooklin Boat Yard is located on Center Harbor, Maine) persuaded me to try fiberglass centerboard trunks, molded in one piece and flanged under the wood keel, and I have never looked back. On the other hand, combining incompatible materials can cause structural trouble. A rigid welded steel web frame at the mast in a relatively flexible fiberglass hull will likely be disastrous, with the hull as it flexes trying to tear itself away from the rigid steel structure.

Now some specifics of the many construction material choices available to you. There will be a general discussion of each class of materials, with sufficient information to allow a reasonably educated assessment of them. There will also be a chart to relate the materials to each other as to desirability. The selection of the basic building material is one of the most important in the design process; make it carefully.

Table 11-1 gives a general review as to how size affects the selection of a material. The chart is made up to suit U.S. practices and standards, and may vary considerably in another country where the labor and material situations may be quite different. Materials should not be used at all for "poor" sizes except experimentally; "fair" materials can be used with care and if extra cost and perhaps lessened performance are acceptable; "good" and "very good" materials are all right to use, with a slight advantage in cost, strength, etc., accruing to very good.

Wood: Wood remains one of the best building materials for small and medium-size boats, up to about 100' (30 m) or more (in 1987 the U.S. Navy began building a series of fine, nonmagnetic minesweepers of wood, 224' (68.5 m) LOA, 1,250 tons displacement). It has good strength-to-weight characteristics, comes in a wide variety of species and forms, is naturally buoyant, and affords excellent heat and fair sound insulation. Modern adhesives and sealers, if intelligently used, allow the combination of relatively small pieces into timbers of any size and physical properties. Wooden craft can be completely modern in every sense.

Table 11-1
Suitability of Construction Materials versus Vessel Size

Length Overall						Ferro-
Feet	Meters	Steel	Wood	Aluminum	FRP	cement
10-20	(3-6)	P	G	VG	VG	P
20-30	(6-9)	P	VG	VG	VG	F
30-40	(9-12)	F	VG	VG	VG	G
40-60	(12-18)	F	VG	VG	VG	VG
60-80	(18-25)	G	VG	VG	G	VG
80-100	(25-31)	VG	VG	G	G	G
100-125	(31-38)	VG	G	G	F	F
125-150	(38-46)	VG	G	G	F	P
150-up	(46-up)	VG	F	F	P	P

P = poor   F = fair   G = good   VG = very good

A case in point: In 1966 I designed 30′ (9.14 m) pulling boats for Hurricane Island Outward Bound (Rockland, Maine) for glued strip cedar construction, with an extra layer of mahogany from the keel to above the waterline for strength and resistance to abrasion when hauled up a beach. These boats are used for extended bay and ocean camping trips with 12 to 14 persons aboard, and all the original boats are still in excellent condition. Periodically, we have explored the possibility of building them in another material, either aluminum or fiberglass (FRP). Each time we return to the wood construction on the basis of performance and cost.

The world over a vast number of boats are built of wood. Although global supplies of timber are shrinking, the relatively high quality timber required for boat construction is usually readily available. Wood boats can be manufactured using relatively simple equipment (90′ [27.5 m] Indonesian cargo ketches are built with axe, adze, plane, chisels, hammer, small saws and pit saws); the skills required are traditional; and a well-built wooden craft will last a long while with reasonable care. Maldive fishing dhonis, built largely of coconut timber, last 25 to 40 years, and many working craft in other parts of the world can boast of being 75 to 100 or more years old. Jacques Cousteau's *Calypso* was built in 1942 as a U.S. Navy minesweeper, and has just had a complete refit (to serve for how many more years?).

Wooden boats are not as archaic as one would think. Wooden yachts are actually coming into increased demand, and many fishing vessels are being built of timber in the United Kingdom and Ireland as well as in other parts of the world. Two modern 85′ freezer shrimp trawlers of my company's design are now building in India. So using the best techniques of wood construction can produce a modern pleasure or work craft with a long and economical life.

A modern wood boatyard could be distinguished from a traditional one by having a gluing facility, and by having no timber stock on hand thicker than 2″ or so. All large pieces required (deadwood, keel, stem, etc.) will be glued up, and all curved pieces will be laminated. This approach is much less expensive than traveling miles searching out large pieces of timber, which will then require a large crew to mill and handle them. Most important, the quality of the final product will be much improved.

For studying wood construction, *Wood: A Manual For Its Use as a Shipbuilding Material* is a must. It can be supplemented by Howard Chapelle's *Boat Building,* or Robert Steward's *Boatbuilding Manual.* There is also *The Gougeon Brothers on Boat Construction* treating molded hull construction, and my own description of glued strip construction, as originally published in *Yachting,* August 1954, and presented as a paper at a Conference of Wood Construction in Copenhagen, Denmark.

Following are descriptions of common methods of building wooden boats (see figure 11-1):

Plank on frame—This is the traditional method of building wooden boats. Starting with a keel in place, with the vertical structure at the bow (the stem) and stern erected, steamed frames or ribs are bent in place perpendicular to the keel at regular spacing. Longitudinal planks, widest amidships and tapering to the ends so that the seams run in fair sweeping curves compatible with the sheer line, are secured to the frames with nails, screws, or rivets. At the sheer a strong longitudinal member, called the sheer clamp or clamp and shelf, runs from bow to stern. The frames are bolted to it as are the deck beams, transverse members spaced about the same as the frames and curved upwards slightly to "crown" the deck so that no water will stand. The decking is of narrow strips of wood about the same thickness as the planking, run fore and aft, and fastened to the deck beams with nails or screws. The seams in the planking and deck are caulked with twisted cotton or cotton and oakum (hemp fibers), and payed with a puttylike compound to render them watertight.

In variations to this type of construction, bent frames can be single pieces or doubled or split to render bending easier, or made up of several laminations glued together. The latter is the best and most expensive; the 224' (68.5 m) nonmagnetic minesweepers building for the U.S. Navy have laminated frames. On large craft frames are most often sawn to shape; sometimes two complete frames are bolted together with joints staggered (double sawn frames), sometimes a single frame only has short butt pieces spanning the joints (single sawn frames).

The most common type of planking is carvel, which is smooth and caulked as described above; the second most common is clinker (lapstrake) in which the planks overlap like clapboards (sometimes erroneously called "shiplap," in which planks are flush, halved onto each other along the seams), riveted together along the laps and to the frames. Clinker construction can be lighter than carvel and in a power-boat the projecting laps act like many spray strips, but with age the rivets work loose and are difficult if not impossible to retighten. Carvel planking can also be double or triple, in which two or three layers of planks are installed with their seams parallel but staggered; a fabric diaphragm is set in glue or compound between the layers. Other forms of planking are: marine plywood sheets (only on V-bottom hulls), glued strip, or molded up of several layers of veneer (see below for details on the last two).

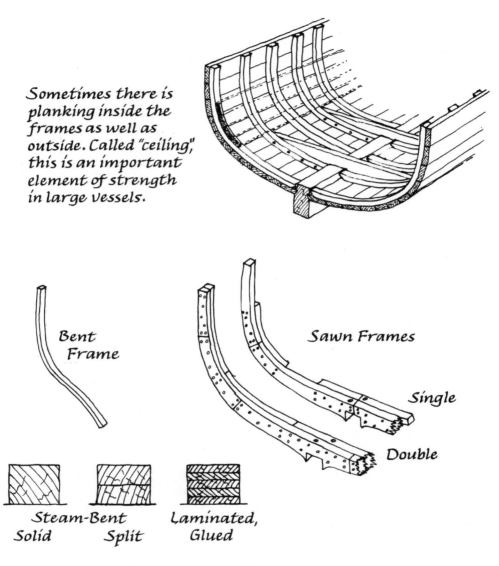

Sometimes there is planking inside the frames as well as outside. Called "ceiling", this is an important element of strength in large vessels.

Bent Frame

Sawn Frames

Single

Double

Steam-Bent Solid   Split   Laminated, Glued

Fig. 11-1. Methods of framing wood vessels

Decks are now generally of waterproof plywood, preferably glued as well as nailed/screwed to the deck beams, and sheathed with fiberglass-reinforced epoxy or polyester resin (FRP). Over the FRP may be laid a deck of teak strips glued down or well bedded and screwed or, on commercial craft, rough wood or other protection. On large craft, laid and caulked decks are still used, but are prone to leaks, and do not provide as much strength and stiffness to the hull as would plywood decks.

Unit hulls—Wood can also be used very advantageously in building unit (monocoque) hulls, that is, hulls in one piece from sheer to sheer. This type of hull depends for much of its strength on the one-piece skin, with framing installed only as necessary to supplement bulkheads, joiner work, etc., in providing strength at points of maximum stress. Being in one piece, with very little framing, the hull is light in weight and has no seams that can leak; building cost and the cost of maintaining the hull in good condition is considerably reduced.

Glued strip planking is a method I have used since 1948. Strip planking is not new, said to have been used by the Egyptians thousands of years ago, and used periodically since then. A century ago the Hampton boats of Casco Bay in Maine were built using strip planking with white lead putty in the seams, and this is the building method of choice for lobster boats on the Northumberland Strait of New Brunswick, Canada.

Following World War II, Ralph Wiley of Oxford, Maryland, used newly developed resorcinol glue to build a number of boats with glued strip planking. Following his lead, I began using it myself. It is a method that uses inexpensive materials, is easy for both professional and amateur builder, and results in a lightweight, strong, long-lived hull. It can be combined with other materials to afford the designer great flexibility in structural design.

Glued strip construction utilizes square strips of wood (cedar is preferred because it glues and fastens well, resists decay, is light in weight, and swells and shrinks very little with changes in moisture content), glued and edge-nailed together to the shape of the hull. The backbone is fairly light and is best laminated. Once the planking is completed, the interior joinery, and such supplementary framing as the designer calls for, can be installed. I still prefer straight resorcinol glue for this purpose.

Variations include double planking, with an outer layer of mahogany strips glued and nailed to the cedar base (a good idea for boats over 45' [14 m] or so); laying up one or two layers of veneer on one or both sides of the cedar base; or sheathing the exterior with epoxy resin reinforced with an elastic fabric such as Vectra (a good idea for extended stays in wormy seas).

Strip planking is to my own knowledge used extensively in Indonesia and the Republic of Maldives for building craft from 12' to 100' (3.5 to 30.5 m) in length. The planking is thicker than normal, and the planks are fastened to each other and to the rather light framing with trunnels (treenails, wooden dowels). Laid in the seams between planks are thin shavings of the lining of coconut shells, which swell in the water to provide watertightness.

Molded plywood (veneer) has been in use since World War II for building boats and airplanes (Mosquito bombers). The hull is built by laying up several layers of veneer over a form, the layers being glued together with an adhesive such as epoxy resin or resorcinol glue. Pressure to ensure continuous contact between the plies can be obtained by nonferrous staples, a vacuum bag (fastened around the perimeter and with the air pumped out of it so that the ambient air pressure forces the plies into contact), or by bagging the hull and inserting it in an autoclave that not only provides pressure but heats the assembly to facilitate the cure of the adhesive.

The designer can apply the same selection method for additional framing and reinforcing to a molded hull as used in the glued strip hull. For maintaining the smoothness of the hull and protecting it, the hull can be covered with fiberglass in epoxy or polyester resin.

(The West System is a method of building hulls from veneer and/or strips developed by the Gougeon brothers. The system refers to a family of materials and tools developed by the Gougeon brothers for making boatbuilding as simple as possible and the boats as strong as possible.)

This cataloging of wood construction methods reveals some of the flexibility and versatility of the material. By taking advantage of modern methods of manufacturing, fastening, sealing, and preserving, wood need defer little to any of the other materials common in boatbuilding and shipbuilding. It may also be just the material that will give you the greatest pleasure and satisfaction in your future boat.

Fiberglass-reinforced plastic: There is no denying the preeminent place of reinforced plastics (called FRP in the United States and GRP in the United Kingdom) in the boatbuilding field. Because it lends itself best of all materials to quantity production (molds for building parts are very expensive but the parts made in them can be produced quickly and cheaply), it has permitted the formation of boatbuilding companies that are large by pre-World War II standards. A customer of this automotive-type industry is more apt to be *sold* a boat because the company is offering it than he is to *buy* a boat because it fulfills his need quite precisely. This is not to say that the average fiberglass boat is not a good boat but that it lacks the personal individuality that has characterized a fully satisfactory watercraft since early men argued whether a long thin log was better than a short fat one. The need for individualism has apparently been recognized because more and more systems for building one-off fiberglass boats are being developed.

Fiberglass-reinforced plastic is an engineerable material; failure to meet performance standards usually stems from inadequate design and poor quality control during production. A wide range of component materials are available for selection when engineering the construction of a hull or other component, so that virtually every requirement can be met in some way. But there are variables in the construction process itself that make the finished product not quite as predictable in performance as something constructed in metal.

The rationale underlying FRP construction is that glass fibers are extremely strong—about 300,000 lb per in^2 (21,240 kg per cm^2) tensile strength as compared with 60,000 to 70,000 psi (4,250 to 5,000 kg per cm^2) for structural steel. This strength is harnessed by encapsulating the fibers in a plastic resin, typically polyester for large objects like boats. Looked at another way, a boat hull is a casting of resin reinforced by glass fibers. The glass fibers come in several formulations and a number of weaves, which are combined in the design to provide the desired characteristics to the finished product at minimum cost.

A major element in *any* FRP boat is coring, in which a stiff or lightweight material such as plywood, expanded plastic, or balsa wood is molded in the middle of the glass structure. The amount of coring can range from plywood pads at locations where fittings will be bolted on to almost the complete boat being cored with foam. It is generally accepted that a solid FRP boat, with pads only as necessary to resist bolting compression, is the strongest construction, but also the heaviest. A hull extensively cored is lighter in weight but more subject to damage and to delamination. Probably the cost difference is small between boats of equal cubic number built by the two methods.

FRP construction is most suitable for quantity production. The basic materials are not expensive, and the labor required to build a hull is minute compared with other methods. The problem is that to build a large number of identical hulls requires a mold that is built, usually of fiberglass, over a male plug built of wood to the shape of the hull. Another mold is required for the deck assembly, and often large units of the interior are molded. The cost of the plug and mold is high—about $140,000 for a 44′ (13.4 m) hull (1985)—and must be distributed over the number of boats built from it.

In recent years, though, several processes have been developed to make one-off construction of FRP hulls economically feasible, so it is practical to have your own sketch design built in FRP. However, one may expect a higher cost than for a stock boat. Many small boat yards are doing very well finishing up stock hulls built by large producers; the sketch designer might consider either of two approaches to taking advantage of such an arrangement: (1) designing his ideal boat and then finding the most suitable hull or (2) selecting his hull and sketch designing the rest of it. The general principles of preliminary design outlined in this book apply in either instance.

From the standpoint of the sketch design, once FRP has been selected as the basic material there is really only one decision that needs to be made—whether it should be solid FRP or cored FRP. There can be many high tech ramifications to this decision but it is not necessary to go into them here. For some insight into FRP construction and what it offers, *Fiber Glass Boats* by John Roberts will introduce you to the subject.

Steel: Next to wood, ferrous metals have been the material of choice for shipbuilding, and, for general use in large sizes of 150′ (45 m) LOA or more, the only practical one. The first ferrous vessels were of riveted wrought iron construction. Wrought iron is a fibrous, soft, malleable iron, not very strong but tough and highly resistant to corrosion. Working vessels of wrought iron over 100 years old are not unusual. Because it is not possible to arc-weld wrought iron satisfactorily, the market for it has about disappeared, and it is now very difficult to find in sheet form.

The development of steel, a refined, granular form of iron, revolutionized the shipbuilding industry. Steel is available in large sheets of closely controlled thickness in a wide variety of alloys to meet almost any requirements, and it is readily arc-welded. Nearly all ships over 100' (30 m) LOA are built of steel, notable exceptions being nonmagnetic minesweepers in the 200' (60 m) range being built of timber in this country and fiberglass in Britain.

Steel has one drawback—it is subject to thinning through oxidation (rusting), or through galvanic corrosion, the loss of material due to electrical currents in an electrolyte such as seawater. For this reason when figuring the scantlings for a steel vessel, a corrosion allowance is added to the plating so that after the vessel has lived out its life expectancy, there is still sufficient steel left for structural strength despite the expected corrosion (see figure 11-2). On

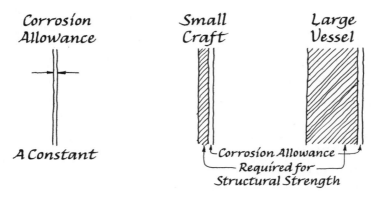

Fig. 11-2. Effect of corrosion allowance on steel plating thickness

a large vessel with thick plating, the corrosion allowance is a very small proportion of the total plating thickness, but on a small vessel it is a large proportion and so adds "useless" weight to the displacement.

Because of this readiness to rust and corrode, steel requires constant attention to maintain its appearance and its structural integrity, at a level increasing over the years. By comparison, wooden and FRP craft can be subject to indifferent attention for appreciable periods without suffering severe damage. I inspected a fleet of shrimp trawlers in a South American country, about half of wood and half of steel construction. All were about the same age (7 to 8 years) and quality of construction, and about half the fleet had been laid up for varying periods due to lack of spare parts. The steel vessels were in a more advanced level of deterioration than the wooden vessels, and were much less suitable for rehabilitation.

Nevertheless, because of its strength, ready availability, and low cost, steel is by far the most popular material for commercial craft over about 60' LOA, and, if the hull is suitably coated, protected from corrosion, and well maintained, should give approximately 20 years of reasonably trouble-free performance before major repair or rebuilding is required. Money spent on what seems like an expensive finishing system for the steel surfaces when the vessel is built, and on touch-ups thereafter as necessary, is probably money well spent.

A decision to be made fairly early in the design of a steel vessel is whether the hull should have round bilges, or single or double chines. Because of the difficulty and expense of building smaller steel vessels with compound curvature in the hulls, they are usually of single or double chine construction. (see figure 11-3). A shipbuilder once told me that for each ton of steel a round bottom hull required 160 man/hours to build, a double chine 150 man/hours, and the single chine 140

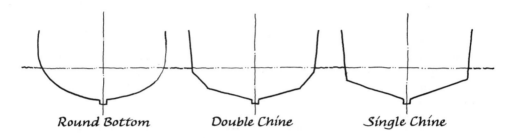

Round Bottom   Double Chine   Single Chine

Fig. 11-3. Steel hull forms (round bottom, double chine, and single chine)

man/hours. The trade-off here is that, for hulls not expected to plane, the round bottom hull is inherently the most efficient (least horsepower required), the single chine the least efficient, and the double chine somewhere between the two. So if long voyages are to be made (or if beauty of hull is important) then the round bottom is worth it, otherwise either of the chine forms will be satisfactory.

Variations—Framing of a steel vessel can be either transverse, with evenly spaced athwartship frames from bow to stern, or longitudinal, with closely spaced stringers (spacing about the same as transverse frame spacing) running fore and aft, supported at intervals by bulkheads or web frames. There is no weight advantage to either system, but there may be a cost advantage; discuss it with your architect.

Aluminum can be used on a steel vessel above the deck if simple steps are followed to avoid corrosion by insulating the aluminum from the steel. At little if any extra cost, the spars, booms, etc., of a fishing vessel can be of aluminum, with a saving of weight, total lack of maintenance, and no concern about weakening the system from rust or corrosion. Aluminum deckhouses share the same advantages.

Recently there has been research on reducing or eliminating hull corrosion and organic fouling by cladding the steel hull plating with copper or by using copper-nickel alloy for the exposed underwater hull members (plating, keel, rudder) to just above the waterline. There has been considerable success along these lines and the prospective owner of a new steel vessel should explore the possibilities, especially if the vessel will be away from shipyards for long periods.

Aluminum: I consider aluminum to be perhaps the best boatbuilding material we now have. It will not corrode (unless dissimilar materials are used with it, thus setting up galvanic currents) or rust; it is lightweight (with a density a third that of steel, aluminum structures seem to weigh about half what a steel structure of similar strength will weigh); aluminum boats can be built in a shop accustomed to building wooden boats with the addition of inert-gas welding equipment and trained welders and, if required, a device for imparting compound curvature to the plates. Aluminum requires a minimum of maintenance (the white powder that forms on unpainted aluminum is an oxide coating that protects the aluminum and should preferably not be removed); aluminum is approved for use with food, so can be used for water (as well as fuel) tanks and for sanitary linings, stanchions, and pen boards of fishholds.

By comparison with iron and steel, aluminum has only recently come into widespread use; most of the wide range of alloys, suitable for virtually every purpose, have been developed since 1940. Even so, a sizable power cruiser built in 1931 of aluminum in England took part in the Dunkirk evacuation and is, so far as I am aware, still going.

In another instance, after about 20 years of use, Geerd Hendel (naval architect of Camden, Maine) gave a thorough precautionary inspection to a 25′ (7.62 m) aluminum sloop he designed in the thirties. While there were no obvious reasons for the examination, he decided on it because the boat was riveted (welding of aluminum was not easily done until the forties) and because the boat was built using the unsophisticated alloys of the day. The examination revealed no structural problems. The only sign of corrosion was on the hull plating adjoining the fir fin keel, perhaps from acids in the wood; although there was still plenty of material remaining, since he already had the keel off an additional plate was welded over the corroded portion before replacing the keel. He also replaced a few rivets that were possibly doubtful.

In a demonstration of the strength of welded aluminum, I was shown a crumpled section of keel cut out of a Stryker powerboat that had dropped onto a keel block when a lifting sling broke. The section was severely distorted, but the metal itself and the welds were completely sound.

Aluminum is stocked in sheets of a wide range of thicknesses and sizes, and a wide range of alloys. Some of the alloys are suitable for welding, some lose their temper (are annealed) when welded. Aluminum is also available in an endless variety of extruded or drawn shapes, from round tubes to very complicated window framing. These can often be used to advantage when building deckhouses and other on-board structures. For the sailboat designer, there is a vast inventory of drawn and extruded aluminum shapes for masts and booms; aluminum spars are lighter and stronger than wood, withstand much rougher treatment, and cost a fraction as much.

As with steel, chine hulls with developed (single curvature) plating are the most economical to build. But unlike steel, which must be heated and rolled to obtain compound curvature, it is quite easy to impart compound curvature to aluminum plates. Two methods are used, both involving cold-working. In one method, a sharp-edged disk is rolled over the surface of the plate under considerable pressure. The groove cut by the disk has the effect of expanding that surface of the plate. If a number of these grooves are cut in different directions in the middle of a plate, the plate will dish somewhat. The other plate-curving method involves two pairs of jaws that grip the metal tightly and then are forced toward each other to shrink the metal or forced apart to expand it. Repeatedly shrink-biting the edge of a plate will cause the plate to dish in the middle to form a compound curvature. Typically, both types of machine are located next to the hull being plated so that the plate can be accurately fitted to the curves of the hull framing by the "cut and try" method.

A drawback to aluminum, although one that can with proper design be avoided, is the volatility of aluminum in conditions of galvanic corrosion. It is a "base" metal, so that it forms the anode from which the current flows to the cathode, and thus loses metal to the more "noble" cathode. The flow of electrons depends upon the electrical potential between the anode and the cathode, and this potential can be high for aluminum in solution with, for instance, copper. Relative area also plays a part in galvanic corrosion. Fastening a copper plate with aluminum screws would be disastrous because molecules of aluminum would be drawn from such a small area relative to the "drawing" areas. However, an unpainted aluminum sheet fastened with copper screws would last a considerable time because there would be so much area of aluminum from which to lose material relative to the area of copper.

Another consideration in using aluminum is that it has virtually no heat-insulating qualities; heat passes very quickly through aluminum, which explains why it is used for cooking utensils. In a boat, this characteristic calls for increased use of heat insulation, not only for personal comfort but also to slow down the transmission of combustion heat from compartment to compartment in case of a fire aboard.

Aluminum offers the boat owner light weight, high resistance to corrosion, low maintenance, and ease of working relative to steel. Since the technology of galvanic corrosion in connection with aluminum is now well understood it no longer need be counted a serious objection to the use of aluminum in boatbuilding.

Building costs in aluminum may run 10% to 25% more than for a comparable craft in steel; aluminum is considerably easier to work than steel, but the material cost per pound is much higher. Also, since aluminum production requires vast amounts of electricity, its cost is sensitive to the costs of electricity. Once built, though, the maintenance and repair costs for the aluminum craft will be much less than for the steel.

Ferro-cement: Ferro-cement, as the name implies, is a combination of cement and steel; the steel provides the tensile strength via an armature or skeleton, on which cement is plastered to provide compressive strength and watertightness. Critical steps in ferro-cement construction include the design of the armature, its erection, holding it in position while plastering it with cement, the selection of the cement "mix," holding the cement to the designed thickness, and curing the cement under proper conditions of time, temperature, and humidity.

(An interesting and apparently successful method of ferro-cement construction has been developed by Michael Iorns of California. A layer of suitable cement is plastered on the inside of a female mold. Into this is pressed one or more layers of expanded metal (like metal plaster lath) and then all is covered with a finish layer of cement. This system replaces the labor of building an armature with the labor and cost involved in building a female mold. Since the mold can be used many times, this method is especially suited for mass production.)

Ferro-cement is not as popular a material as it could be. This may stem from the mistaken idea that building a cement boat is no different from building a funny-shaped sidewalk, and that therefore it is too simple to be any good. But in fact just as much care must be taken in designing and building a boat of ferro-cement as of any other material if only because once cured it is a very intransigent material to work with. While to make a hole, remove or add a major component, or even lengthen the hull or change its shape in most other materials is not a major problem, it is extremely difficult or impossible to carry out these changes with a ferro-cement hull; at best it is nasty, discouraging, dirty work.

One problem that does not seem to have been solved (except by building in a female mold) is getting the exterior of the hull fair and smooth. While unimportant in commercial craft, this can be a factor in the appreciation of a ferro-cement pleasure boat.

The following case histories may be helpful in avoiding the pitfalls of ferro-cement construction, and in making a factual and rational evaluation of the material for your craft.

1. I was called upon to advise on problems with a 40' (12.2 m) ferro-cement sailing yacht which had just been launched. It floated too deeply and trimmed considerably by the stern, whether through poor design or construction I never found out. Normally in such a situation, the best measure would be to remove some of the ballast, whether inside or outside, and so reduce the vessel's weight and relocate its center of gravity so the the craft would float as close to her lines as possible. In this yacht, however, the ballast of steel punchings in cement had been poured before launching, and was completely impossible to remove. The only possible corrective action was to add a small amount of lead ballast way up in the bow; while this sank the boat a fraction of an inch deeper, it trimmed the bow down and the stern up by several inches, so that at least the vessel floated nearly level. My guess as to how this weight problem arose is that through inadequate control while building the hull,

it was too thick and hence too heavy. In addition, some of the the ballast should have been left out to allow trimming after launching.

2. In Jamaica as a fishing vessel consultant, I recommended the development of a fleet of ferro-cement fishing craft, since the Jamaicans had mountains of limestone and plenty of labor. My idea was adamantly rejected. Inquiry disclosed that a ferro-cement boat had been tried and that it had been too heavy and had sunk. Further questioning revealed that very little expertise had been available for the project, so that the boat was much over-built. I also learned that a second boat had been built and was fishing very successfully. Also in Jamaica was a 50′ (15.3 m) British-built ferro-cement research vessel which had been trouble free for 10 years of heavy use. This incident reveals how irrational some of the objections to ferro-cement construction can be.

3. Much of Cuba's small-craft fleet is of ferro-cement. I have seen a 70′ (21.3 m) lobster boat, and sizable river freight boats built in Cuba which were doing yeoman service.

4. A skilled and boatwise friend of mine designed and built a lovely 40′ (12.2 m) tops'l schooner in ferro-cement. He did everything just about right, and the boat is a great success.

The potential for ferro-cement construction is high, but don't turn to it because you think it will be faster, easier, or cheaper, or require less skill in design and construction.

Displacement is about the single most important characteristic of vessels; upon it depends their performance, roominess, and cost. It will vary somewhat according to the major material used in their construction. To be precise about these variations must wait for the naval architect's final weight calculations. However, for the purposes of sketch designing, tables 11-2 and 11-3 have been prepared to help in estimating displacement.

Table 11-2
Approximate Indexes of Displacement for Different
Materials of Equal Strength

Material	LOA = 50′ (15.25 m)	LOA = 200′ (61 m)
Steel	100	100
Aluminum	81	81
Wood, sawn frames	105	NA
Wood, bent frames	90	90
Wood, strip or molded	75	*
FRP, solid	86	90
FRP, cored	75	80
Ferro-cement	101	*

*Data not available.

Table 11-3
Relative Displacement of 90′ (27.4 m) Fishing Vessel in Long Tons

Steel	Wood*	Aluminum	FRP	Ferro-cement
300	315	243	264	303

* Sawn frame construction.

To sum up, all the materials cited above can be used to build good boats. Whether the boats *are* good will depend upon care in selecting the component materials, care in design, care in building, and care in maintenance. The best material can be ruined by inconsiderate use, yet some primitive societies build very good and long-lived boats from materials we would consider inferior.

In your role as conceptual designer, one of your most important decisions is to select the basic material of construction. Take great care in doing so, but once done exploit the advantages of your choice to the limit.

12. Powering

IN all watercraft in forward motion, there are two sets of opposing forces at work. There are those that hold the vessel back and those that drive the vessel ahead. We will first discuss those holding the boat back. This has already been touched on in chapter 5, but we will review it here with specific reference to powering. Then we will look at the forces that can be applied to overcome the hold-back forces.

Hold-back forces: There are two major components tending to restrain forward motion of a vessel—frictional resistance and wave-making resistance. (A third component, wind resistance, is relatively unimportant and extremely variable. Except in very high speed craft it is ignored.) Frictional resistance is caused by the "stickiness" of water in contact with a hull that tends to hold it back. Wave-making resistance represents the work required to create wake waves; normally included with wave-making resistance are minor sources of resistance such as eddy-making around shafts, struts, rudders, etc., the complete package being known as residual resistance.

The naval architect states this in the simple equation:

Total resistance = frictional resistance + residual resistance
$$R_t = R_f + R_r$$

The rationale for separating these can perhaps be better understood by thinking of a submarine. On the surface a submarine makes an impressive wake, so that R_r will be a sizable component of R_t. When deeply submerged, however, there are no gravity waves so R_r becomes much smaller, consisting of "form" resistance and eddy-making. But R_f becomes considerably greater because the wetted surface now includes the entire submarine. So the contributions of these two sources of resistance are in different proportions when the submarine is submerged and when it is on the surface.

When a vessel's model is tested for resistance in a towing tank, total resistance is measured. Given the vessel's length and speed, and the wetted surface area, the frictional resistance can be calculated with good accuracy. Knowing the frictional resistance, it is then possible to find the great variable, residual resistance, as follows:

Residual resistance = total resistance − frictional resistance
$$R_r = R_t - R_f$$

In order to find the total resistance of the full-size vessel, from which we can calculate the required shaft horsepower, its frictional resistance is calculated as described above. The ship's residual resistance is found by expanding the model residual resistance by the ratio of vessel displacement/model displacement. Adding the two resistances gives the total resistance for the full-size vessel.

$$R_{ts} = R_{fs} \text{ (calculated)} + R_{r\,m}\text{(measured in towing tank)} \times$$
$$\text{displacement}_s/\text{displacement}_m$$

Figure 12-1 suggests what a typical speed/power curve may look like for a displacement-type craft.

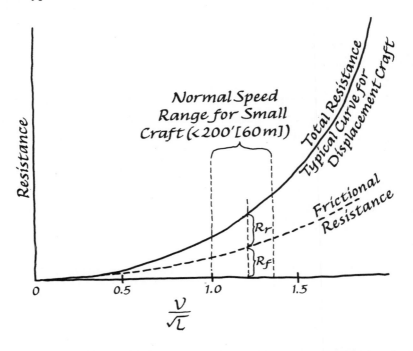

Fig. 12-1. Typical speed/power curve for a displacement craft, showing the division between frictional and residual resistance.

From these curves we can draw some useful conclusions:

1. At very low values of speed-length ratio, (SLR), all resistance is frictional, with a bit of eddy-making included. No waves have yet been generated.

2. At cruising speeds, SLR = 1.2 to 1.4, the wave-making resistance has become noticeable so that frictional and residual resistances are about equal.

3. As speeds go beyond SLR = 1.4 the curve of frictional resistance continues a conservative upward sweep, but the effects of wave making cause the curve of residual resistance, and hence total resistance, to rapidly head for the stars. In this range, adding quite a bit of horsepower causes very little increase in speed.

138 : Preliminary Design of Boats and Ships

Resistance of smaller craft is usually expressed in terms of pounds of pull required to tow the full-size vessel at various speeds. This "towbar pull" is the actual force required to tow the plain, unpowered boat at those speeds. Converted into horsepower by the following equation, it is known as effective horsepower (EHP).

$$\text{Effective horsepower} = \text{total resistance} \times \text{feet per second}/550$$
$$= \text{total resistance} \times \text{knots}/326$$
$$= (\text{kilowatts}/746)$$

Effective horsepower is the precise amount required to overcome the resistance of the vessel at the given speed. However, an engine sufficient to provide that EHP—to give the thrust to overcome the resistance of the hull—must have additional power to compensate for inefficiencies and losses in the propulsion system. This relationship, effective horsepower/shaft horsepower, is called the propulsive coefficient, or PC, and for a first approximation can be taken as = .5, that is, half the engine's shaft horsepower is taken up with overcoming losses so that the other half can drive the boat. Therefore, using a preliminary PC of .5 we can estimate SHP as follows:

$$\text{Shaft horsepower, SHP} \approx \text{effective horsepower, EHP}/.5$$
(The symbol, $\approx$, means "approximately equal to.")

Large vessels, with PC of about .6, are more efficient than smaller craft which can have a PC as low as .4. This concept of propulsive coefficient is used in connection with mechanically powered craft, but the resistance pattern illustrated in figure 12-1 applies to all craft, and inefficiencies are present in other powering methods such as oars and sails.

Go-ahead forces: There are three major sources of propulsive power for causing a boat or vessel to move ahead against its resistance: human power, via oars or pedal-driven propellers or paddle wheels; the wind, via soft or rigid sails, rotors, kites, or air propeller to water propeller; heat working through steam or the internal combustion engines driving screw or cycloidal propellers, paddle wheels, water jet pumps, or as yet uninvented devices. A more visionary source of power is gravity; for instance, it is entirely possible to translate the work of pitching, rolling, and heaving in gravity waves into a propulsive force, perhaps through submerged driving elements that function like fish tails. Eventually we may bypass the oceans completely with vehicles in tunnels drilled in a straight line from continent to continent; building up speed coasting downhill for the first half of the trip, their momentum carrying them up the second half nearly to their destination. No doubt in a thousand years nauticians will regard our poor and inefficient propulsion efforts with the same condescension with which we are apt to view ancient craft driven by a single baggy square sail.

Human power—Oars and paddles have no doubt been with us since Mr. Cro-Magnon pushed his log into water too deep for poling, and found that by properly wielding the pole in the water he could keep the log moving in the desired direction.

Rowing is surely one of the most effective and pleasurable exercises there can be, and must share with the bicycle the honor of being the most efficient form of personal transportation there is. Supporting this view is the fact that other translations of human power into forward vessel motion—paddle wheels and screw propellers—have never graduated from the swan pond, whereas there are many examples of entirely oar-powered craft crossing the Atlantic and Pacific oceans.

Twenty years ago there would have been no justification for including oars in a discussion of propulsion; except for trying to manhandle an 8′ (2.44 m) pram out to the mooring, most rowing was confined to the highly specialized field of racing shells. But that is all changing now, with recreational rowing for pleasurable exercise increasing, geometrically it seems. (Lying in lovely Christmas Cove on the Maine coast one quiet misty morning, I was treated to a look at the future. Around a point came a smart lapstraked peapod, with a handsome young couple rowing four oars and with a small child in the stern sheets. The rowing was perfect, the oars in complete synchronization and perfectly feathered on each stroke. After circling the harbor observing the boats anchored there, the vision disappeared again around the point. This "made my day!" in a much more pleasing and wholesome way than any Clint Eastwood action.)

The design of oars (also known as sculls or sweeps) for converting human energy most efficiently into propelling a boat may not be as difficult as one might think. After all, Africans rowing with simple poles are working as hard in the right direction as are racing shell oarsmen pulling sculls of complex design and construction. If the work applied by the rower to the end of the oar is the same in quantity and direction, it is going to have the same propulsive effect. Probably the most useful improvement in oars is in how and where they are supported and balanced to optimize the relationship among the natural stroke length and speed established by your physiology, the height of the rowlock above water level, the proportions of the oar inboard and outboard of the rowlock, the speed of the oar blade, and the resistance characteristics of the boat. Also important is the ease of feathering and the reduction in wind resistance when feathered. Despite this technology, if you chance to lose your oars a pair of matched, trimmed alder or cedar trees will probably do just about as well.

In designing rowing boats, there are several characteristics of oar power that should be kept in mind:

1. Rowing boats are slow in terms of speed-length ratio. Even racing shells, because they are so long, travel at speeds of not much more than $V/\sqrt{L} = 1$, and most ordinary rowing boats go at speeds of $V/\sqrt{L} = .7$ or less. So wave making is not of great importance, which means that most resistance is frictional. So keep the bottoms smooth and free of eddy-making projections and corners!

2. Oar power is applied intermittently. For about one-third of the stroke cycle time the oar blades are out of water and not only not producing forward thrust but in a head wind may even be undoing some of the work you just did on the power

stroke. This fluctuating power is reflected in speed variations; the relationship is shown schematically in figure 12-2.

3. There is a bow-down pitching moment during the power portion of each stroke. Figure 12-3 illustrates how the forward thrust applied at the rowlock, well above the center of resistance, creates a moment tending to rotate the bow downward, causing a trim by the bow. In very light low-freeboard boats this pitching moment should be counteracted by a wider deckline forward.

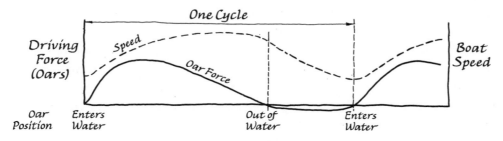

Fig. 12-2. Graphical representation of rowing force and boat speed

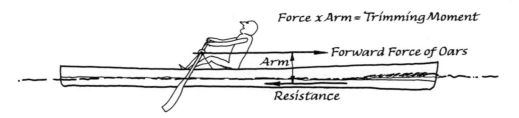

Fig. 12-3. Rowing force in relation to boat resistance

4. The maximum power available from oars is small, and it doesn't take much head wind and sea to make forward progress impractical. Rowing boats should therefore be designed to be as sea-kindly as possible in adverse conditions, and with safety in mind when conditions are severe enough to halt forward progress.

There have been attempts to transmit human power through propellers instead of oars. This doesn't seem to have proven very efficient, as the the only applications I know of are (1) park pond swan boats and (2) lifeboats. Probably the popularity of both of these applications stems from the inability of an untrained person to operate oars properly or for an extended period of time.

However, all is not lost. *Scientific American* for December 1986 has an article describing a human powered, propeller driven, hydrofoil lifted catamaran which, with one man aboard, can beat a single shell by 10 seconds over a 2,000 meter course at speeds to 10 or 11 knots. An interesting picture of both craft side by side suggests the reason for this exceptional performance. The hydrofoil, once its hulls are lifted clear of the water (at about 6 knots), has much less wetted surface and virtually no wave making compared with the shell. In addition, the propeller system seems able to absorb much more of the operator's power at low speeds than does the oar system, presumably giving the hydrofoil better starting acceleration.

Wind power—Wind power has its own unique set of problems. Highly variable in velocity, ranging from zero knots to hurricane force (65+ knots), and over all points of the compass, it almost never blows exactly in the direction you are traveling. As a result, its application as propulsion power to a vessel is so complex as to defy exact evaluation. Years ago I started a list of the forces, vectors, and relationships involved in sailing craft performance with the idea of sorting them out by some sort of systems analysis or symbolic logic. When the list reached 40 items, though, I realized that the problem was unsolvable and gave it up. It is precisely this ever-changing complexity that makes sailing such an engrossing challenge to the modern sailor in a day when so much of our decision making is done for us electronically.

It is not the purpose of this volume to reveal all the secrets of wind power, for which I recommend to the serious student *Aero-Hydrodynamics of Sailing* by Marchaj. Rather, I am assuming that the sailboat sketch designer has had enough experience with sailing to know in general how sails work, what the difference is between a stable and a tender boat, and the effect of weather and lee helm. In this chapter wind power will be discussed in rather general terms; its application to specific craft will be discussed in chapter 15.

Wind power is energy extracted from wind blowing past the extraction device. There are a number of different such devices: soft sails, hard sails (wings, for instance), kites, propellers, Flettner rotors. All work on the same principle: low pressure on one side, high pressure on the other, resulting in a net force vector in the approximate direction of travel. The air flow and pressure field about a single sail are shown in figure 12-4. It is easy to see that the net force vector (the sum of all the local vectors shown on the sketch) of the sail will point toward the top of the figure.

Figure 12-5 is a schematic representation of the sail forces and their relationship to the boat. The resultant wind force is the sum of all the vectors acting on the sail in figure 12-4, and this in turn can be broken down into whatever vectors will be of use to the designer. Usually, as shown in figure 12-5, these are the driving force that propels the boat forward and the lateral heeling force causing leeway and heeling. If the forces shown here were the only ones involved in sailboat performance, with no counter-reacting forces, our boat would increase in speed to something approaching the velocity of light and fly off the earth into outer space, and in a sideways direction at that! To prevent the loss of our boat to the galaxies, there are water forces acting on the keel, rudder, and hull that are equal and opposite to the wind forces to satisfy the requirement of equilibrium, in which the boat will hold a steady course and speed.

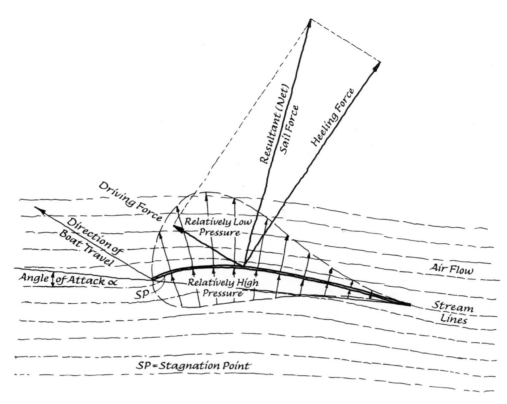

Fig. 12-4. Diagram of wind forces acting on a sail

Figure 12-5 shows the boat hull, the wind and water forces working on it, and their effect on its speed and direction. The resultant wind force is separated into its forward (driving) and sideways (heeling) components, the latter being manifested in the heeling of the boat and in the leeway it makes. Also shown is the wind force vector diagram by which the apparent wind (the wind as actually felt on the moving boat) speed and direction are found by adding the true wind vector and the boat speed vector.

If the boat is to hold a steady course, then the resultant water force must be equal to, and directly opposite, the resultant wind force, as shown by the vectors on the diagram (fig. 12-5). Usually the water force vector on the fixed hull (the force on the hull and fixed keel assembly) vector is not lined up with the wind force vector, but is forward of it as shown, causing the bow to swing to windward. To counteract this tendency, known as weather helm, the rudder must be turned to provide a counter force. When the rudder is turned just the right amount, the net water force vector is moved aft until it is exactly opposite to the wind force vector and the boat sails in a straight line.

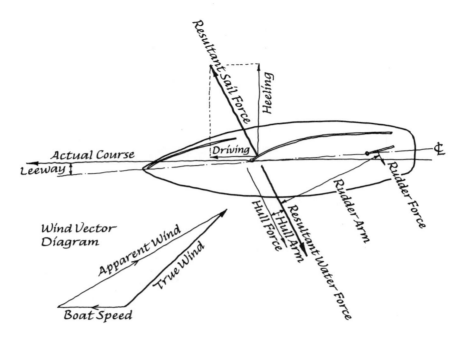

Fig. 12-5. Wind and water forces acting on a sailboat

It might be helpful to look at the vectors affecting our sailboat when it is hit by a puff as it sits becalmed. Becalmed, the values of both wind and water vectors are zero. When the puff hits, the wind force vector almost immediately is as shown (although since the boat hasn't begun to move the apparent wind vector is not yet as shown) but the water force vector is still zero. Thus, the system is not in equilibrium, so the boat begins to move ahead and a bit to the side (leeway). It accelerates in both directions until the resultant water force is equal and opposite to the resultant wind force. The system is then in equilibrium and will remain that way until the apparent wind changes its direction or velocity, when the system must readjust itself to attain equilibrium.

Figure 12-6 gives a bow-on view of the wind and water forces, showing how the heeling moment of the wind on the sails (heeling force × heeling arm) is exactly balanced by the righting moment (displacement × righting arm). If the wind force increases, the boat will heel more, increasing the righting arm sufficiently so that the righting moment again equals the heeling moment, although both will be greater and thus put more strain on the rigging and spars.

The side wind force affects sailboat performance negatively. The area of sail exposed to the wind is reduced, the attitude of the sails to the wind is not as favorable, and the point of application of the driving force is well off to the lee side. In addition, the heeled hull making leeway is considerably less efficient than the upright

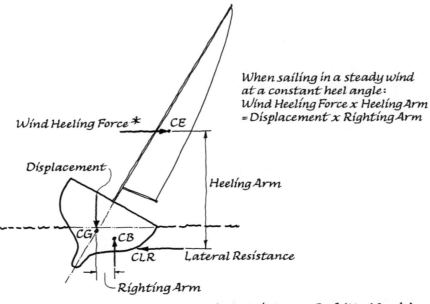

When sailing in a steady wind
at a constant heel angle:
Wind Heeling Force x Heeling Arm
= Displacement x Righting Arm

Wind Heeling Force *

CE

Displacement

Heeling Arm

CG

CB

CLR   Lateral Resistance

Righting Arm

* WHF = Sail Area x Cos² (Heel Angle) x psf

Fig. 12-6. Sail heeling forces versus hull righting forces

hull. In general, one can assume that sailboats begin to lose speed when the heel angle exceeds 25° for wider boats, 30° for narrower craft.

The task of the designer is to select the best mix of characteristics: minimum frictional and wave-making resistance, acceptable leeway and heel angles under ordinary conditions, an efficient rig supported on a stable and sea-kindly hull. The difficulty of achieving a suitable synthesis of these often conflicting requirements in a design that must fulfill a host of other needs is the reason that sailing yacht design is far from an exact science. The racing yacht designer depends heavily on towing tank testing to resolve some of the conundrums. Fortunately the less demanding tolerances of recreational sailing yachts allow the designer to achieve suitable results by less expensive means. These considerations will be explained in detail in chapter 15.

The sails we have been discussing so far are the familiar bright white dacron sails seen pointing their triangles in many directions against a blue sky. There are other types of "sails" that should also be discussed. The explosion of oil prices in the seventies has made the idea of commercial sailing craft worthy of reviving. Mostly these efforts have been aimed at "sail assists" for conventional fishing craft, freighters, tankers, etc., and in certain applications these have demonstrated some practicality. Many applications utilized familiar fabric sails, but there has been some infusion of reasonably high technology in fitting sails to commercial craft. (The subsequent lowering of oil prices lowered the economic encouragement of commercial sail assist, but it seems certain that prices will rise in the future and the encouragement for sails will return.)

Two configurations have received the most attention: rigid or semirigid wing sails, and the Flettner rotor or variations of it. Wing sails (fig. 12-7), are analogous to airplane wings, mounted vertically on pivoting masts. Usually the only control

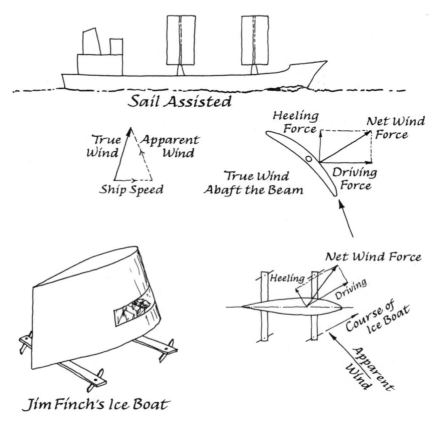

Fig. 12-7. Sails on a tanker, and an unusual ice boat

they require is rotation of the masts to give the best angle of attack; they are furled and reefed by aligning them with the wind, either restrained in a feathered position or allowed to weathercock. Wing sails can provide significant power to large vessels, and can be handled entirely from the bridge, an advantage with crews who are unknowing about sails and unenthusiastic about the extra work in sail handling. Inventive ingenuity (see Jim Finch's flying wing ice boat in figure 12-7) has a field day with wing sails trying to solve such problems as: how to make more efficient sails by incorporating asymmetry that can be changed as the wind comes from first one side of the boat and then the other; how to adjust the size and/or shape to increase power absorption in light airs and reduce it in heavy winds; how to make the wings light yet strong.

The Flettner rotor (fig. 12-8) a concept of Dr. Flettner based on the Magnus effect, was tried in 1924. Nearly a hundred and fifty years ago, Heinrich Magnus, a German physicist, discovered that a rotating cylinder with air flowing over it sets up high and low pressure zones that provide a force vector at 90° to the ambient wind flow. Therefore, by using a very small amount of power to rotate the rotors, quite good thrust characteristics are obtained and the vessel moves ahead. Adjust-

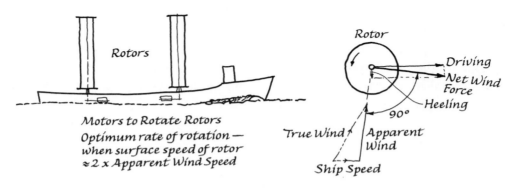

Fig. 12-8. Flettner rotor ship

ing the size of the rotor to the wind velocity of the moment is a real problem, as is luffing since of course there is no thin edge to present to the wind. It does, however, seem possible to have a reefing rotor, with two or three cylinders nesting within each other like a portable radio aerial. Various devices have been tried, by Jacques Cousteau for one, to improve the efficiency of rotors.

The application of sail assist to commercial craft is not a simple problem, involving how steady the wind is in force and direction, and the economics of installing, maintaining, and operating the sails. A look at the wind vector diagram (fig. 12-5) will show how rapidly the apparent wind speed and direction can be changed by a small change in true wind speed or direction when a vessel is steaming at a considerable powered speed. The consequent difficulty of maintaining the sails at optimum attitudes suggests why sail assist may be viable only in trade wind conditions. The installation cost is considerable, and the rig will be uneconomical if this cost plus maintenance is not recovered in saved fuel within a reasonable period. For fishing vessels, sail assist is especially questionable because of the frequent changes of course required when fishing and because the massive top-hamper of a fishing vessel makes it a problem to find space for an efficient rig. In addition, fishermen are worked very hard; a lack of enthusiasm for messing with sails would be understandable.

One area of great potential for the use of sail is in developing countries. Along the Windward and Leeward islands in the Caribbean with continuous easterly trade winds, or the Republic of Maldives in the Indian Ocean with southwesterly and northeasterly monsoons blowing across the long axis of that island country, sailing craft such as catamarans could very well provide fast and reliable passenger, mail, and light freight service at a fraction of the cost of modern steel motor ships.

Sail, not long ago a quaint anachronism, is again receiving attention as an economically viable propulsion method, as well as providing some of the best recreational sport in the world. Tapping the inexhaustable and free power of the wind is a tantalizing goal.

Mechanical power: A mechanical marine propulsion system is made up of three major subsystems: the prime mover (engine); the transmission method (clutch, transmission, shaft, etc.); the propelling device for translating engine power to forward thrust, propeller, jet pump, etc. (see figure 12-9).

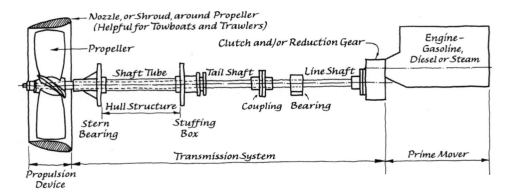

Fig. 12-9. Mechanical marine propulsion system

Prime mover—This may be a gasoline or diesel internal combustion engine, a steam engine, or a steam or gas turbine. Steam engines are rarities and are physically and operationally unlike the others, so will not be considered here; for further information, one of the amateur steam engine societies may be approached. Power is obtained from a gasoline engine by the explosion of a mixture of air and vaporized gasoline introduced into the cylinder and ignited by an electric spark. In a diesel engine a fine mist of fuel oil is ignited by heat generated by the compression of air in the cylinder by the piston to 1/20 of its free volume. Engines have two-stroke or four-stroke cycles (also called two-cycle and four-cycle). Figure 12-10 shows how engines function. It may be taken as a general rule that when a choice is possible diesel power is to be preferred over gasoline power.

Gasoline, diesel, and steam engines are of the reciprocating type. That is, as shown in figure 12-10, power is exerted on pistons—by the expansion of exploding gas or of steam—whose linear motion is transformed into rotary motion for use in turning propellers, generators, pumps, etc.

In addition, there are two types of prime movers that function in rotary motion, the steam turbine and the gas turbine. These are in effect large fans with a great number of blades, rotated by high pressure steam or from the expanding gas of combustion; power is extracted directly from the fan shaft. While turbines are very light in weight for the power they produce, their operating speed is so high that the reduction gears required to reduce the high turbine revolutions per minute (RPM) to practical output RPM are often larger than the turbines themselves.

The steam turbine was the first power source able to achieve high vessel speeds; in 1895 the 100' British motor torpedo boat *Turbinia* reached the unprecedented

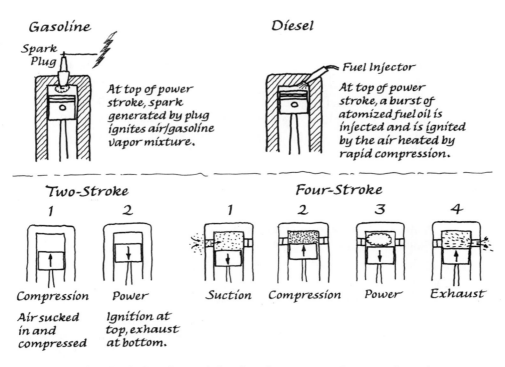

Fig. 12-10. Gasoline and diesel engines compared; two-stroke and four-stroke engine action illustrated

speed of over 32 knots. Since then the steam turbine has been popular in large military craft the world over and, in the United States until recently, in commercial ships. The current high cost of liquid fuel and the inefficiency of steam propulsion by comparison with the diesel engine has all but halted the use of the steam turbine in ships.

The gas turbine is also less efficient than the diesel engine, but its light system weight for the power produced (no boilers, condensers, etc., are required) has caused it to be used increasingly in military craft as a supplemental power source when operating at flank speed. Recent developments in ceramic components, which can allow operation at much higher temperatures and hence with greater efficiency, suggest that in the not too distant future gas turbines may equal diesels in fuel efficiency. At that time they will become a very attractive option for general marine powering. In this book, only gasoline and diesel options will be considered.

In choosing between gasoline and diesel power, the following considerations may be of help.

1. The horsepower range available:

Outboard motors	less than 1 to 250
Gasoline engines	10 to 1,000
High speed diesel (1,800-4,000 RPM) engines	7 to 2,200
Medium speed diesel (700-1,700 RPM) engines	100 to 10,000
Low speed diesel (100-600 RPM) engines	500 to 57,000

2. Weight of engine and gear:

Outboards	2-4 lb/HP
Gasoline engines	3-8 lb/HP
High speed diesel engine	6-20 lb/HP
Medium speed diesel engines	15-35 lb/HP
Low speed diesel engines (direct reversing)	25-100 lb/HP

3. Relative usefulness of advertised power, in terms of work continuously available for driving a displacement-type craft:

Diesel, continuous (commercial) rating	100%
Diesel, pleasure boat rating	85%
Gasoline, inboard or inboard/outboard	60%
Outboard motor	40%

(For instance, an outboard motor of 25 HP may be required to replace an inboard gasoline engine of 17 HP and a diesel of 10 HP.)

4. Safety: At relatively low temperatures (less than 110° F.) gasoline can vaporize after a leak or a spill and mix with air to form an explosive mixture with disastrous possibilities; it is virtually impossible for this condition to occur with fuel oil in normal operations. Nevertheless, the use of gasoline is perfectly safe if the entire machinery installation and fuel handling procedures are done in accordance with safety standards such as those of the American Boat and Yacht Council.

5. Cost: Diesel engines are about twice as costly per horsepower as gasoline engines, but have a much longer life, and are more efficient users of fuel (18-20 HP per hour per U.S. gallon versus about 12 HP per hour per U.S. gallon of gasoline).

6. Other considerations: The rapid evaporation of gasoline causes it to be less of a pollution threat and less of an assault on the olfactory nerves. The smell of diesel oil lingers for a long time and is very offensive and nauseating to many people.

If you have doubts about which type of prime mover to select, your best bet is to seek out similar vessels that use the two types and interrogate the operators. Ask the question, "If they had it to do over again, would they install the same kind of power?"

Transmission method—In addition to the typical transmission system shown above, there are many other ways of getting power from the engine to the driving device (see figure 12-11). These include outboard motor, inboard/outboard (I/O) drive, Z-drive (a commercial version of the I/O), diesel-electric drive, and hydraulic drive. The first four drives are in common use and, if properly made, installed, and maintained, are inexpensive and reliable. Diesel-electric is only valuable where precise control of propeller speed is desirable (since a diesel normally idles at about one-third full RPM, the idling speed sometimes produces more ship speed than is desirable, as in research vessels); plenty of electricity means the whole vessel can be electrical, often an advantage. Hydraulic drives allow location of the engine anywhere in the vessel, but a hydraulic drive system results in about 70% loss of power between the prime mover coupling and the propeller. Which method of transmission you select depends on the end use, on whether it fits well into the vessel, on the cost you are willing to pay, and on availability of parts and repair service.

Propelling device—All propelling devices accelerate the fluid (water or air) in one direction; the reaction to moving this mass of water is what provides the force driving the boat in the other direction. The familiar *screw propeller* is far and away the most common means of transforming marine prime mover power into forward thrust. Under ideal conditions, it can have an efficiency of 70% or better, but variations in load and boat speed, or wrong propeller selection, can affect that considerably. Propellers can have two to four blades on smaller craft, three to six on large vessels. For craft working under load—displacement craft, towboats, trawlers—it is generally true that the larger the propeller the better. For great variations in load, such as between a towboat steaming free and pushing several barges, it is desirable to surround the propeller with a shroud or nozzle; this not only helps the propeller to work efficiently under heavy loading, but the nozzle itself contributes some forward thrust. A nozzle can increase pull on a towline by as much as 20%. Variations on the solid fixed propeller include the controllable-pitch propeller (CPP), in which the angle of the blades can be adjusted from the control panel to give the most favorable pitch for the existing conditions; and feathering and folding propellers which present very little frontal area for sailboats under sail.

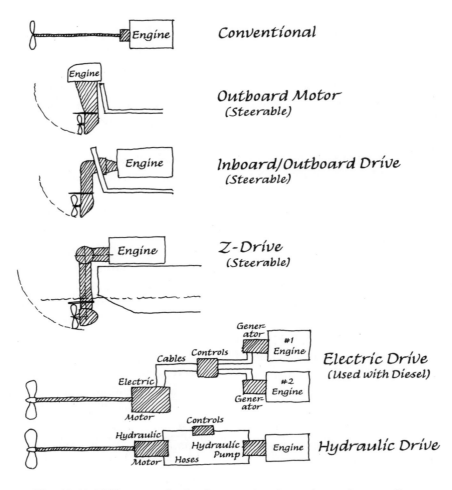

Fig. 12-11. Different methods of connecting the engine to the propeller

Other devices the designer may resort to under special circumstances are shown in figure 12-12. The *water jet* provides thrust by sucking in water, accelerating it, and ejecting it out the discharge; turning and reversing are accomplished by vanes or scoops that divert the discharge. The water jet is generally restricted to high speed craft; it has the great advantage of requiring no projections below the hull for either propulsion or steering. The *cycloidal propeller* can provide thrust in any direction instantaneously by altering the angle of the blades as the base plate rotates (the blades are shown in the neutral, or stopped, position); although subject to mechanical problems, the cycloidal propeller may be the best solution for position holding and omnidirectional thrusting (tugs, drilling vessels, research craft), but should be protected from damage and mechanical problems. The *paddle wheel* is coming back into use as river-vessel replicas are built for dinner cruise vessels, trading off a bit of con-

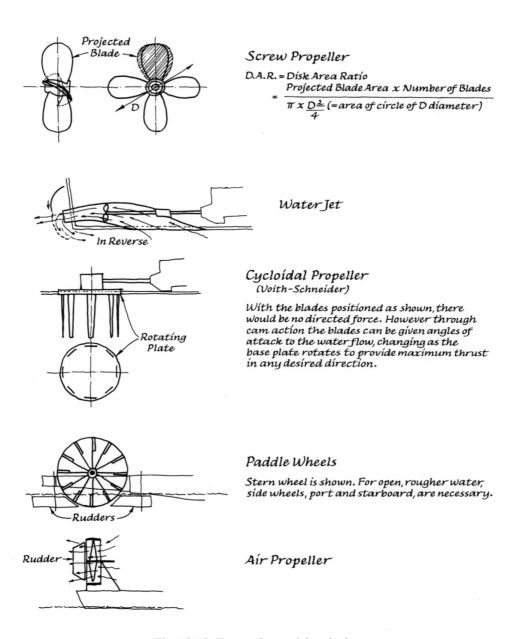

Screw Propeller

D.A.R. = Disk Area Ratio

$$= \frac{\text{Projected Blade Area} \times \text{Number of Blades}}{\pi \times \frac{D^2}{4} \, (= \text{area of circle of } D \text{ diameter})}$$

Water Jet

Cycloidal Propeller
(Voith-Schneider)

With the blades positioned as shown, there would be no directed force. However through cam action the blades can be given angles of attack to the water flow, changing as the base plate rotates to provide maximum thrust in any desired direction.

Paddle Wheels

Stern wheel is shown. For open, rougher water, side wheels, port and starboard, are necessary.

Air Propeller

Fig. 12-12. Types of propulsion devices

venience and efficiency for picturesqueness; one nice feature is that the size of the wooden paddles—length, width, and submergence—can be very easily fine-tuned after the vessel is in commission. Paddle wheels are usually hydraulically or electrically driven, and stern wheels can be split into two independently driven wheels to give excellent controllability to the vessel. The *air propeller* is used on Florida swamp boats and on surface effect craft such as the Hovercraft; its effectiveness is strongly affected by the ambient wind direction and velocity. On small craft the elevated propeller and rudder thrust causes a considerable outward-banking effect in turns, and with very little hull under water skidding turns are standard.

An important propeller phenomenon, which need not however be considered here, is cavitation. If the vacuum on the low pressure side of the propeller blades exceeds the vapor pressure of the water, bubbles or sizable cavities rapidly form and collapse. These bubbles erode the metal of the propeller and are a source of noise. Cavitation is not to be confused with ventilation, in which a propeller close to the surface sucks air into its stream, greatly diminishing propeller efficiency.

In this book only the screw propeller will be considered. If the reader wishes to apply one of the other propelling devices to his design, there is ample literature to refer to, and manufacturers of the particular device will gladly provide any needed assistance.

The side thruster is a fairly recent development that can be extremely useful in maneuvering powered vessels in tight quarters. What it does is provide side thrust either to port or starboard as desired, moving the bow (or stern) sideways with no forward motion. Usually installed only in the bow, for special service they are also used at the stern.

Generally the thruster is a tube through the hull well below the waterline; in the tube is mounted a propeller driven by its own independent prime mover or by a hydraulic or electric motor driven from the main engine. The thruster is controlled from the bridge, and the propeller can be reversed to give thrust to either side.

There are other designs of side thrusters, but the function of all of them is the same—to move the vessel sideways with no forward motion.

Some side effects of mechanical power sources are not helpful. Among these are heat and noise. Excess heat is relatively easily carried away by fans and pumps or can be insulated against. Noise, which can be defined as unwanted sound, is much more pervasive, often is difficult to identify and stop, and has much greater effect on our mental and physical welfare.

Noise originates in the clatter of all the small parts, in air turbulence in the exhaust, in the vibration of moving parts transferred through the foundation, and from the propeller as it repeatedly passes in and out of turbulent water zones. Noise can be transmitted through the structure of the vessel and through the air. If any part of the boat, such as a bulkhead, deck, or standing shelter, has a natural frequency in harmony with one of these vibrations, it will vibrate, sometimes violently, and amplify the source noise like a drum head. Machinery noises can be reduced to acceptable levels around the boat by methods such as these:

1. Machinery clatter—Insulating the engine compartment or room with high-mass or vibration-absorbing materials. Especially important are surfaces interfacing with spaces where people will live and work.

2. Foundation vibration—Use heavy, or at least very stiff, engine foundations, well secured to the vessel at bulkheads, frames, etc.

3. Exhaust noise: Install a good muffler. A wet exhaust is generally quieter than a dry one.

4. Propeller noise—Carefully fair the sternpost to feed solid water to the propeller. Have the propeller tips clear the hull by 15% of its diameter and clear the skeg by 10%.

5. Vestigial noise—If after taking these steps there is still noise at unacceptable levels in living and working spaces, the vibration characteristics of surfaces can be changed by adding stiffeners. Also, once noise is in a compartment, its reflection

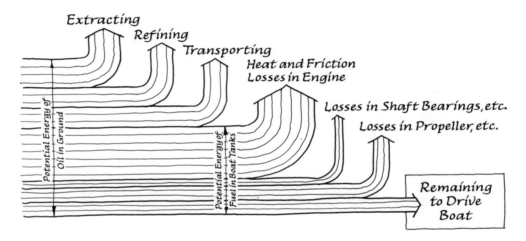

Fig. 12-13. What happens to the potential energy of oil in the ground
on its way to actually providing thrust to a vessel

from surfaces can be mitigated by the installation of accoustical tiles or other materials such as carpeting that will minimize the reflection of sound waves back and forth within the compartment.

Some general comments on mechanical power: The rumbling roar coming out of the exhaust pipe started as a thick black liquid thousands of feet below ground level—crude oil. Lying there, each gallon of crude has a store of potential energy locked in its molecules. But only a small amount of this potential actually ends up doing useful work, such as overcoming the resistance of a vessel. Figure 12-13 shows approximately what happens to the potential energy locked in the crude oil as it passes through the various processes on its way to moving a boat. Note that only about half the original potential energy goes into our tanks, and only about 17% of *that* ends up as push overcoming resistance of the craft to forward motion.

The purpose of the machinery system is to transform the fuel's energy into useful power efficiently and safely (see figure 12-14). The output from this system, measured at the engine coupling, is called horsepower. Tables 12-1, 12-2, 12-3, and 12-4 summarize useful power definitions and equations.

Table 12-1

Distance and Speed Equivalents

Knots (nautical miles* per hour)	= fps × .5925
Feet per second (fps)	= knots × 1.689
Feet per second (fps)	= MPH × 1.467
Miles (statute†) per hour (MPH)	= fps × .682
Kilometers‡ (km) per hour (KPH)	= knots × 1.853

*1 nautical mile = 6,080 ft
†1 statute mile = 5,280 ft
‡1 kilometer = 3,281 ft

Table 12-2

Horsepower Defined

$$\text{One horsepower} = \frac{\text{force} \times \text{fps}}{550} = \frac{2 \times \pi \times \text{torque}_{(\text{lb ft})} \times \text{revolutions/second}}{550}$$

$$= 746 \text{ watts} \approx .75 \text{ kilowatts (kw)}^*$$
$$= 2{,}545 \text{ British thermal units}\dagger \text{ per hour}$$
$$= \text{amount of work a good horse can do}$$

*Power is now quite universally expressed in terms of kilowatts. To find horsepower approximately, divide kilowatts by .75.
†British thermal unit (BTU) = heat required to raise 1 lb of water 1° F.

Table 12-3

Types of Horsepower

Brake HP (BHP) = actual HP measured at output coupling of prime mover.
Shaft HP (SHP) = BHP with accessories and gears.
Propeller HP (PHP) = power actually delivered to propeller hub or, conversely, the power absorbed by the propeller. Due to bearing losses, PHP ≈ 97% SHP.
Effective HP (EHP) = actual resistance of vessel, measured at towline.
Bollard HP = tension on towboat towline. Bollard pull is maximum when towing speed is zero, and is zero when vessel is free-running.

Table 12-4
Horsepower Ratings, Diesel Engines

Pleasure boat—Full power for not over 15 minutes per hour. Average load factor over any 24-hour period not to exceed continuous rating.

Light, or intermittent, duty—Full power not over 8 hours in any 24-hour period. Average load factor equal to or less than continuous rating.

Continuous duty—Indefinitely continuous uninterrupted service at full throttle.

Note: These ratings can be obtained from the same basic engine by selection of the injector nozzles and governor setting. See figure 12-15 for a graphic description of these ratings.

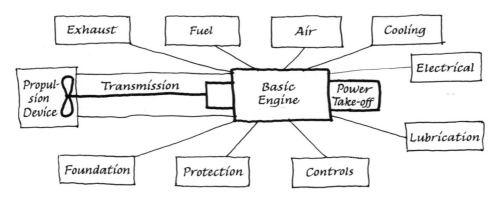

Fig. 12-14. Subsystems making up the propulsion engine system

Horsepower, which represents an empirical quantification of the work an average horse can do, has been the basis for many energy concepts, expressed not only in mechanical terms but also in terms of heat and electricity. The power rating of an engine is given in terms of kilowatts (1 HP = 746 watts [U.S.]) as well as in brake horsepower, BHP.

Note also that diesel engines are often given three horsepower ratings—pleasure boat, light commercial duty (intermittent), and continuous. These are matched to the loads experienced in various services and are the result of using different nozzles and governor settings on the engines.

Diesel engines produce 18-20 horsepower per hour per U.S. gallon of diesel oil, gasoline engines about 12 horsepower per hour per gallon of gasoline. There is no way to beat these numbers. So when someone tells you he burns only 5 gallons of fuel per hour in his 250 HP diesel, you can tell him with the greatest assurance that he is actually getting only 90-100 horsepower output at the coupling.

The graph in figure 12-15 illustrates the relationship between engine RPM and BHP for a typical diesel engine at the various power ratings, and between engine RPM and horsepower absorbed by the propeller in normal use. If the propeller is

Powering : 157

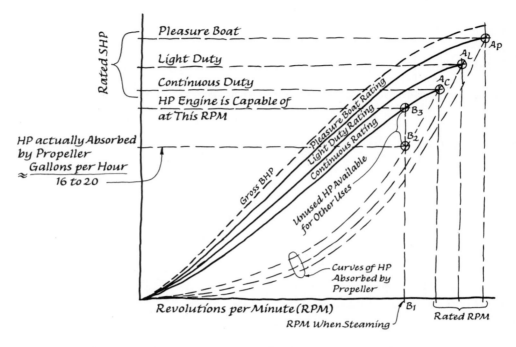

Fig. 12-15. Typical diesel power curves for various duty ratings

selected to allow the engine to develop full rated HP at its rated RPM when the vessel is free-running, then at any RPM below that, assuming no added conditions such as towing nets, the HP absorbed by the propeller will be less than the engine is capable of putting out. This unused HP is available for acceleration, for driving a winch, or for towing gear or a barge.

The ideal propeller will just allow the engine to turn the full rated RPM (points A_P, A_L, A_C on curves) when the boat is clean and normally loaded. A propeller actually absorbs power in proportion to $RPM^{2.7 \text{ to } 3}$. Therefore, if the throttle is set when steaming to give B_1 RPM, then the actual power absorbed by the propeller is B_2. However the engine at B_1 RPM is capable of putting out B_3 horsepower. The unused HP between B_2 and B_3 is thus available for turning a winch, accelerating, or doing other work.

We have dealt with the three basic subsystems of the machinery system that create the power and transform it into useful thrust (the prime mover, transmission, and propelling device), but there are a number of other subsystems each of which the designer must consider in his design. Figure 12-14 is a road map of a machinery system showing the subsystems that must be incorporated in the design of a vessel, and will help ensure that no subsystems are overlooked in the planning process.

Powering system decisions: There are a number of decisions concerning the powering system of a vessel which can and should be made early in the design process. It is assumed that, in the conceptual stage—before anything has reached paper—a determination has been made as to whether the vessel is to be all sail, sail with auxiliary power, all power, or power with auxiliary sail. The desired speed pattern (displacement mode, semidisplacement, planing) that fits the projected use of the vessel has been selected, the waterline length has been derived from the envelope sketch, and the displacement estimated. With all this basic information in hand, it is a good time to make all basic powering decisions, with the knowledge that on succeeding passes around the design spiral these decisions may need to be revised. In the final analysis your naval architect will review the powering needs as he develops the final design. Tables 12-5 and 12-6 offer some crude guidance in overall power system selection.

Table 12-5
Representative Physical Comparisons among Marine Engines

Type	BHP	RPM	Cubic inches (Cubic centimeters)	Pounds (Kilograms)	Base cost (1987) $ per rated HP
Outboard	10	4,800	13 (213)	60 (27)	125
	135	5,500	100 (1,640)	345 (157)	50
Inboard, gasoline	10	3,000	33 (540)	145 (66)*	200*
	130	4,400	181 (2,960)	633 (287)	38
	375	4,600	454 (7,400)	1,000 (454)	18
Inboard diesel†	10	3,000	29 (475)	200 (91)	200
	130	2,800	354 (5,800)	1,000 (454)	65
	375	2,800	636 (10,400)	2,500 (1,134)	60

*Estimated information.
†Diesel data are for pleasure boat rating.

Table 12-6
Performance Comparison among Major Engine Types

Engine type	Compression Ratio	Fuel consumption HP/gallon (U.S.)/hour	Equivalency Index*
Outboard, gasoline	6-8	12	100
Inboard, gasoline	6-8	12	67
Inboard, diesel	≈ 20	16-20	47

*To approximately equal the effective power of a 47 BHP diesel may require an inboard gasoline engine with an advertised rating of 67 HP and an outboard with an advertised rating of 100 HP.

Checklist—machinery decisions: (Note: In doing this exercise, follow the design spiral game plan. Run through it once rather quickly, then go back over it carefully as many additional times as are necessary until all the selected elements of the total system are suitable and compatible. In the process described below, only mechanical power is considered; sail power will be dealt with in chapter 15.)

1. Speed desired (in knots)—Top speed, _____ knots; cruising speed, _____ knots. Define any special requirements such as towing speed or pull (trawlers, towboats) or very low speed (research vessels must be able to operate over the range from zero knots to top speed as well as hold position on a station).

2. System choice (preliminary)—Inboard, inboard/outboard, outboard, twin or single screw.

3. Horsepower requirement—Estimate shaft horsepower required to achieve top speed or towing demands, whichever is greater. Since engines nowadays are relatively small, lightweight, and low cost, it is prudent to increase this estimated power by 10% or so to cover any unforeseen power needs. For first-pass estimates of engine size, use figure 12-16 for craft operating at $V/\sqrt{L}$ of 2 or less and figure 12-17 for craft operating at $V/\sqrt{L}$ greater than 2 (see page 165 for information on estimating SHP for sailing craft).

4. Fuel selection—Gasoline or diesel. The safety, reliability, efficiency, and long life of modern diesels make them the first choice over gasoline engines despite considerably greater initial cost and approximately double the weight. For initial economy, cleanliness (spilled diesel oil smells and takes forever to evaporate), ease of repair, and light weight, gasoline would be the choice; a proper installation may be considered completely safe.

5. Prime mover selection—If you have a preferred make of engine, stick with it if it can provide the required performance. Familiarity with a particular manufacturer and availability of parts and service are important factors in picking an engine. Virtually every established engine will deliver the promised service if properly used and maintained, so no matter how enthusiastically someone praises it don't pick some obscure make that doesn't have good backup in your area.

Review the offerings of the selected manufacturer and choose the engine that conservatively will provide the required performance. For a gasoline engine, select one which, at 50% to 60% of the rated horsepower, will drive the boat at the desired cruising speed. For instance, if it is determined that cruising speed requires 100 SHP, select an engine rated at 180 to 200 BHP; when turning about 75% of rated RPM, this engine/propeller combination will provide the necessary 100 propeller horsepower. Moving the throttle to 85% of rated RPM (the maximum at which a gasoline engine should be operated for more than moments) will provide 130 propeller horsepower and increase the speed about 15%.

If diesel is selected, determine from the definitions in tables 12-1, 12-2, 12-3, and 12-4, in which mode you will operate your vessel: pleasure boat rating, light commercial (intermittent), or continuous. If there is any doubt about which class your vessel falls in, go to the next most arduous one; it will return dividends throughout the life of the engine. Be sure to use the horsepower curves for the appropriate use rating.

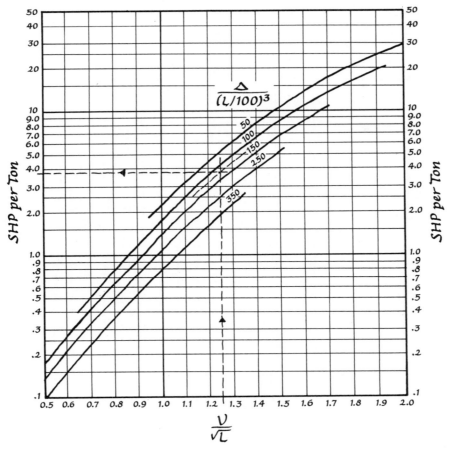

Example: Given: L=100', Displacement=125 Tons, and V_S=12.5 Knots

$$\therefore \frac{\Delta}{(L/100)^3} = 125 \text{ and } \frac{V}{\sqrt{L}} = 1.25$$

From graph, $\frac{SHP}{Ton} = 3.8$

$$\therefore SHP = 3.8 \times 125 = 475$$

These curves are intended to suggest the size of engine installed in displacement craft designed to a specified speed. This is helpful in determining the size, weight, and cost of the propulsion engine(s), and for estimating fuel capacity needs. The actual SHP required will be calculated by your naval architect.

Multiply $\frac{V}{\sqrt{L}}$ in meters by .554 to get $\frac{V}{\sqrt{L}}$ in feet, Multiply Froude Number, $FN = v\sqrt{gxL}$, by 5.67 to get $\frac{V}{\sqrt{L}}$ in feet.

Fig. 12-16. Approximate installed horsepower per ton versus speed-length ratio for displacement craft

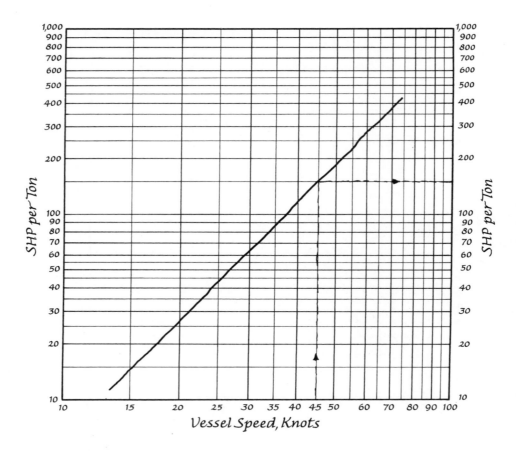

Example: Given LWL =32', Beam =11', Δ =7.5 Tons, V_S =45 Knots

$$\frac{SHP}{Ton} \text{ from graph} = 150$$

Total SHP = 7.5 x 150 =1,125
(Two engines, each of 565 HP)

Do not use when $\frac{V}{\sqrt{L}}$ less than 2.0

These curves are intended to suggest the size of engine installed
in planing craft with a specified design speed. This information
is helpful in determining the size, weight, and cost of the
propulsion system, and for estimating fuel capacity. The actual
SHP required will be calculated by your naval architect.

Fig. 12-17. Approximate installed horsepower per ton
versus speed for planing craft

6. Transmission system—Determine propeller diameter from figure 12-18 and optimum propeller revolutions per minute from figure 12-19. Select straight shaft drive or Z-drive, reduction gear ratio, with or without clutch, or diesel-electric or hydraulic drive.

7. Propulsion device—Fixed-pitch propeller, controllable-pitch propeller, feathering or folding propeller (sailing craft only); fixed or steerable nozzle (shroud) around propeller; water jet propulsion; cycloidal (Voith-Schneider) propeller; paddle wheel, stern or side. For other devices, refer to the literature or to manufacturers' recommendations.

8. Fuel system—Tank capacity = _____ U.S. gallons (liters). This is based on the desired steaming range or endurance (number of days vessel can operate without taking on supplies), the pattern of engine use in terms of horsepower for each hour during the trip, and the specific fuel consumption (number of horsepower per hour per gallon); the capacity developed this way should be increased by 20% to 30% to provide a safety cushion. The distribution of the tankage is important; as fuel is used, the fore-and-aft trim of the boat should not change, which requires that fuel and water tanks be more or less equally distributed fore and aft about the longitudinal center of flotation. Straight-line fill pipes into the tanks allow direct sounding of fuel level. If deck plates are on the weather deck any spillage can be easily cleaned up (but *not* allowed to drain overboard!). Select type of fuel level meter.

9. Exhaust system—Dry exhaust or wet exhaust? Muffler size _____ diameter × _____ length. Use a dry exhaust where freezing is apt to occur and for most commercial purposes. Use a wet (water-cooled) exhaust where a stack and its heat and noise would be objectionable.

10. Cooling—Air or liquid cooled? If liquid, seawater or fresh water/coolant? If fresh water/coolant, heat exchanger or keel-cooler?

11. Electrical system—Voltage: direct current (DC) of 12, 24, or 32; alternating current (AC) of 110, 220, 440, or other. Is standard engine-mounted generator sufficient? If not, use standard oversize engine-mounted generator, additional engine-mounted generator, auxiliary generator driven by gasoline or diesel prime mover? Batteries: starting, _____ 20-hour rate; service, _____ 20-hour rate.

12. Ventilation—Engine aspiration air intake area, _____ square inches (cm) clear ($1/2$ in^2 [3.25 cm^2] per maximum total installed horsepower). Engine room ventilation, _____ total in^2 (cm^2) intake + discharge; natural or forced (fan) ventilation?

13. Controls—Hydraulic, air, push-pull, rod and crank? Number of stations _____ and location(s). Warning devices: oil temperature, oil level, water temperature, exhaust temperature, high engine room temperature (fire), high bilge water level, shaft temperature.

14. Bow/stern thrusters—Required? How much thrust needed? Driven independently or via hydraulic or electric drive?

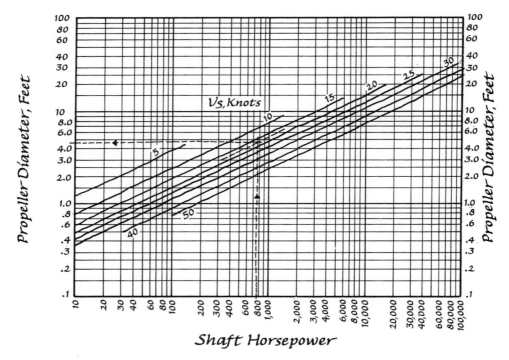

Example: Given SHP=750, Vs=17 Knots
From graph, Diameter=4.6'=55"(1.40m)

The propeller diameters given by this graph are approximately the optimum. Propeller design is a very complex and arcane skill, involving a host of interrelated parameters. This graph can only take them into consideration in a general way.

Diameters can be decreased by 5% to 10%, but with some loss of efficiency.

The diameters given by this graph are for standard three-blade propellers with a .5 disc area ratio (DAR). For two-blade propellers, increase diameter by 5%, for four-blade reduce by 4%.

To find diameter in meters, divide diameter in feet by 3.281.

For SHP in multiple screw installations, use the total SHP divided by the number of propellers.

Fig. 12-18. Estimated propeller diameter versus shaft horsepower and speed

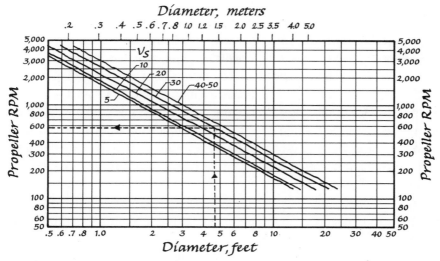

Fig. 12-19. Optimum propeller revolutions per minute versus
diameter and vessel speed in knots

Note on sailing craft: There is no similar figure for sailing craft because all my efforts to produce it came to naught. Despite working with several reliable methods of calculating shaft horsepower to give selected speeds, I could get no results that matched reality. Furthermore, I could find nothing in the literature that dealt specifically with sizing auxiliary power for sailing craft.

Finally I tabulated dimensions and diesel powering of some 200 sailing yachts with waterline lengths ranging from 18′ to 63′. There was no correlation between the installed SHP per ton and LWL or displacement-length ratio. However, the vast majority (about 85%) fell within 3 and 6 SHP/ton. In my opinion, the lower values are suitable for operating in smooth water conditions, the highest values for near motorsailing operation.

I suggest that for a first approximation of adequate diesel power for normal auxiliary use, a value of 4.5 SHP/ton be used. If you expect to be able to punch into a fresh head wind and sea, I would suggest 5.5 to 6.0 SHP/ton or even higher. If you will be motoring only in calms, 3.0 to 3.5 SHP/ton may be adequate.

Having selected the diesel SHP/ton that suits your sailing habits, multiply it by 1.4 if you will have a gasoline engine, and by 2.0 for outboard auxiliary power to achieve the same performance.

The rated horsepower of the selected engine should equal or exceed the SHP/ton × displacement in tons.

If your boat is an out-and-out motorsailer, use the displacement craft powering curves, increased by about 15% to account for increased wetted surface, wind resistance of the rig, and the possibly less efficient placement of the propeller.

The reason for the discrepancy between powering needs for sailing craft and for displacement power craft probably lies in a combination of factors. Certainly the added wind resistance of the spars and rigging is an appreciable element. Other contributors may be increased frictional resistance due to greater wetted surface, the inclination to keep propeller size down for lower resistance under sail by using higher RPM, and the frequent location of the propeller in an aperture that may not have good fairing.

This has been a long chapter, but the power system of a watercraft, whether oars, sails, or machinery, is the single most complex and important element of a vessel and must receive close and careful attention commensurate with its importance. In following through the steps of the checklist, you will undoubtedly find yourself involved in considerable research and study, sometimes tedious, often fascinating. You will appreciate every minute of that when your vessel is built and operating.

13. Economics

THE economics of having a boat or vessel built, and of operating it, are often not given adequate attention during the vessel planning and design phase. Yet these costs are crucial to the success of a commercial venture. Typically, the annual cost of owning and operating a fishing vessel can be broken down to 20% to 25% for interest and principal on vessel cost; 35% for crew costs, including insurance, taxes, etc.; the balance for other operating costs. A vessel tied up all year will still cost about 30% to 35% of what it will cost while operating, an illustration of the importance of keeping the vessel working. To insure profitability, a rough approximation suggests that a fishing vessel should have a gross revenue each year of not less than 50% to 60% of its replacement cost.

But cost can also have an overwhelming impact on yachts and institutional craft. The character who strides into an architect's office proclaiming that he "wants the best, cost is no object" is kidding himself. Cost is *always* an object, usually more rather than less so.

So this chapter on economics should be read as diligently as the more appealing ones about the fun parts of naval architecture.

Cost of construction of boats and ships is nearly proportional to the overall size of the boat if the boats are in the same service and of the same quality. Unfortunately, many people think the "size" of a boat is adequately described by its "length"; one frequently hears learned remarks about a particular craft costing so much "per foot (meter) of length." This is completely meaningless, if one thinks about it. For instance, while a 25' (7.62 m) boat may indeed cost $25,000, or $1,000 per foot ($3,280 per meter) to build, obviously an 8' (2.44 m) dinghy is not going to cost $8,000 nor a 1,000' (305 m) vessel $1,000,000; more likely numbers are $600 and $200,000,000 respectively.

The very simple truth is that the cost of boats is a three-dimensional function; it may be calculated by weight, as with a steak, or by the volume of the craft. The most easily determined, and very accurate, measure of size is cubic number. This is defined for watercraft as:

Cubic number (CUBE) = LWL × beam × depth amidships

(This same type of cubic measure versus cost relationship works equally for houses, holes in the ground, and diamonds.)

The same relationship pertains to costs of ownership. E. Farnham Butler (proprietor of Mt. Desert Yacht Yard, Inc.), in an article in *Rudder* magazine cited his storage yard records to demonstrate that annual yard bills for a sizable sample of yachts of all types and sizes came out to a fairly constant number of cents per pound of displacement, which translated into about 7% of the replacement cost of the yacht. John Proskie, a Canadian economist who did much valuable work on the economics of the Canadian East Coast fishing fleet, showed that annual maintenance and repair costs for fishing vessels is 12% to 14% of replacement cost. Overall annual costs of ownership for yachts average out to about 22% of replacement cost, including crew cost if any, and about 20% for fishing vessels exclusive of crew costs.

One cannot speak of construction or operating costs in absolute or precise terms. Too many factors—inflation, condition of the shipbuilding industry, building site—enter into this complex subject to enable definite statements to be made. Nevertheless, the numbers given in this chapter are useful as a starting point for estimating costs, and for comparing the economics of two or more possible craft.

One of the greatest causes of friction among owner, designer, and builder is the surprise and shock associated with unexpected costs; this surprise usually is sprung at the time of launching or delivery, when everyone's expectations and emotions are at a highly charged peak. To avoid this unpleasantness, in your role of conceptual designer and eventual owner it is important that you arrive at realistic estimates of the cost of building and operating the proposed craft. These costs may be of only academic interest to you, or they may be absolutely vital to the success of the project. In any event, it is well to have an idea of the costs that will be encountered so that *you* won't be surprised, even though your naval architect and builder are. The prudent person will also have in the back of his mind (and in his bank balance) a cushion of 10% to 20% over the estimate to cover unforeseen eventualities such as inflation or a late decision to increase the size of the engines.

New vessel construction costs: What you are looking for is the total vessel cost (TVC), which is the cost of the complete vessel, at your dock or mooring, all rigged and equipped, ready to perform its function. Prices when listed in advertisements, stated in the press, or quoted off the cuff are virtually useless if you are after a reasonably accurate estimate of what you will have tied up in your craft when you take it out on its first trip. Therefore you will probably be well served to use the estimating methods described here; in order to increase precision you may wish to have a builder help you fill in some of the numbers.

The construction cost of pleasure craft can be safely and easily estimated on the basis of displacement. The displacement is very near to being a constant for a particular boat since there are no large variables such as cargo, wide variations in number of passengers, etc. Generally speaking, the designed displacement is the proper figure to be used as it represents the weight of the vessel in its average operating condition.

Displacement of commercial craft may change significantly from day to day, even hour to hour, due to variations in cargo and the amount of fuel aboard. Therefore the designed waterline (DWL) shown on the plans is assumed to be nominal only, used as a datum plane for making measurements, etc. Since the displacement is a variable, but the cubic number (CUBE) is a constant, CUBE should be used as the measure of size of all commercial craft. Using the same measure of size, CUBE, permits useful comparisons to be made between commercial craft whether or not they carry cargo and independent of their hull proportions. (Watch out for the news stories that report a vessel as "weighing" so many tons; the actual number they quote is usually the gross tonnage, a measure of volume, not weight—see chapter 3.)

Estimating the building cost of institutional craft, as with yachts, can be carried out on the basis of displacement, which tends to be pretty constant. But displacement is a figure that is often not available, so here again cubic number is a more convenient measure of size.

Two other less used bases for cost computation are light displacement (weight of the vessel structure, with no cargo, consummables, crew, or passengers), which is the most accurate measure of the weight of the structure actually built by the shipyard but is also the most difficult number to get; and gross tonnage, a measure of internal volume that is fairly readily available but, because of many exemptions, is not very accurate.

Pleasure craft—In 1987 the list prices of pleasure boats ranged all the way from about $6 to $20 or more per pound of displacement. An average list price for pleasure boats can be estimated at $10 per pound. These are base prices, to which should be added 10% to 30% for design, extras, delivery, and other goods and services. To estimate current prices these numbers should be increased by the amount of inflation (consumer price index).

What causes such a wide variation in list prices? Quality of material and workmanship, type and degree of finish, amount of gear installed, complexity of the electronics kit, size of engines or sail outfit are all involved in estimating cost. Another important factor is how busy the shipyards are. If they have long backlogs, there is no pressure to fine-tune their quotes. On the other hand, in slack times sharp competition causes a drop in prices.

Off-the-cuff estimates of vessel building costs can be made using the above approximate costs per pound. But a more precise determination can be made using the graph in figure 13-1. The important feature of the graph is not the values represented by the curves, but the fact that the curves are parallel straight lines. This means that, if you can get an accurate current cost figure for boat A, of similar quality and design to the one you propose, it is possible to plot that point, A, and draw a line parallel to the curves shown. On this new curve, pick out the point B corresponding to the displacement estimated for your new boat, and find the estimated cost on the left-hand scale.

Commercial and institutional craft—With somewhat less accuracy, rough estimates of building costs for commercial/institutional craft can be made on the basis of displacement, either using a simple dollar value per unit of weight or by the method illustrated in figure 13-1. However, table 13-1 gives examples of a more accurate method of estimating building costs for three types of nonpleasure vessels—Atlantic trawler, cruise vessel, government patrol craft. The dimensions have been worked out so that all three have the same cubic number (CUBE), 30,000 ft³ (850 m³). Although the proportions differ, all three are directly comparable because CUBE is the same. Note that the primary elements of this method of cost estimat-

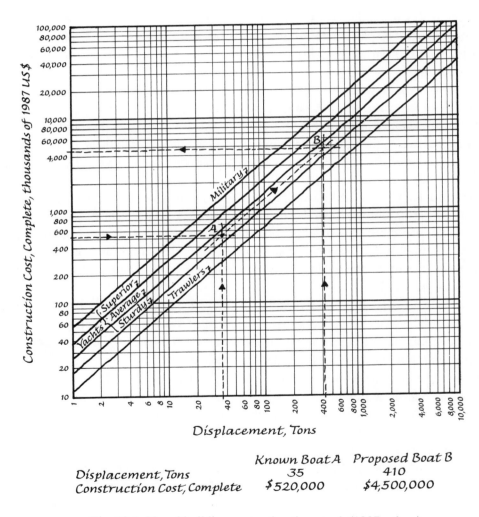

	Known Boat A	Proposed Boat B
Displacement, Tons	35	410
Construction Cost, Complete	$520,000	$4,500,000

Fig. 13-1. Vessel building cost estimating graph (1987 values)

Table 13-1
Vessel Cost Comparisons

	Atlantic trawler	Cruise vessel	Patrol craft
Vessel characteristics:			
Cubic number, CUBE	30,000	30,000	30,000
= LWL × beam × depth	81 × 26.5 × 14	90 × 30 × 11	100 × 25 × 12
Propulsion horsepower	800	450	2,000
Auxiliary horsepower	100	200	300
Total horsepower, TOTHP	900	650	2,300
Number of passengers, NUMPAS	0	25	0
Cost per CUBE, COSCUBE*	$38	$28	$76
Cost per installed HP, COSHP*	$160	$135	$250
Cost per passenger, COSPAS†	0	$13,000	0
Vessel cost analysis:			
Basic vessel cost, CUBE × COSCUBE‡	$1,140,000	$840,000	$2,280,000
Machinery cost, TOTHP × COSHP × 2§	$288,000	$176,000	$1,150,000
Passenger quarters cost, NUMPAS × COSPAS	0	$325,000	0
Specialized electronics, installed	$100,000	$20,000	(install only) $150,000
Specialized gear and equipment, installed	$125,000	$30,000	(install only) $150,000
Net vessel cost, NVC	$1,653,000	$1,391,000	$3,730,000
Design fee, % of NVC	@4% $66,000	@6% $83,000	@6% $224,000
Total vessel cost, TVC	$1,719,000	$1,474,000	$3,954,000

*Cost is subject to influences of inflation, amount of work in shipyard, type of vessel, etc.

†Includes per passenger cost of stateroom/personal furnishings, public rooms, galley, and structure above the main deck.

‡Basic vessel, complete except for machinery and mechanical systems but with basic electronics, etc.

§Cost per HP, COSHP, is obtained from manufacturers; times 2 provides for machinery installation, tanks, electrical system, etc.

ing are only two: CUBE, and the total installed horsepower, TOTHP; specialized elements required for the particular application should certainly be included, as shown, but do not normally constitute an overwhelming portion of the final total vessel cost.

After you have determined the size, shape, and general specifications of the vessel you will be sketching up (having been through the preliminary decision block of figure 8-3), it would be wise to visit a shipyard that builds that type of craft and check out with them the current values of the various elements used in the cost calculations. Engine prices can best be obtained from the local distributor of the engines you will use; in pricing engines, be sure that all the necessary accessories (suitable reduction gear, heat exchanger, extra alternator, power take-off, etc.) are all included in the price, as well as delivery to the shipyard and sales taxes.

The cost figures input to table 13-1 are approximations, but probably fairly representative of 1987 practice. As with any numbers given to you by someone else, check them out for yourself. If possible, find an owner who has just had a vessel of your type built and who is willing to give you his actual cost figures, not sales figures from a builder trying to induce a sale.

Note that, while the cost factors for the two commercial vessels are similar—the difference reflecting the more arduous service required of the fishing vessel—the factors for the institutional vessel are much higher. In general it is probably true that military craft, including U.S. Coast Guard vessels, will cost about twice as much as commercial craft of the same size (CUBE). Nonmilitary institutional craft, such as research vessels and pilot boats, will cost perhaps 25% to 50% more than commercial craft.

In costing out anything as complex and variable as a vessel, which furthermore is to be produced by a boatbuilding industry noted for its variability, one should allow plenty of tolerance. It is wise to hold out at least 10% or 15% of your available resources above the total vessel cost as a cushion to compensate for errors—yours or those of others.

Used boat costs: Ignorance of the factors involved in buying and owning used boats has probably caused more frustration, disappointment, and financial loss than any other single area of boat ownership. While as a conceptual designer you will be thinking in terms of new construction, there are two possible situations when the information given here on used boats can be helpful. First, as a business precaution you may wish to balance the cost of a new boat against the cost of a used boat; this is a useful exercise and if it does nothing more it will settle the question in your mind once and for all—to choose new or used. Second, you may have a used boat and wish to use your newfound designing skill to plan some rebuilding and rearrangement, in which case a knowledge of the cost structure will give you perspective on what is economically feasible and what is not.

It is my opinion that *any* used boat, when it has been brought up to grade, outfitted as desired, and commissioned, will cost 75% to 80% of what a new boat similarly prepared would cost. Whereas a relatively new used boat, at a high price, will presumably require little expenditure for commissioning, an old boat purchased for a small sum will likely require a good deal of expenditure in hull repairs, system replacement, machinery overhaul, and the other steps required to meet the above conditions. Keep in mind, too, that the used vessel is closer to the end of its useful life than is the new boat. So if the inherent and unfixable drawbacks that will inevitably exist in a craft built some time ago for someone else are not more than counterbalanced by the 20% to 25% saving in "ready to go" cost, then that vessel should be discarded as a possibility.

Of great significance in considering a used boat is the cost of operation. As stated below, the cost of operation of any watercraft is a function of its replacement cost which in turn is a function of size. I have known people who, rejecting a new boat as being too expensive in the size of their choice, have succumbed to the lure of a larger used boat at an initial price they can afford, only to find that they cannot afford the costs of maintenance, repair, and operation, costs that unfortunately go on year after year long after the "attractive" purchase price is forgotten. While this sad tale is by no means unknown among yacht owners, it is especially poignant when it happens to a commercial fisherman because it usually spells the end of his taking the leap into owning his own vessel.

Even more distressing is the fisherman who purchases a used boat with the intention of fishing it to earn the money required to bring it up to grade. I cannot think of a single instance in which this tactic is successful. To begin with, the fisherman who must adopt this tactic is usually right on the edge of his financial capabilities. Then, because the vessel is inevitably old, fishing time is lost as gear, machinery, or the hull itself fails under the stress of ordinary use, so that the vessel will be costing money in repairs instead of earning it on the grounds. Thus begins a downward spiral that continues until all the owner's resources are used up.

Should you decide to explore the used boat route as one of the viable options open to you in getting the boat you want, I strongly suggest that the following steps be carefully followed:

1. Estimate what a new boat, designed and built to your specifications, will cost, delivered and ready to use.

2. If you find an existing boat that seems to fill your needs, look it over carefully to get some idea of its general condition and whether with a reasonable amount of work it can meet your specifications. If it meets this test, then—

3. Have the vessel surveyed by a competent surveyor. He should provide you with his estimate of the market value of the vessel, what needs to be done to bring it up to grade (help him make up this list of things to do), and how much that work will cost. He should also render an opinion on the suitability of the vessel for your

purposes. *This survey and report is the most important step of all; do it no matter how competent you feel as a surveyor.*

4. Calculate the cost of the completely refurbished and revised vessel, at your dock or mooring ready for use. The following checklist may be helpful:

Total price paid for vessel	$###,###
Survey and other fees	#,###
Cost of correcting deficiencies	##,###
Yard bills	##,###
Revisions to fit your specifications	##,###
New equipment, installed	##,###
Painting, refinishing	#,###
Delivery to your dock or mooring	#,###
Taxes, insurance during work, etc., if any	#,###
Contingencies (add 5% to 10% of total above)	##,###
Total "ready" cost	$###,###

5. Calculate the cost of ownership for the new and used vessel as outlined in the following section over a period of, say, ten years. Include in the used vessel cost the replacement cost of any items, such as a generator, which the surveyor estimates will not last the ten years. Add as income the market value of each vessel at the end of the ten-year period.

6. Compare the annual cost of ownership of the used boat and a new vessel. (In making this comparison, include a factor for the gain or loss of commissioned time when the vessel cannot be used while it is being built or refurbished. Also include your labor during that time.)

7. Decide whether the new vessel or the used vessel better fits your needs. The final judgment must be largely subjective, and only you can make it. But based on the factual cost data outlined here, the decision is very apt to be a good one.

Cost of ownership: Cost of ownership is the total cost required to own the vessel and keep it in operation for one year. Table 13-2 itemizes the various elements of this cost and suggests how some may be estimated; not all categories will be applicable to all vessels, but the list includes the elements necessary to calculate the annual cost of virtually any vessel.

Profit: The measure of success of a commercial vessel is whether over time it generates an adequate return in the form of a "profit." But there are a number of different ways of defining profit. The operator's profit is simple: if the total income from the vessel exceeds the total costs by enough to satisfy the operator, then the enterprise is profitable. The banker's criterion (known as return on investment, ROI) is different: if the net income (excess of revenue over total cost) is sufficient to pay off the TVC as planned, then it is neutrally profitable; any excess over payments against principal and interest accrues to the operator or owner as *his* profit. These two approaches are not quite as simple as they seem, but there are other even more difficult methods. Probably consultation with a trusted CPA familiar with marine economics would be well worth the small expense.

Table 13-2
Estimating Cost of Ownership

Fixed annual costs:

Insurance (2.5% or 3% [?] of TVC)	$ ##,###
Administrative costs (10% [?] of TVC)	$ ##,###
Cost of principal and interest per year*	$###,###
Total fixed annual costs	$###,###

Variable annual costs:

Maintenance and repair (10% to 14% of TVC)	$ ##,###
Fuel (1 U.S. gallon per 17 horsepower-hours [diesel])	$###,###
Other consumables (food, lube oil, ice, bait)	$ ##,###
Crew costs (total annual wages × 1.25)	$ ##,###
Miscellaneous costs (gear repair, port fees, taxes)	$ ##,###
Total variable annual costs	$###,###

Total annual cost = annual fixed cost + annual variable costs

*Total interest to be paid can be estimated as follows:
Total interest = .632 × TVC × years to pay off × interest rate
Cost of principal and interest per year = (TVC + total interest)/years to pay

To calculate profit requires an estimate of income or revenue. To guard against the frequent error of over-optimism use as many hard data—based on your own experience or that of others, for instance—as possible, and develop three scenarios: worst case, best case, and probable case. You should be capable of surviving the worst case (for instance, if your target fish disappear for one year) for a year or two in order to have a secure enterprise.

A final word on vessel economics: Economics seems a cold and lifeless subject. Many don't have the gumption to face up to a true picture of the costs involved in their fishing vessel or yacht: "Don't confuse me with the facts; my mind is made up." But the wise person will examine carefully the financial side of the marine operations equation, and therefore will make decisions that are more likely to be wise ones than the person who doesn't study the economics.

My advice is that, once you have gone through the exercise described in this chapter and have determined that the vessel you have in mind is economically practical for you, forget all the details and pursue the course you have laid out.

But don't succumb to the lure of getting something "on the cheap." Stick to your original high standards; you have already decided that you can afford them. Because guess what? The cheap little fuel filter, piece of bargain rigging, or unknown electronics, is not going to fail when you are alongside a dock crawling with repair trucks loaded with spare parts. It is going to let go when that beautiful flat sunlit sea has in a few hours become a succession of towering breaking seas roaring at you from the blackness, and you are rolling your heart out beam to the seas because you fell for "just as good" fuel filters for $15 less.

So when the vessel arrives on your mooring you should have pride and confidence in every small and large detail. It makes economic sense as well as satisfying your inner being.

14. Power Yachts

G ENERALLY speaking, the function of pleasure power craft is to get from point A to point B and back again. This may be done with the major consideration speed of passage, or fun, or minimum discomfort, or occasionally transporting things. Point B may be an island cottage, a favored fishing ground, a pleasing and quiet bit of marine-land, or even the next television hookup. Compared to sailboating, in which the pleasure is derived from being under sail, getting from A to B in a powerboat is rarely as enjoyable. It may be relaxing or exciting, even scary sometimes, but it seems to the sailboater-author that the appeal of a powerboat lies in its ability to cover ground at a reasonably consistent rate, which is one, two, or more times the average sailboat speed. Boating is a very subjective avocation, and no one can tell another what he should enjoy. While my power craft preference is for the good seaboat of moderate speed (one of my favorite visual memories is watching a round-bottom 42′ Mathews cruiser slice smoothly through a steep head sea at 10 or 12 knots), the desires of others are satisfied by craft verging on houseboats (once described to me by a Maine boatbuilder as "sixteen straw decks and a glass bottom"), to those that pound over the waves at a liver-wrenching 50 knots.

Design comments: But everyone to his taste, and the role of the naval architect is to satisfy any taste as economically, fully, and safely as he can, whether he sympathizes with it or not. He can be personally judgmental, but not professionally so. Some of my most satisfying designs have been power craft for exceptionally fine people.

Incidentally, this and the following three chapters are written on the assumption that you have at least browsed through the preceding chapters and have studied chapter 8, "The Design Process," in detail.

Operating modes—Power craft can be placed into three categories according to operating modes: displacement craft, planing craft, and semidisplacement craft. The boundaries between these modes are not sharp, and there is some disagreement among naval architects as to the location of the boundaries. At the extremes the differentiation is clear. A heavy, round-bodied fishing vessel or tugboat is obviously a displacement vessel, while the hydroplane at 150 knots is clearly planing; in between is a large group whose mode is neither pure displacement nor pure planing.

A rigorous physical definition of the three modes is easy to conceive but difficult to put into practice. The change in vertical position of the center of gravity of a power-boat as it increases its speed from zero to a high speed is plotted in figure 14-1. The VCG actually drops somewhat as the speed increases from zero—probably due to the decreased pressure under the hull resulting from (1) the longer path of the water resulting in increased velocity and reduced pressure (Bernoulli effect), and (2) the greatly increased velocity of the water along the hull above the propeller(s). As speed increases dynamic lift begins to overcome the Bernoulli effect at point A until at some speed, B, at about speed-length ratio = 1.5 the VCG has returned to its at-rest

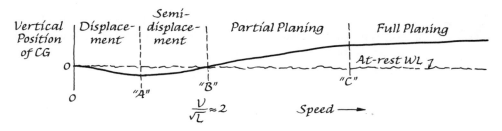

Fig. 14-1. Change in a powerboat's vertical position of
center of gravity with change of speed

level. Between zero speed and B, because the VCG is below its at-rest position, the virtual displacement of the boat may be said to be greater than the actual weight; beyond speed B the VCG lies above its at-rest position, indicating that due to dynamic lift the virtual displacement is *less* than the actual weight. At some point C the full weight of the boat is supported by dynamic lift; there is then close to zero displacement in the sense of there being little or no hole in the water and the CG can rise no more. I describe this state as "full planing." This history of the VCG position could be divided into four modes as shown: displacement, semidisplacement, partial planing, and full planing. This is a highly theoretical division because the changing position with speed of the VCG is virtually impossible to establish on a full-size boat; however, it does provide a useful conception of what is occurring over that speed range.

More perceptible but less precise descriptions of planing include: when the water clears the transom; when the water clears the topsides of a chine boat; when the speed-length ratio, $V/\sqrt{L}$, exceeds some level such as 2.5. The distinction is further blurred by a variation of absolute speed with vessel size; a 25' boat at speed-length ratio = 1.0 is traveling at only 5 knots, unacceptably slow, while a 1,200' tanker at the same low speed-length ratio would be traveling at 35 knots, twice the speed at which these vessels can economically steam.

Figure 14-2 is a schematic plot of the horsepower versus speed curves for boats operating in the three modes. At very low speeds, when nearly all resistance is frictional, the curves are nearly concurrent. As wave- and eddy-making become a factor, the displacement hull will have the lowest resistance up to the point where the $V/\sqrt{L}$ = about 1.2 or 1.3, above which the limiting effect of length becomes apparent as its rounded shape tries to climb out of the wake wave hole it has made. The straighter lines of the semidisplacement boat allow it to climb out of this hole, even if struggling a bit, and then at the higher speed-length ratios to show a distinct improvement; nevertheless its curve, too, continues to rise rather steeply. The planing

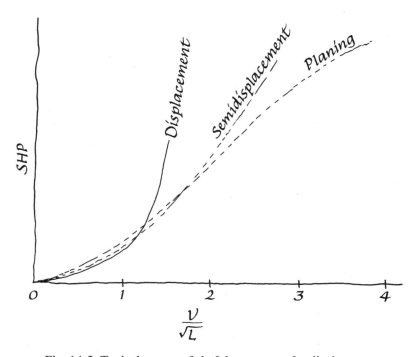

Fig. 14-2. Typical curves of shaft horsepower for displacement,
semidisplacement, and planing craft

boat, the worst performer in the early stages of wave- and eddy-making, soon benefits from being dynamically lifted clear of the wake waves so that at high speeds its curve has a very flat rise.

There is another fundamental factor in the performance of planing craft that is directly related to boat size. Analogous to the lift a wing provides an airplane, the dynamic lift acting on the hull can be described mathematically as the pounds of lift per square foot of water plane area. Since the laws of similitude require that the water plane area increases as L^2 while the displacement increases as L^3, the load per square foot increases directly with scale as can be seen in figure 14-3. Each square foot of water plane area of boat II must therefore take twice as much load as on boat I, thus requiring twice as much dynamic lift to support each square foot of boat II over boat I. Since, other things being equal, dynamic lift per square foot on a planing surface is a fixed amount for a given speed, the only way to achieve *similar* planing in a large vessel is to increase the speed in proportion to $\sqrt{L}$. It is for this reason that naval destroyers are not planing hulls, and why there is an upper limit for such lift-dependent craft as hydrofoils. In figure 14-3, boat II must travel at 28.3 knots to

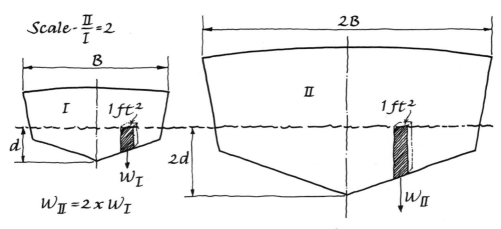

Load per square foot of waterplane area
for Hull II = 2 x that for Hull I.

Fig. 14-3. Increase of bottom loading on planing boat with increase of boat size

lift the same proportion of its displacement as does boat I at 20 knots. Both boats will be operating at $V/\sqrt{L}$ = 2.83, LWL = 50' (15.24 m) at 20 knots and LWL= 100' (30.5 m) at 28.3 knots, respectively.

Another solution to this size problem would be to lighten up the larger boat so that it displaces half as much as boat II. But if one assumes that boat II was reasonably efficiently designed in the first place, it would be difficult or impossible to lighten it up by anything approaching one-half.

Pounding (slamming)—Because of the speed at which powered vessels travel, and the fact that, unlike sailing craft, they can travel directly into a sea, pounding (also known as slamming) is an important aspect of power craft design. It is desirable to minimize pounding as much as possible to improve the comfort and safety of people aboard and to reduce the stresses on the hull.

Obviously the finer a powerboat is in the forebody, the less it will pound, but fineness is difficult to achieve in a planing hull. John Hacker maintained that to avoid pounding, the deadrise at station 2 should not be less than 25° (fig. 14-4); I have used this rule in my powerboat designs and have been satisfied with their performance in a sea. I also avoid wide transoms, which tend to drive the bow down with considerable force and thus increase the pounding pressures.

When all has been done in that direction that can be, there must be assurance that the hull is strong enough to withstand any foreseeable stress; this aspect will be addressed by your naval architect as he develops the construction plans for your boat.

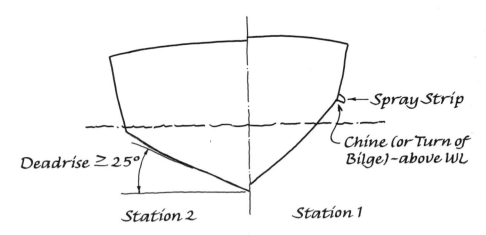

Fig. 14-4. Forebody features to improve powerboat sea-kindliness

Peripheral to the pounding question is that of spray generation and deflection. It is desirable to keep spray away from the deck and pilothouse of the boat as much as possible without hampering overall performance. A constant cloud of spray is an unpleasant nuisance at best, and at worst can significantly interfere with the vision necessary for safe operation.

I use two features to cope with this problem (see figure 14-4):

1. At station 1, I like the turn of the bilge or chine to be clearly above the water-line. This helps knock down the bow wave and also helps prevent broaching when operating in a steep quartering sea.

2. Spray strips significantly improve dryness and seem to provide some planing lift in faster boats. On a chine boat, locate the strip at the chine. For a round bilge boat, it's helpful to operate the boat without the strips and note where the bow wave peels away from the hull; locate the strip at or slightly below that locus. The lower surface of spray strips should be square with the hull and about 1½% of the overall beam in width; strips should run from the stem to about amidships at least.

Displacement—Having stipulated the operating speed of your craft and developed the overall dimensions via the envelope sketch, it is time to determine the displacement. Your naval architect will calculate this precisely, matching up the displacement with his calculated weight of the vessel, but you will need to make as close an estimate as you can in order to sketch the hull realistically.

In estimating a preliminary displacement for your design, it is best to do it in a particular order to avoid the need for tedious backtracking. When in doubt, make the boat too heavy rather than too light; nobody ever minded a boat that floated above her lines, but when the boot top disappears on launching day there are bound to be frowns and frets.

1. Select a preliminary length-displacement ratio (LWL/cube root of displacement in cubic feet or meters) according to the type of boat you have sketched so far, built to ordinary standards and scantlings for the type. Roughly speaking, a value of 5.7 will give the displacement for high performance craft to operate at speed-length ratios of up to 5 or 6; 4.8 will give the displacement of the ordinary cruising boat designed for a top speed-length ratio of 2.0 to 2.5; 4.2 will give the displacement of a heavy, fisherman type of yacht with a speed-length ratio of 1.4 or less.

(Note: Length-displacement ratio is used here instead of the displacement-length ratio common in the U.S. because the former is nondimensional and can be used with either the English or metric measurement system or any other consistent measurement system; see chapter 3 for a discussion of these important ratios.)

2. If your design has unusual proportions—for instance, long and narrow or short and broad—use the cubic number, CUBE, instead of length as the basis for selecting the base displacement (see table 14-1).

3. If you are using nonstandard construction, adjust the base displacement according to the indexes in table 11-2.

4. If you have unusual weights on board, such as fuel capacity for 20 days endurance, increase the displacement appropriately.

Hull proportions—It is time to shape the hull. In doing this, the primary consideration is the speed-length ratio, $V/\sqrt{L}$. Obviously hull forms for planing boats will be different from those for displacement boats, with semiplaning boats having some of the characteristics of each. Picture four vessels, with LWLs of 1,000', 300', 65', and 22' (304.8 m, 91.4 m, 19.8 m, 6.7 m). All are traveling at the same velocity, 15 knots. But the speed-length ratios are respectively 0.47, 0.87, 1.86, and 3.20, so that, while the 1,000' (304.8 m) vessel is apparently moving quite slowly and making a relatively modest wake, the 22' (6.7 m) launch is flying along on top of the water. The two largest vessels are in full displacement mode, the 65-footer (19.8 m) is entering semiplaning mode, and the launch is approaching a full plane. Since the three modes each require a different hull form, it is easy to see why the speed-length ratio really dictates the hull form.

Table 14-1
Representative Ratios of Displacement Volume to CUBE

Tankers	.56
Freighters	.40
Containerships	.33
Ferries	.44
Research vessels	.34
Tugboat	.54
Fishing vessels—trawlers, etc.	.46
Naval vessels—corvettes, etc.	.29
Planing	.16 ±

Multiplying CUBE by the values listed here will give a first approximation of the displacement volume. To get tons, divide volume by 35.

One of the important parameters of hull form is the prismatic coefficient, C_p; sometimes called the fineness coefficient, the prismatic coefficient is described in chapter 3, and table 3-2 lists optimum C_p against $V/\sqrt{L}$. The prismatic coefficient is related to the wave-making character of the hull, an important element of total resistance at $V/\sqrt{L} = 1.0$ to 2.5 or more. If LWL, displacement, and C_p are known, then the midsection area can be calculated:

$$\text{Midsection area below LWL, MA} = \frac{\text{Displ}_{vol}}{(\text{LWL} \times C_p)}$$

For a displacement craft with a $V/\sqrt{L}$ of 1.1 or 1.2, the desired C_p is about .55, giving a hull that tapers from a sizable midsection in sharply toward the bow and stern. For low values of $V/\sqrt{L}$, C_p can be quite high without loss of efficiency because the residual (wave-making) resistance at low speeds is an increasingly smaller proportion of total resistance (see figure 12-1). It is for this reason that very large tankers can be efficient with hulls shaped like long boxes rounded off at the ends, with a C_p on the order of .9.

Other useful proportions are L/B (= LWL/beam), B/D (= beam/depth), and B/T (= beam/draft). Values for these proportions vary rather widely depending on size and use of vessel; they can be derived easily from published material on vessels of the type you are sketching.

Hull shape: It is obvious from the foregoing that the same hull will not be equally suitable for all three operating modes. Figure 14-5 illustrates hulls for each mode; to improve the comparison all three boats have the same displacement and waterline length. Please understand that these hulls are illustrative only so don't spoil your fun by copying them. Let your imagination create hull shapes that reflect your own concepts; your naval architect will advise you of any flaws that may creep in.

Displacement craft—This vessel, designed for only 7 knots, will seem impossibly passé to a U.S. yachting public accustomed to 60-knot speedsters. But while sketching it, I was reminded of seeing a similar hull lying-to in a 20-knot wind in the middle of the North Sea a hundred miles from the nearest shore. (I was aboard the 530′ (161.5 m) training vessel *State of Maine,* making the crossing in great comfort.) She was a lapstrake fishing vessel with a riding sail, of just about the size shown, and it was a pleasure to see how nicely she rode, lying about 6 points off the wind. As we steamed past it, two men came out of the companionway and waved at us, perfectly comfortable and enjoying a rest before the sea quieted down and they could start fishing again. This type of hull is not for the summer coastwise sailor, who is unlikely to meet severe weather and usually has a port to make for if he does, and who is better served by a little more than 7 knots speed. But it would do well for a cruise around Newfoundland and Labrador, or the Aleutian Islands, and points north, areas where it is more often wise to stay out in bad weather than to seek a doubtful haven.

A great virtue in sea-kindliness is to have both ends of the boat somewhat similar as in the displacement hull. One can imagine the hull in the sketch running before a quartering breaking sea with virtually no tendency to broach or to pitchpole.

This hull form is also much kinder when steaming directly into a chop. The fine stern allows the bow to rise easily and quickly, and does not force it back down in a hard pitching motion after the crest has passed. Also the finer waterline shape with its lower transverse moment of inertia will give a more comfortable rolling motion.

Planing craft—At the other end of the speed scale is the high speed full planing boat. Note that the after 60% or so of the hull is essentially a prism in which the midsection shape is carried right back to the transom. This has been demonstrated to be the most efficient shape for high speed; actually a flat bottom would be even more so, but the deadrise makes for a softer riding boat. The hull shown here has really no upper limit of speed although at some very high speed there will be a tendency to heel and ride on only one side of the bottom. Essentially, though, the upper limit on speed will be dictated by the amount of power installed and the controllability and sea-kindliness of the hull in the sea conditions of the moment.

High speed operation places great stresses upon the hull, so that the construction material and the scantlings must be selected to provide adequate strength without excessive weight. Very likely welded aluminum would be the material of choice, although specialists in exotic materials (composites with carbon fiber, etc.) might argue the point.

These high speed craft in any kind of a seaway often leave the water, and the impact of the return to the waterborne state, measured in g's of acceleration, can be extremely high. If the acceleration due to pitching reaches a maximum of 1g, everything in effect weighs twice as much at the moment of impact. Accordingly, foundations for engines, tanks, and any heavy components must be extremely strong and tied in well to the entire hull so that they don't tear themselves loose.

Planing boats of any size invariably have twin screws, sometimes triple screws, and small balanced spade rudders, supported entirely by bearings within the hull.

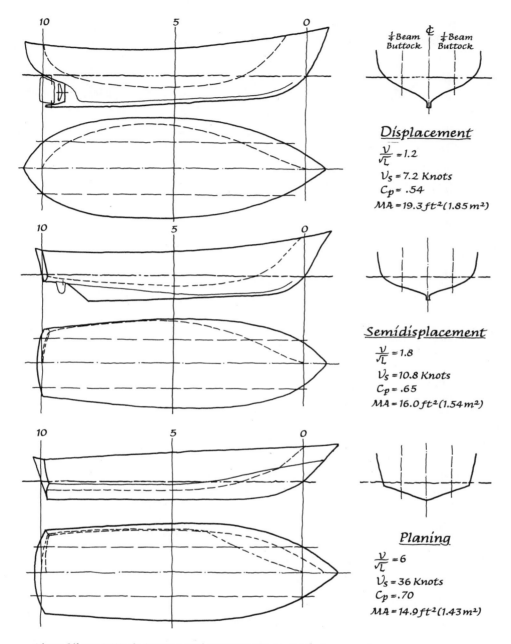

¼Beam   ₵   ¼Beam
Buttock   Buttock

Displacement

$\dfrac{V}{\sqrt{L}} = 1.2$

$V_s = 7.2$ Knots

$C_p = .54$

$MA = 19.3\,ft^2\,(1.85\,m^2)$

Semidisplacement

$\dfrac{V}{\sqrt{L}} = 1.8$

$V_s = 10.8$ Knots

$C_p = .65$

$MA = 16.0\,ft^2\,(1.54\,m^2)$

Planing

$\dfrac{V}{\sqrt{L}} = 6$

$V_s = 36$ Knots

$C_p = .70$

$MA = 14.9\,ft^2\,(1.43\,m^2)$

Note: All are 36' LWL (10.9 m) and 24,000 lb (10.9 mt) Displacement.

Fig. 14-5. Representative hull forms for displacement,
semidisplacement, and planing powerboats

Skegs and external keels are eliminated because of the resistance they offer; this is fine when conditions are good, but when, as can happen, the crew or the boat can no longer operate in the planing mode, these are poor craft. Undoubtedly they are safe enough, in part because their great power allows them to respond quickly and fully to sudden hazards, but they won't hold a candle to the displacement boat described above when things get really bad.

Semidisplacement craft—This hull will operate at a speed between the displacement hull and full planing hull. It tends not to be as efficient as the others at its designed speed in terms of miles traveled per gallon of fuel. Nevertheless, it combines for the recreational boater an acceptable speed with a nicely shaped hull for comfort and good handling qualities. The ubiquitous Maine lobsterboat hull is of this general class, and the best of those are as able and handy as one can find if they are not heavily loaded. Transom width should be about 85% of maximum beam, and the waterline shape forward should not be too fine; a triangular-shaped waterline plane can be hard to control in a quartering sea, with a tendency to uncontrollable broaching.

Arrangement: The accelerated motion of powerboats and the increasing severity of pounding in the higher speed ranges, suggest a few rules about how the contents of the boat should be arranged.

1. Put those accommodation areas where the most waking hours will be spent well aft in the boat. This includes the helm and lounging areas.

2. Berths can go well forward. It is surprisingly easy to relax in a bunk in an area of the boat where it is difficult or impossible to cook, lounge comfortably, or even stand up for any length of time because of the motion.

3. Galleys should be at or astern of the pitching pivot point (about $4/7$ aft).

4. The faster the boat, the farther aft should be loose gear that can be tossed about and heavy weights (tanks, machinery, etc.) which with repeated high accelerations may actually pound the hull apart.

5. Although some may disagree, toilet rooms are used a small proportion of the time at sea, so can often be located at the very bow as long as all the contents can be secured from jumping about.

Typical arrangements are shown for our three sample craft in figure 14-6. These are presented only as a basis for discussion; the reader is urged to experiment with the many possible arrangements before selecting one. Remember that after selecting the basic arrangement pattern it is usually very difficult to make any significant changes without going back to the beginning and starting over again.

Displacement craft—This arrangement was actually used on a motorsailer for a family with four girls. They slept forward while Mom and Dad slept in the deckhouse; note that the toilet room is accessible from either sleeping area without disturbing the other. This is an example of specific needs for the boat calling for a departure from the general rules set forth above, since the toilet room could use space more efficiently were it in the bow.

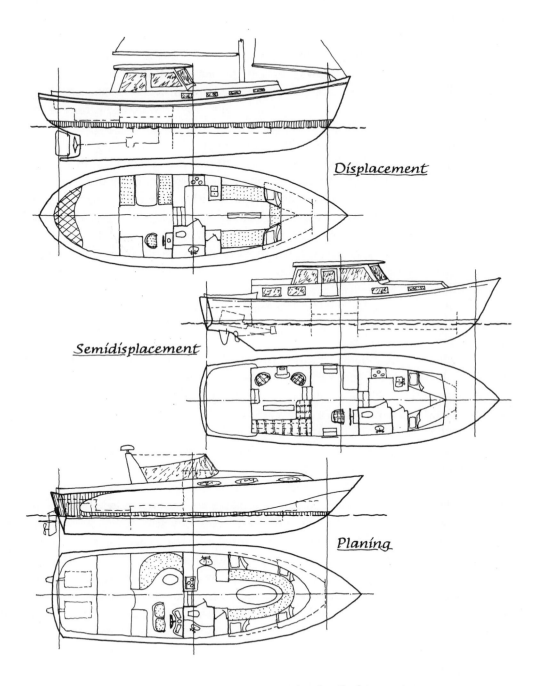

Fig. 14-6. Possible arrangements for displacement,
semidisplacement, and planing powerboats

The engine is located under the pilothouse for easy accessibility (there should be one small hinged hatch for ordinary maintenance access), but the deck should be sound-insulated. Fuel tanks could be outboard of the engine and, because water and fuel would be used at about the same proportional rate, would be balanced as far as trim is concerned by a sizable water tank under the foremost berths.

With a metacentric height, GM, of 1.5' (.46 m) or so this would be a remarkably comfortable boat in any seaway and on any heading. If desired, a modest rig of 250-300 ft² (23-28 m²) would have a nice steadying effect in a beam sea, allow throttling back a good deal in a favoring breeze, and provide welcome variety to the boredom of powerboat passages.

Semidisplacement craft: I used the arrangement shown here on a successful 39' (12 m) strip-planked power cruiser. The purpose was to have the living and lounging area aft, separated from the sleeping-cooking-toilet area by the bridge.

The boat was one of the first moderate-speed fairly heavy craft to be driven by outdrives; despite some doubts, the drives held up better than the engines. The engines were located under a sizable clear after deck, isolating much of the noise and smell from the rest of the boat, and the compartment was easily accessible through large hatches. Fuel and water tanks were ideally located, under the bridge near the center of flotation.

The hull form was designed for sea-kindliness, sacrificing a little efficiency at the upper end of the speed range ($V/\sqrt{L}$ = 1.8) but below that being very efficient. This was a wonderful sea boat.

Full planing—Although I confess to not being an expert in this specialized field, I would design the interior something like that shown in figure 14-6. The bouncy and bangy part of the boat would have all the berths, the bedding (and occupants!) of which could be strapped down easily. Aft of the berth and lounge area would be the galley and toilet room, close to the pitching axis. Passenger lounging would be in safety seats opposite the conning station, and on any sybaritic cushions the owner wished to distribute about the cockpit.

Engines would be well aft, driving propellers through V-drives or outdrives. This would permit the fuel tanks to be in a separate compartment close to the center of flotation and balanced by the modest water tank forward.

Catamarans: Catamarans (not to be confused with the lashed-log katumarans of India) were first conceived in the western world about 200 years ago. Although one thinks of them as sailing craft, their first use was as powered vessels. The twin hulls provided stability, a large deck area, and a central protected location for the paddle wheel driven by the new-fangled steam engine. The catamaran idea kept reappearing, culminating in an English Channel steamer, but was never economically successful because the early low-powered engines had difficulty overcoming the excessive skin friction of two hulls; the vessels were therefore slow and, despite the advantages of the type, never caught on.

Another drawback was that two hulls joined by a wing tended to be very heavy when built of the materials of the day. (This is still true today, and catamarans should be built of light materials like aluminum, not steel.) Nevertheless it is significant that my studies of catamarans have never turned up an instance in which the hull-wing assembly failed structurally, excluding high performance craft built to the limit of the material.

The advantages of the catamaran still pertain: high stability and great deck area. These days, with light materials and low-cost, high-power engines available, power catamarans are again becoming popular. Two types are of interest in this chapter—the high performance planing craft, and the displacement mode cruising or workboat.

The motion of catamarans may take getting used to. Very stiff in the transverse direction, their pitching characteristics are about the same as a monohull of the same length. The combination of the two motions sometimes imparts a corkscrew motion to the vessel in a quartering sea which some people find unsettling.

However, fishing my own 34′ (10.36 m) catamaran off the Maine coast in winter (only a few trips because the shrimp had left by the time we got out there) demonstrated her to be a superior sea boat for her size.

High performance catamarans—The high speed catamarans seem to have two advantages over the conventional monohull speedboat. It has greater stability than the deep-vee monohulls, which can occasionally and disconcertingly drop off onto one side of the bottom. Also, the air trapped between the hulls seems to provide some lift and cushioning effect. Developments in lightweight building materials have made it possible to design this rather weak hull form to be strong enough to take the terrific impacts such a craft is subject to.

Cruising or working power catamarans—When a catamaran is large enough for full headroom in the hulls—from about LWL = 30′ (9.14 m)—its advantages become very noticeable. Compare, for instance, the accommodations in the sketched catamaran (fig. 14-7) with those of the average 42′ to 45′ (12.8 m to 13.7 m) cruiser of equal displacement. In addition to the big-ship bridge, spacious lounge, and large convertible stateroom on the main deck level, the design includes a complete galley and and toilet room in the port hull and a sleeping space for two or four in the starboard hull. Note also that the engines, with the noise and smell, are entirely clear of the accommodations and are easily accessible for maintenance or for major repair, even removal. (Travelers along the East Coast may encounter a slightly smaller version of this craft—the 37′ (11.28) LOA *Janthina,* designed for Howie and Willa Eckles.)

There is no single answer to things nautical, but many of the problems people face in finding a compatible boat can be solved by the catamaran.

Nowadays even small powerboats can be highly complex, with a whole host of goodies undreamed of in the thirties. Along with the machinery subsystems

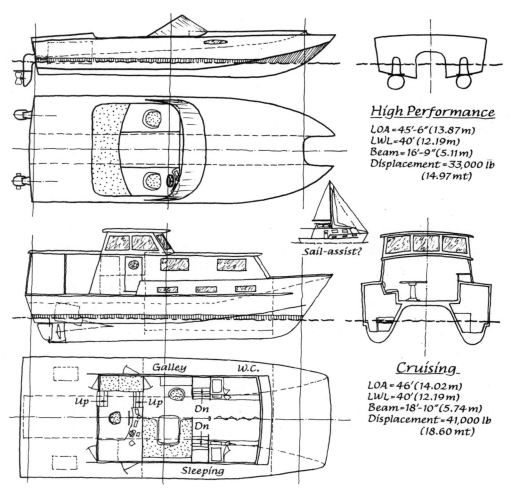

High Performance
LOA = 45'-6" (13.87 m)
LWL = 40' (12.19 m)
Beam = 16'-9" (5.11 m)
Displacement = 33,000 lb
(14.97 mt)

Sail-assist?

Cruising
LOA = 46' (14.02 m)
LWL = 40' (12.19 m)
Beam = 18'-10" (5.74 m)
Displacement = 41,000 lb
(18.60 mt)

Galley   W.C.
Up   Up   Dn
Dn
Sleeping

Fig. 14-7. High performance and cruising types of powered catamarans

described in figure 12-14 one may expect to find auxiliary generators; mechanical refrigeration; 12 VDC and 110 VAC electrical systems; pressure hot and cold water systems; sewage treatment or holding capability; air-conditioning/heating; electronics, including depth-sounder, UHF and VHF radios, Loran-C, radar, speedometer, satellite navigator, hi-fi. The more of this there is, the more care must be taken in fitting it all in so the components do not interfere with one another, are conveniently located for use and servicing, are safe from damage, and don't adversely affect the trim or stability of the boat. To exercise this care requires much early planning via mental design and envelope sketches, so make sure you go around the design spiral enough times to have done all the necessary revising and cross-checking.

15. Sailing Craft

THERE is a mystique about sailing craft that doesn't apply to any other type of watercraft. In an Iowa farmhouse where one would not be apt to find a picture of a tanker or an ocean liner there may very likely be an oil painting-by-the-numbers of *Constitution* or a print of *Mayflower*. And thousands who wouldn't give a nickel to ride on a modern trawler pay to sail on *Spirit of Massachusetts,* a replica of the Gloucester fishing schooner *Fredonia.* Sailing craft have an appeal that is somewhat akin to the appeal of the ocean itself, an appeal that Rachel Carson ascribed to an atavistic desire to return to the sea, womb of our mammalian beginnings.

I knew a man who, growing up wealthy, had tried everything for excitement. Auto racing, flying, speedboating—none had given him more than a brief thrill. But in sailing he finally found the challenge for which he had been searching much of his life, and so far as I know he kept at it to the end. I do know that his money made him fair game for every gadget and electronics salesman with the result that every available cubic foot of his cutter was stuffed with something other than bread and beer. Finally, after finding that he spent most of his time keeping this gadgetry repaired, he pitched it all overboard and went back to the basics—a simple sailing craft that he could enjoy.

And surely the sailors of today, whether perched on an 8′ dinghy becalmed in the middle of a lake, or struggling through a Cape Horn gale in the single-handed race around the world, or repairing a tack seizing on a high yard in a rolling sea, are not doing it in search of the easy life. Each in his or her own way is endeavoring to recapture the challenge faced by the Phoenicians heading into the unknown through the Pillars of Hercules, or by Columbus's crew wondering if indeed they would find the edge of the earth. Every time we set out for a sail, we are reliving that challenge in a small way, by entering a world of uncertainty in which we must work with the vagaries of nature, using our own wits and strength to make good our intended course and distance.

In the wealthy Western world we can afford to buy this mystique, but it exists in the developing world also, not as a luxury to be purchased but as a major fact of life. The fishermen of the Maldives assign one crew member the task of propitiating the gods of the sea. Rough but sturdy sailing lighters, built entirely by hand on the river bank at Kakinada, India, are launched with appropriate ceremony, coconuts cracking on the stem. And the oculus (an eye painted on each bow), found in so many marine cultures, suggests that a god-like quality is invested in the vessel carrying them.

In designing a sailing craft, whether for racing, cruising, or carrying passengers or freight, we must recognize this special quality that the completed vessel will engender and include it in our planning. We should neither pretend it doesn't exist and try to hide it under a cold high tech creation of carbon fibers and super winches nor fancy ourselves as Captain Hornblower cruising the Spanish Main in search of a Panama galleon. But, somewhere in between, we should include in our thinking the realization that a sailboat isn't only for getting from point A to point B, that it has a higher function than merely fulfilling the old saw about "getting there is half the fun."

In chapter 12, we learned something about the resistance forces that hold a sailboat back, the driving and heeling forces of sails, and some of the unconventional "sails" used to extract a driving force from the wind. In this chapter only conventional sails and rigs will be considered; if the reader wishes to become involved in a fascinating if complicated field, he can join the small but increasing band of investigators exploring old and new rigs and sails and their applications. It is difficult to imagine that a free source of energy like the wind will not come into its own in the future in commercial as well as recreational uses. And looking out into "empty" space, there are winds of photons and subatomic particles waiting to be harnessed to drive spacecraft.

This chapter deals with all sailing craft, whether used for pleasure or profit and including everything from speed-seeking catamarans to passenger-carrying schooners and school ships. It will thus be divided into three sections: sailing craft in general, sailing yachts, and working sailing craft.

Sailing craft in general: Two characteristics of all sailing craft loom very large: stability and balance. Measured as the amount of helm required to hold a vessel on course as wind velocity and direction change, balance is largely a matter of pleasure and convenience, but stability is a vital factor that can mean life itself.

Stability—Stability is the power the sailing craft has to resist the overturning moment of wind and sea, and may be divided into two levels: operational and ultimate.

Operational stability relates to day-to-day heel angle with an upper limit of 20 to 30 degrees of heel, above which the boat performs less efficiently. The stability of a boat, as explained in chapter 6, is a function of the height of the center of gravity in the vessel and the position of the center of buoyancy; for a given CB location, a high CG will give less stability but a more comfortable motion, a lower CG greater stability but a more violent motion. Working to overcome the stability is the sail side force; the higher and larger the rig, and the stronger the average wind force, the more the boat will heel.

Matching up the size and type of rig with a given hull's stability characteristics is not a pat and rigorous process, although a simple method of estimating sail area is given later. Quite apart from the fact that it is difficult to represent precisely the wind and wave conditions in which the boat is operating, the match depends upon several rather subjective considerations: the sailing habits and preferences of the owner and his family; the average conditions of the vessel's home waters; whether the boat will be raced, and if so whether casually or seriously and under what rating rule. You should answer these questions before starting your sketch design. Also, transmit the answers as precisely as possible to your naval architect so that he can match your boat closely with you.

Figure 15-1 illustrates how the center of gravity (CG) and the center of buoyancy (CB) are tied to each other in the righting moment (RM) which is the quantitative measure of stability. Also shown is a typical plot of the righting arm, GZ, against heel angle; from this graph it is seen that this particular boat has positive stability to about 160° of heel.

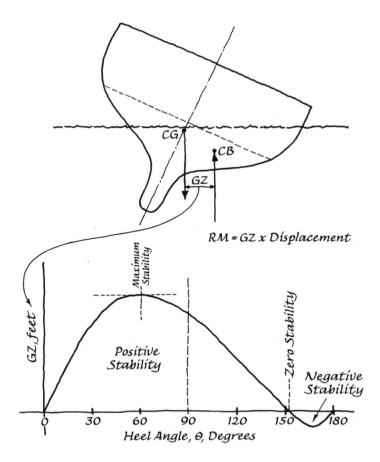

Fig. 15-1. Sailboat operational stability

With respect to ultimate stability, it is an interesting exercise to see how your boat would look if heeled to 90°; the maximum heel angle from wind force alone is probably not over 80°. Sketch the full midsection heeled to 90° and adjust the water plane, which will be parallel to the center plane of the hull, so that the area under it equals the upright midsection area plus 10% to 15% (see figure 15-2). This is only a rough depiction of a boat blown over to this angle because it does not take into account such things as the fore-and-aft shape of the hull, trim, or the depressing effect of the wind and/or waves.

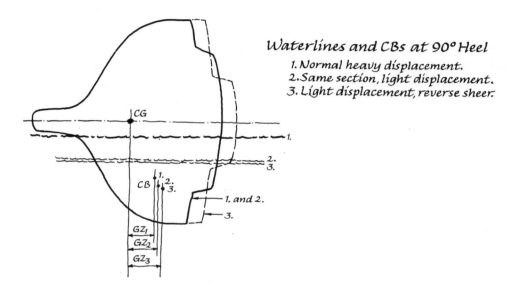

Waterlines and CBs at 90° Heel
1. Normal heavy displacement.
2. Same section, light displacement.
3. Light displacement, reverse sheer.

Fig. 15-2. Sailboat ultimate stability, comparing light and heavy displacement and conventional and reverse sheer

Some conclusions can be drawn from this exercise, however. For truly arduous service, all openings should be concentrated as close to the centerline as possible so as to be above the 90° waterline; a light displacement boat will float higher and thus have less chance of flooding through hatches, etc., than a heavy boat; reverse sheer would further improve the chances of a boat in a knockdown.

The naval architect does the best he can to forestall disaster at sea. But the disturbed air/water interface is no respecter of modern technology, and its extremes often mock our earnest efforts. While totally inadequate craft can survive seemingly overwhelming conditions, large, modern, well-equipped and ably handled vessels still disappear without a trace. Everyone who ventures afloat, whether in a 10' dinghy or a 1,000' tanker should be aware that absolute security does not exist at sea, that there is no guarantee against hazard to life and property.

Balance—In figures 6-11 and 6-12 we took a look at how the rudder acts upon the hull to hold a course or to maneuver. The steering and course-keeping for a powered craft is relatively simple; the propelling force is centrally and consistently applied and the rudder forces can be accentuated by placing the rudder directly in the accelerated stream of water coming from the propeller. However, when we examine the application of sail power to a vessel, illustrated in figures 12-5 and 12-6, the picture becomes very complicated. In addition to the variability of wind velocity from zero to hurricane velocity and of bearing from dead ahead to dead astern, the sailboat heels and makes leeway, and the apparent wind vector (the wind actually felt on the boat) is a combination of the vectors of true wind speed and direction and boat speed and course. In a word, the complications are monumental. In the face of them, it seems almost impossible to design a sailing craft that can be held on course under all conditions.

Nevertheless, it is entirely possible to design a well-balanced sailing craft that will hold its course with little effort on the helm, even in variable winds. This requires that the resultant wind vector be exactly balanced in direction and magnitude by the net resultant water force; in the well-balanced boat this will require only small movement of the rudder. Our instinct is to ensure a balanced boat by properly locating the rig—designing it to have a certain "lead." Lead is defined as the amount the center of the sail area, the center of effort (CE), is forward of the center of the underwater profile, the center of lateral resistance (CLR). This is an approximation because the geometric centers of sail and underwater profile do not correspond with the actual aero- and hydrodynamic centers. If we also consider the fact that water is 800 times as dense as air, and that the very influential bow and stern waves are far apart at the ends of the boat, we can begin to understand why hull form is of vastly greater importance to balance than is the rig. In fact, an unbalanced hull will always be inherently unbalanced, no matter what is done with the rig and the sails; the only way to correct an unbalanced boat is to rebuild a portion of the hull to a correct shape.

A boat with a weather helm resulting from an unbalanced hull can usually be adjusted to steer reasonably easily in constant conditions by adjusting the trim of the sails, but will tend to sheer sharply into the wind in a puff, and off the wind when the puff lightens. This is not only uncomfortable and inconvenient, but can be hazardous when the sheering effect is too great to be overcome by the rudder. (I saw a fleet of L-16 sloops, running along a rocky shore with spinnakers set; they were hit by a fresh puff, broached, and sailed onto the rocks. I say I "saw" them —actually I was around a point and we only heard the deep "bongs" as the molded plywood hulls took to the granite. It's a credit to the construction that so far as I know none suffered any real damage.) A boat with a lee helm will bear off in a puff and come up when it lightens, the reverse of the weather helm.

In my view the ideally balanced boat has just a touch of weather helm, not enough to be a physical problem for the helmsman, but enough so that the boat will round up into the wind if the helm is left unattended. This small weather helm means the rudder is providing a slight but useful side force to windward like a flap on a plane's wing, a help when working to a weather mark. But whatever happens, avoid a lee helm like the plague. It is most uncomfortable, and can be dangerous to boot. The 11th commandment might have been, "Thou shalt not inflict upon thy fellow man a lee helm."

Fortunately there is a very quick and simple means of ensuring that a sailboat design will have a reasonable helm. This system, shown in figure 15-3, has served very well on all my designs in which it was used. I cannot guarantee that at some time it will not fail for someone, but I wouldn't think of turning out a design that didn't pass the test.

If the shift aft of the center of flotation (center of gravity of water plane) between 0° and 25°-30° heel angles is more than 1 percent LWL, there is probably more weather helm than desired. If there is no shift, or the shift is forward, there will be no helm or a lee helm, both undesirable. Filling out the forward sections and/or fining up the after sections will move the heeled CF forward; filling in aft and taking away forward will move CF aft.

For me, to be pleasing a boat *must* be well balanced. You can trust it, knowing that it will be responsive and well behaved under all conditions, and that nothing is holding it back from reaching its speed potential. It's a major goal I always strive for in my designs.

Monohull versus multihull—While we think of the multihull sailing craft as being a recent invention, it probably dates all the way back to the beginnings of water transport. A log, even if shaped and hollowed out, is not a very stable craft. It must have soon occurred to the earliest boatbuilders to improve stability with another log or bamboo pole supported some distance away from the main hull. In some cases, as in the South Seas, the logs were the same size and the result was what we call a catamaran. (The katumaran of the Indian East Coast is formed of a number of solid logs lashed together and fitted with a seat and a single leg-o'-mutton sail. These little craft are launched through the surf, sail 10-15 mi (18 to 28 km) out on an offshore breeze, fish all day, and return on the afternoon onshore breeze. After landing through the surf, the lashings are taken off and the individual logs are carried up the beach; drysailing keeps them from becoming waterlogged. The jacaranda is a similar type of craft, built of bamboo and native to Brazil.)

There are two types of multihull—the catamaran, composed of two similar hulls with an overall beam somewhat less than 50% of the length, and the trimaran, consisting of a main central hull and two smaller side hulls with an overall beam somewhat greater than 50% of the length. Each has its minor advantages, but none that I consider makes one superior. Since in general they have the same functional characteristics, I will ignore the screams of outrage from partisans of the two types and lump them together.

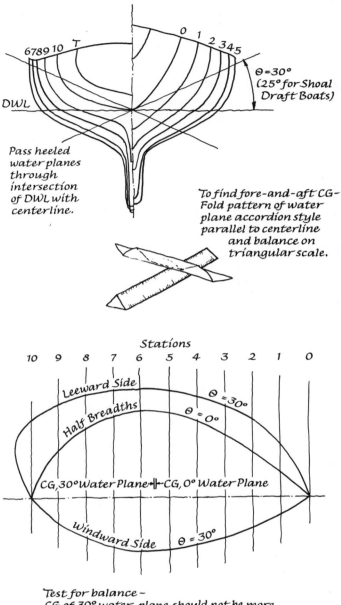

0 1 2 3 4 5

6789 10 T

$\Theta = 30°$
(25° for Shoal
Draft Boats)

DWL

Pass heeled
water planes
through
intersection
of DWL with
centerline.

To find fore-and-aft CG—
Fold pattern of water
plane accordion style
parallel to centerline
and balance on
triangular scale.

Stations

10   9   8   7   6   5   4   3   2   1   0

Leeward Side

Half Breadths

$\Theta = 30°$

$\Theta = 0°$

CG, 30° Water Plane —||— CG, 0° Water Plane

Windward Side $\Theta = 30°$

Test for balance –
CG of 30° water plane should not be more
than 1% LWL aft of 0°CG.

(Lay out water plane offsets on
cross-section [graph] paper.)

(CG of water plane is same as
Center of Flotation, C.F.)

Fig. 15-3. Method of ensuring balance of a sailboat hull

What separates multihulls from monohulls is the way they achieve stability. The multihull is stable because of the spread of the hulls, which gives very large righting arms at normal operating heel angles (10° or less). The monohull, without that hull spread, has a relatively small righting arm. The ability to carry sail is a function of righting arm (GZ) × displacement, so the multihull, with a large GZ, can achieve equal stability with a much smaller displacement than the monohull. When the differences of displacement and wetted surface as they relate to residual and frictional resistance are sorted out, the multihull will be on average faster than the monohull of equal sail area. Indeed, this is the major reason multihulls exist—because they are faster than monohulls, as has been demonstrated in a number of ocean races and in speed trials.

But there are drawbacks to the multihull. Because of its light displacement, a multihull has very little momentum so it forereaches, or coasts, very little, a situation not helped by the large wetted surface inherent in multihulls. Coming about, going from one tack to the other, must therefore depend a good deal on speed, which means sailing the boat about. If the speed is lacking through light airs or from a succession of maneuvers or if there is a chop, the multihull becomes pretty unmanageable without the help of oars or engine.

The stability curve of a multihull, figure 15-4, suggests another problem, the questionable ability of a multihull to remain upright in extreme conditions. The catamaran has much less, perhaps half as much, "stability energy" for resisting capsize than does the monohull. It is therefore not surprising that there are numerous examples of multihulls capsizing at sea from the wind force, from wave action, or from a combination of both; fortunately, being unballasted they float upside down, but such an experience is guaranteed to spoil one's sailing fun. By contrast, there are many instances (read the report on the 1979 Fastnet Race) in which monohulls have been rolled completely over and returned to an upright position.

One might say that the more conservatively a multihull is designed, that is, the closer its displacement and sail area are to that of a comparable monohull, the safer it becomes, but at the expense of super performance. At the other extreme, radically designed high performance multihulls are among the fastest (and most exciting) sailing craft ever built, frequently achieving speeds exceeding 30 knots.

If you the reader are considering changing from a type with which you have had considerable experience to the another type, investigate it well to make sure you won't be disappointed in the results. An excellent idea is to charter one of the new type for a week or two to give it a real test.

Displacement—It is possible to have a considerable range of displacement among sailing craft of the same size, covering a range of perhaps 20% above and below "normal" displacement. This range of vessel weight results from the selection of a building material, and how the material is designed into the boat.

One reason boats are heavy is because there is a lot of material in them. Many believe heavy scantlings indicate a strong vessel, but this is not necessarily the case. If the material is not of good quality, if it is poorly assembled into the boat, or most importantly if the designer has not matched its use in the hull to the local stresses set up in that locality, then there is much weight in the craft that is not only not contributing to strength but is unnecessarily loading the rest of the structure. Ironically, this over-building not only doesn't make the vessel safer, but the cost of every useless pound of material is money down the drain.

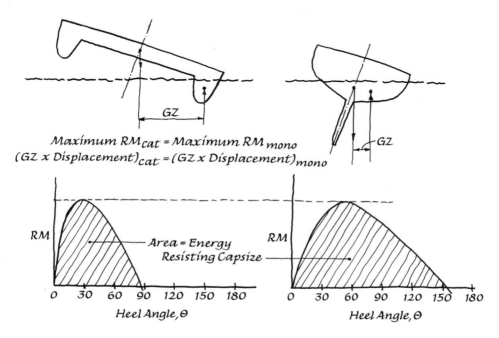

Fig. 15-4. Catamaran and monohull stability compared

When determining the scantlings for the Hudson River sloop replica *Clearwater* I resorted to the best information I could find. Most of this was not available to the builders of the original sloops in the first half of the nineteenth century, although they were remarkably handy at evolving good practices on their own. I believe that her excellent condition after 18 years of hard use justifies her scantlings (as well as demonstrating the intense and capable attention paid to her maintenance). Over-built vessels are needlessly carrying around useless weight, and underbuilt vessels risk high maintenance and rebuilding costs in the future, or even failure under duress. So mass of material doesn't necessarily mean a strong vessel (except when the function of the vessel requires it, as in the case of such craft as *Hero,* built by Mr. Gamage in South Bristol, Maine, many years ago for use in the Antarctic and still in service there).

Other things being equal, my own preference is for light displacement rather than heavy. (Light displacement cruising boats suffer from guilt by association with light displacement high tech racing machines. A bad hull is a bad hull whether it is of light or heavy displacement.)

The advantages of light displacement over heavy include the following: the vessel responds more readily to wave action, so is drier and has a smoother motion; it floats higher in a 90° knockdown; the sails and ground tackle are smaller and lighter, a factor for single- or short-handed sailing; building and maintenance costs, being proportional to displacement, are lower; acceleration, both starting and stopping, is more rapid; the vessel is more responsive to helm; pitching action can be controlled by longitudinal distribution of weights; the excellent record of light displacement craft in heavy weather suggests they are somewhat more seaworthy as a class.

A rather paradoxical advantage of light displacement is that it generally permits a greater latitude in loading a boat (with passengers, cargo, equipment, machinery) over its designed level than does the average heavy boat—the lighter boat has a larger water plane area over which to distribute the additional weight. Table 15-1 gives examples of three boats each of 16,000 lb (7,260 kg) designed displacement. Boat 1 is of the *Controversy* type, of glued strip construction, and with moderate ends. Boat 2 is a typical yacht of conventional wood or fiberglass construction, with normal overhangs. Boat 3 is a character boat, of stout wood construction and with short ends. Note the greater number of pounds required to sink the *Controversy* type 1"; in addition to this factor, the lighter construction permits a greater freeboard like the reverse sheer of the *Controversy,* giving a greater allowable number of inches of sinkage available.

Table 15-1
Comparison of Three 16,000 lb (7,260 kg) Sailing Yachts

Displacement Classification	Light	Conventional	Heavy
General Description	Controversy	Cruising Club of America	Cutter
Length overall	41.0 ft (12.5 m)	32.5 ft (9.9 m)	28.9 ft (8.8 m)
Length, waterline	33.0 ft (10.1 m)	27.5 ft (8.4 m)	26.8 ft (8.2 m)
Beam	10.42 ft (3.2 m)	9.25 ft (2.8 m)	10.47 ft (3.2 m)
Draft	5.58 ft (1.7 m)	5.76 ft (1.8 m)	4.85 ft (1.5 m)
Displacement	250 ft^3 (7.08 m^3)	250 ft^3 (7.08 m^3)	250 ft^3 (7.08 m^3)
Sail area, 100% fore triangle	693 ft^2 (64.4 m^2)	584 ft^2 (54.3 m^2)	627 ft^2 (58.2 m^2)
LWL area (LWL × beam × .7)	241 ft^2 (22.4 m^2)	178 ft^2 (16.5 m^2)	196 ft^2 (18.2 m^2)
Weight to sink 1" (1 cm)	1,285 lb (229 kg)	950 lb (170 kg)	1,045 lb (187 kg)
Cube	2,390 ft^3 (66 m^3)	1,780 (50 kg^3)	1,570 (44 kg^3)

The major problem for the newcomer to light displacement is that the lighter boat forereaches, "shoots," a considerably shorter distance than the heavy boat; this ceases to be a disadvantage when one becomes accustomed to it. The obverse is that light displacement boats accelerate more rapidly in a puff.

Whatever type of boat you select, estimating the displacement is one of the most important design decisions you will make. Upon it depends overall dimensions, the space within the boat, the sail area and engine power required, and the scantlings. So use all the information you can find, including the text later on, to help make the estimate accurate.

Arrangement considerations—A major factor separating the design of sailboat accommodations from those of power craft is that sailing craft often sail for extended periods of time at heel angles of 25° or more. This means that sea berths, as opposed to berths used only in harbor, must go essentially fore and aft. Also, some kind of restraint is required to keep a windward berth from losing its passenger; wooden bunk boards are the norm, but my preference is for the more comfortable canvas "boards," trapezoidal in shape, hooked to the overhead when rigged and stowed under the mattress when not. Quarter berths, of which a third to a half is in a cave under the cockpit, are very secure-feeling, are a great place for cameras, sweaters, and tiny children during the day, and can in effect add 2′ to 3′ to the length of a small boat.

To allow its use when the boat is heeled, a doorway, passage, or hatch must be wider than is required on a powerboat. A full height doorway should preferably be 30″ (75 cm) wide, 24″ (60 cm) minimum, and a passage 36″ (90 cm) wide, 30″ (75 cm) minimum. Companionways should be 30″ (75 cm) wide as a minimum, and the ladders should be *wide* enough (16″ [40 cm] minimum, 20 ″ [50 cm] good, 24″ [60 cm] if possible), especially at the bottom. Obviously in small craft these standards cannot all be met, but everything should be done to ease the effects of heel angle on life aboard.

Heel angle has a great effect on laying out the galley. Things roll, spill, clank, and become chaotic unless the design imposes order. Compartmentalize spaces— ice boxes, dish lockers, countertops, food storage lockers, etc.—so that things and liquids can never go far. If the boat is large enough, a U-shaped galley seems best, with the opening inboard and the stove across the outboard bottom of the U; the stove must be there if it is gimballed. ("Gimballing" means that an object is hung in pivots so that it can swing to accommodate the current heel angle.) On large craft, which are slower in their motion, have more room below, and don't usually heel as much, the long axis of the stove or range can be athwartships.

Sometimes the dining table is also gimballed to fit the current heel angle. The table is pivoted high up at the fore-and-aft ends and lead weights are suspended below it. The theory is that the tabletop will always be level, an unquestioned desideratum. The problem is that the table can go into a pendulum action in a rolling sea and do great damage to shins, not to mention making a lottery out of spooning up your oatmeal. So I suggest cutting down on the weights, and having stout clamps to secure the tabletop at the best average angle for the conditions.

Ventilation is one of the most important factors in small boat design. Hot, rainy weather, with supper cooking and a half dozen relatively unwashed people sitting around below, makes for a rather fuggy atmosphere. Add to this a bathroom in one corner of the living room, and the need for good ventilation under all conditions is obvious. Because of heel, there should be *no* opening ports or windows in the top- sides unless there is a fail-safe indicator system warning when any one is not closed. If there are opening windows in the cabin trunk, they should be closed except in port. All-weather openings, such as Dorade (baffled and drained) vents, stove pipes, tank vents, hatches normally open, and engine room vents should be in a band down the center of the boat if the boat expects to do much offshore cruising; a frequent cause of sailing vessels foundering is downflooding in a knockdown through open- ings that are not, or cannot be, shut off.

Sailing yachts: There are a great number of decisions to be made before begin- ning finally to put your ideas on paper. Even before the envelope sketch stage, some general decisions must be made. In making them, keep all options open as you take a turn or two around the design spiral. For instance, if you start by picturing your- self in a character vessel but then determine that your real interest is in racing, then the character concept must go. But before going back to "start" on the design spiral, consider the following:

1. What type of craft: character, cruising, cruising/racing, racing?
2. What rig: catboat (traditional or high tech), sloop, cutter, yawl, ketch, schooner?
3. Light or heavy displacement?
4. Type of underbody: full keel, keel/centerboard, full centerboard?
5. Arrangement: this should be worked out with repeated envelope sketches. Make yourself do some even after you seem to be satisfied; it is surprising what a little tinkering can do to improve an arrangement.

Type of craft—The question of whether you want a character, cruising, cruis- ing/racing, or straight racing sailboat is the first, most personal, and most important question to be answered before you have firmed up in your mind's eye the boat you will sketch. The feelings about sailing craft are highly subjective and thus difficult to state precisely, and are apt to change with time; a striking photograph, or a sail on someone else's boat, or the shifting currents of one's imagination or pocketbook can change one's yearnings drastically. And we must never forget that making this and other decisions takes more than an absent minded, "Yes, dear" from the chair on the other side of the fireplace. There must be full understanding and agreement on this and the other impor- tant questions among all who will be directly involved in the craft.

In order to provide some measure of objectivity to answering this question, I have drawn figure 15-5, with sketches representing each type. Some of these are im- aginary, some based on actual designs, both mine and those of others. Displaying them all in an equal format may permit a person to better evaluate his own feelings and discuss them with someone else.

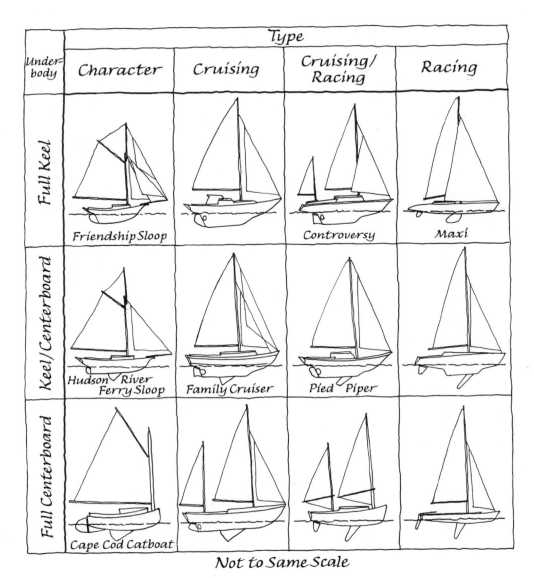

	Type			
Under-body	Character	Cruising	Cruising/ Racing	Racing
Full Keel	Friendship Sloop		Controversy	Maxi
Keel/Centerboard	Hudson River Ferry Sloop	Family Cruiser	Pied Piper	
Full Centerboard	Cape Cod Catboat			

Not to Same Scale

Fig. 15-5. Sailing yacht types illustrated

Rig—Closely related to the boat type is the rig it will have. Obviously a character boat must have a rig in character. Generally speaking boats for racing have sloop rigs, with either masthead or fractional forestays; what separates the competitive boat from the cruising sloop are not only the tall, narrow rig and spartan accommodations but also the use of high tech in winches, spars, vangs, backstay tensioners, and a host of other devices that are expensive but are intended to improve performance the fraction of a percentage point necessary to make a winner.

It is the cruising person who has the widest scope for selecting a rig. Often the choice is made on the basis of rather undefined views based on personal experience, what was learned at father's knee, and the talk at the yacht club bar. It may therefore pay to sort out some of the pluses and minuses of the various rigs. My comments are as objective as I can make them but inevitably include my own prejudices.

What do we ask of the rig of a cruising sailboat? That it drives our boat at reasonable speed over a wide range of conditions, that it be easily handled by the available crew (one person in the case of the single hander and of many two handers), that it cost what we can and will pay, that it be as simple as possible while still fulfilling the other aims, and that it not clutter up the boat unnecessarily are all normal expectations. No rig answers all these needs, or is suitable for all sizes of craft; some compromising judgments must be made in selecting *your* rig.

Any rig, even the allegedly inefficient ketch or schooner, can be fitted to a hull to drive it at acceptable cruising speeds. The modern high aspect ratio sails (short boom, long hoist) permit even ketches to go to weather in acceptable fashion. And anyone who has had the venerable *Niña* steam past them on a reach can attest to the occasional potential of the staysail schooner. Therefore, while there are inherent differences among rigs, the differences should not be of overwhelming importance to the cruiser; they are pretty well taken account of in the various rating rules if one is inclined to take in an occasional race. So the major consideration lies with the second requirement—that the rig be easily handled by the available crew.

One average man is supposed to be able to handle a sail of 400 ft² (37 m²) under most conditions, and a strong able person about 600 ft² (56 m²). Not counting headsails, which presumably would not be set in times of emergency, and assuming that at some time on any boat that does not have a paid crew one person will have to take in or reef the boomed sails, then the largest sail should be restricted to that range of sizes depending upon one's assessment of his own ability. (Anyone who has read Richard McMullen's 1877 account in *Down Channel* of taking two days to get his 48′ (14.6 m) yawl under way in Cherbourg after firing his crew and then sailing it alone to Dover will understand that these limits are only guides.) Therefore, whatever else, the rig should not have individual sails larger than the limit you set for yourself.

A divided (multimast) rig can have several advantages. The sails are broken up into smaller pieces, the rig is lower and spars shorter, and, by careful trimming, an unwelcome helm (God forbid we should have one on our boat!) can be adjusted out. Shortening sail can be done effectively and quickly by dropping the mainsail (foresail on a schooner) but be sure the mizzenmast is sufficiently strong to carry a heavy load. Nevertheless, on boats under 30′ to 35′ (9 m to 10 m) LOA the added mast and rigging sometimes just plain get in the way. My preference on boats over 35′ to 40′ (10 m to 12 m) is for the yawl (a mizzen staysail set on a yawl or ketch is a helpful and easily handled reaching sail); as the mainsail goes beyond its size limit, the yawl becomes a ketch.

Between about 25' (7.5 m) and 35' to 40' (10 m to 12 m) LOA I favor the cutter rig, defined here as having two headsails. A successful arrangement I have used is to have in effect a fractional rig, with a very strong forestay and jumper stays but with no headstay. The jib is set flying on roller furling gear (the old kind without all the extrusions) from the masthead. Shortening sail from full sail (roller jib, boomed staysail, mainsail) is done very easily, in this order: roll up the jib from the cockpit, leaving an efficient rig with much of the load taken off; single reef the mainsail, which can be done while jogging under the staysail; double reef the mainsail; drop the mainsail entirely, either sailing under the staysail alone or if desired setting a storm trisail. Note that it is not necessary to go forward of the mast during any of these exercises.

A revolution in rig design and construction was wrought by the advent of aluminum masts. These are light, strong, resistant to damage, and inexpensive; I cannot imagine having a wooden mast except to stay in character. (However, I rather like a wooden boom because it is so easy to fasten various useful doodads to it.)

More recently, the composite fiberglass/carbon fiber mast has made practical another type of rig. The basic unit is the mast, unstayed and rotating in a deck bearing. Instead of a boom there is a "wishbone" hinged partway up the mast and bowing aft on both sides of the sail to the clew, allowing the sail to assume an efficient jib shape. Reefing is done from the bottom and the sail drops into lazy jacks when it is dropped. Using this basic rig, boats are rigged as catboats or as cat ketches. With a single halyard led aft, it would seem an extremely simple rig to sail. A disadvantage is the difficulty of setting light sails or coping with very heavy winds.

Displacement—The benefits and flaws of light and heavy displacement are discussed above, and you have presumably by now made up your mind where in the displacement continuum your boat will lie.

What does that mean in actual pounds for your boat? Figure 15-6 is a plot for many boats of all types of displacement against "L" (defined as [LOA + 2 × LWL]/3, which helps in comparing short ended and long ended boats). From this plot you can see the range of displacements that can apply to a boat of your "L," and select that which suits your concept.

Because sail area and displacement are closely linked, the plot also includes sail area versus displacement. A range is shown to help you select the value that best suits your design. These are average values of sail area; increase by about 10% for a light weather area like San Diego, reduce by about the same for blustery conditions like Buzzards Bay or San Francisco Bay.

Companion curves are shown for multihulls, with catamarans and trimarans being lumped together as promised.

Type of underbody—A major decision is what kind of underbody the boat will have. For character boats, this is usually determined by the model it is following. However, sometimes the design does not slavishly follow the original but, as with Murray Peterson's lovely *Coasters,* incorporates modern concepts of hull form

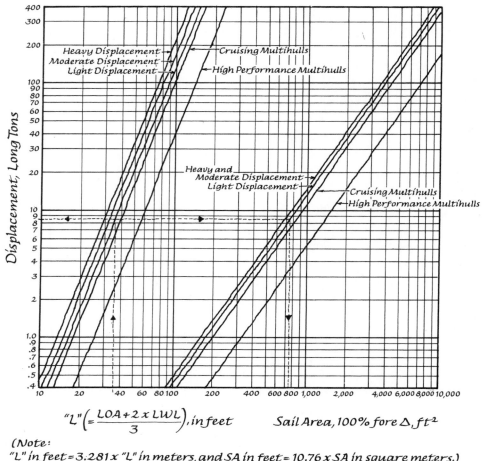

"L" $\left(= \dfrac{LOA + 2 \times LWL}{3}\right)$, in feet　　　Sail Area, 100% fore △, ft²

(Note:
"L" in feet = 3.281 x "L" in meters, and SA in feet = 10.76 x SA in square meters.)

Fig. 15-6. Graph for estimating displacement and sail area
for various types of sailing craft

while preserving the character appearance of the original. In this instance, the character boat slips over into the cruising boat column. "Character" is not achieved by sticking a figurehead or clipper bow onto a modern hull; many so-called "Friendship sloops" bear no resemblance to the real thing.

The out-and-out racing boat must be purely pragmatic in concept. If the rating rule forces you to do something you know to be stupid (not unheard-of), you must still do it to be competitive. Beyond that the laws of physics must be obeyed, most especially fluid mechanics as applied to the hull form, appendages, and rigs. The serious designer of a one-off racing yacht must count on extensive tank testing to evaluate his hull form and to refine the hull to achieve ultimate performance. ("Ultimate performance" has no place in a naval architect's vocabulary, although some still think in those terms. John Bertrand reports that Ben Lexcen claimed *Australia II* would win races by 20 minutes. In actual fact, *Australia II* won the America's Cup because of superior preparation, support, and crewing, not through any miracle of hull or keel.)

Figure 15-5 illustrates most of the underbodies in common use. The shape of the hull itself, the "canoe body," is pretty much determined by the laws discussed in chapters 3 and 6. The fun begins with selecting the appendages to the canoe body that will best do their jobs—resisting the side force of the sails, providing a place for ballast, and assuring satisfactory handling characteristics—with the least drag possible.

The drag in this case is largely frictional (the wave-making resistance is generated by the bulk of the canoe body), so our aim should be to reduce wetted surface to a minimum. At the same time, we must have sufficient underwater profile area of a suitable shape to limit leeway to an acceptable level. And finally we must have a configuration that combines suitable alacrity in maneuvering with good course-keeping qualities.

These qualities are met in the racing configuration. The hull is a separate entity, designed to support the weight of the boat and to have the most efficient form. The fin keel, another entity, is designed for the greatest efficiency (high lift-drag ratio) by using an optimum NACA (National Advisory Committee on Aeronautics) section on a high aspect ratio lifting surface, yet there must be enough volume of lead to provide stability. The control surface, the third entity, consists of the rudder, with or without a skeg, as optimally shaped as the fin. This is best located well aft and clear of the fin keel to give a long turning arm; it must, however, be tucked far enough under the hull to avoid ventilating or even lifting clear of the water at high heel angles. So why not use this configuration on cruising boats?

There are a number of practical considerations for avoiding the racing configuration on everyday boats. A hull with a fin keel attached has no bilge to hold bilge water so that any bilge water slops back and forth, sometimes wetting things high up the sides (although it is possible to install baffles that hold the water in the center of the boat). In addition, the hull/keel connection is weak. If the boat is not carefully propped up when hauled out, the keel can push the hull upwards. And the keel is also subject to loss under way (remember the maxi which lost its keel off the south coast of Britain?), especially if it has been weakened by going aground.

Also, in an effort to be efficient, the lower end of a fin keel is often designed short and curved. While one doesn't anticipate running aground, it does happen, and a pinpoint landing gear like a sharp fin keel could make it a scary and hazardous experience. Difficulties can also arise if the boat must be grounded out alongside a wharf, or hauled out without benefit of slings. For me, it all adds up to an unseaman-like arrangement for the average sailboat, especially because the benefits in speed, while vital for winning races, will hardly be evident when cruising.

My own preference for the cruising sailboat is the keel/centerboard configuration, which combines the best of the full keel and full centerboard worlds. With the centerboard housed a keel-centerboard boat will, due to having less wetted surface, generally outperform a full keel boat when reaching and running. Yet, unlike the full centerboard boat, in shoal water it can also go to windward quite well with the board housed. The centerboard is completely beneath the cabin sole so it in no way interferes with the arrangement, and if the centerboard pendant is run directly upwards, its pipe container forms a most helpful handhold. Stability is achieved with ample outside ballast so the centerboard itself needs only enough negative buoyancy that it will drop under any conditions; for a 30′ (9 m) boat I specify about 150 lb (68 kg) of negative buoyancy. The long flat keel provides excellent stability for voluntary or involuntary groundings, and even in sizable craft the draft is low enough so that in a grounding one can jump overboard to arrange stabilizing props or even, in smaller craft, put a shoulder under the bilge and heave. Also the external ballast of the keel-centerboard configuration is low enough to provide significant righting advantages over the full centerboard boat, yet both rolling and pitching are softer than in a full keel boat. And finally there are occasional opportunities for a bit of one-upmanship by steaming past the keel boats all jammed together in the deep pool to anchor in lonely splendor at the shoal end of the harbor. The advantages of the keel/centerboard configuration carry a price tag—an added 2% to 3% on the cost of the boat—but in my view this is a bargain.

I learned to sail on the South Shore of Long Island, New York, surrounded by full centerboard boats, the only type that could fully exploit the many square miles of very shallow water there, so my negative bias against centerboarders is not based on ignorance. However, conditions in Maine (or in most other sailing areas) don't require this extreme, the disadvantages of which were illustrated in a scene in a Camden shipyard. A sizable, modern, fast full centerboard sloop was hanging in the slings with 6 or 8 feet of skinny and slightly bent centerboard hanging out. She had been down east and bent the board in contact with a ledge. Unable to house the board so that she could be hauled by a down east boat yard, or even grounded out, she had to return to Camden before finding a travel lift that could handle her—not my idea of a seamanlike craft!

A centerboard arrangement you might consider, especially for longer runs, is two centerboards. In addition to the usual board, close to amidships, there would be another smaller one as far aft as it could be installed. The reports are that, with the main board housed and this board down according to need, a boat can be made to self-steer on a broad reach. A very nice feature, but again at a slight extra cost.

A most important component of a sailboat is the steering system—the rudder, stock, support, steering gear. Your naval architect will work out the engineering details (press him to use a fat safety factor; experience has shown that steering gears are a major source of weakness and failure), but you must give him a configuration to work to. Figure 15-7 shows three common ones. Pick either *a* or *c*; in *b* the turning arm is so short (remember that the turning power is the side force on the rudder times the turning arm; see chapter 6) that the boat will be unmanageable at times.

Several points that might be helpful in working out the rudder details are described below:

1. The rudder area should be 8% to 10% of the underwater profile area, for larger and smaller sailing craft respectively—better to have it a little too large than too small.

2. To eliminate trimming effect when the rudder is turned, slope the rudder stock so that it is perpendicular to a line connecting the center of pressure of the rudder and the center of flotation of the water plane. If the stock is perpendicular or slopes aft downward, when the rudder is turned there will be a force trying to lift up

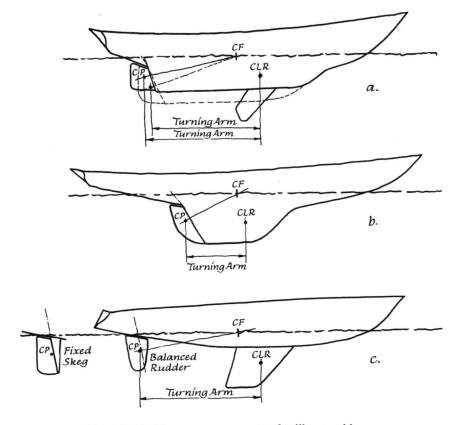

Fig. 15-7. Different arrangements of sailboat rudders

the stern of the boat, the amount depending on the departure of the rudderstock from the rule given above. This lifting force must come from work done by the sails so it is not helping the boat move ahead and is thus wasted.

3. In c two different configurations of separated rudders are shown. For racing the balanced rudder is best because it has less drag and more side force when maneuvering; the balance (area forward of the rudderstock) should not exceed 17%

of the total rudder area. The rudder with a fixed skeg is better for course-keeping and is stronger, but will significantly slow the boat down when, say, short tacking; it is best for cruising and casual sailing. Since the skeg helps the rudder, the rudder/skeg combination needs to be only slightly larger in area than the balanced rudder alone.

4. For a steering gear, I consider the faddy pedestal steerer an abomination in anything under 50′ to 60′ (15 m to 18 m) LOA. I can never get comfortable at one. If I stand up, it's too low, so my back gets tired, and I occasionally receive a surprise bang on the head from the boom. If I sit down behind it, my knees get in the way of the wheel so I am forced to lean way forward, and the compass is difficult to see. Sitting alongside the wheel is not bad, but I don't want to have only one position from which to steer. And in any event you are either fighting the feedback from the rudder, or must put the brake on which increases the effort of moving the wheel.

I sailed with tillers for many years; I prefer a tiller for small boats and am comfortable with one on large boats (although steering the 75′ (22.9 m) Hudson River sloop replica *Clearwater* with a tiller is *hard* work). Then Farnham Butler introduced me to his steering wheel and seat arrangement, the wheel turning the rudder through an Edson worm steerer. Figure 15-8 illustrates this arrangement, showing the many comfortable positions from which one can steer. For long stretches, it is hard to beat the seat, which is rounded and saddle-like to permit the helmsman to slide around to windward as the boat heels. Note how the wheel slants in over the lap to permit steering from a relaxed sitting position. The compass, using all the lubber lines, is easily viewed from all the positions, and the compass pedestal can also hold the engine controls and the main sheet. To top off, the easy-working Edson worm steerer, probably one of the most reliable pieces of equipment ever made for a boat, does not transmit the rudder forces back to the helmsman; the wheel stays where you put it, but can be moved with the greatest of ease. For the cruising or cruising/racing boat I have never seen anything that came close to this arrangement for comfort and convenience.

Arrangement—A major, often ignored, consideration in laying out cruising sailing yacht arrangements is that the people on board each day normally spend 8 to 12 or more hours on deck. These people should have reasonable comfort on deck, a variety of different places they can lounge in without interfering with the operation of the boat, and as much protection as possible from the weather (sun down south, wind and spray up north).

There must also be space below for the entire complement to lounge, have meals, play games, etc., at night and when the weather is foul. And finally, there should be adequate sleeping arrangements for the entire complement; this is often done with very comfortable permanent berths for two couples and temporary berthing for the occasional brief overload. If a crew is to be carried, provide comfortable sleeping, toilet, and lounging facilities completely separate from the owner's party.

Location of the galley is a major decision. For owner-operated craft, the galley should be aft to (1) minimize the motion, and (2) allow the "galley slave" to still be a member of the party. If a professional crew will be carried, the galley should be forward just aft of the crew quarters so as to segregate the noise, smell, and bustle of meal preparation. In smaller craft—25' to 35' (7.5 m to 11 m) LOA—the galley is often located right at the companionway; because of beam limitations, anyone

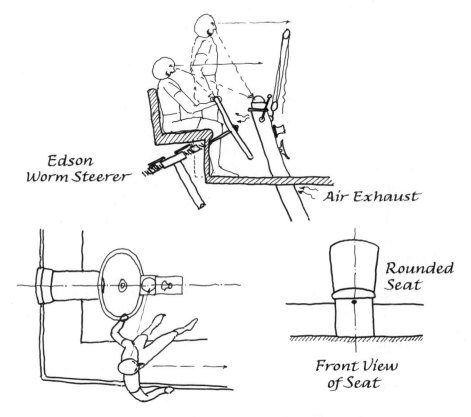

Fig. 15-8. An ideal steering arrangement for sailing craft

working in the galley must be on or close to the centerline of the boat, right in the way of all traffic to or from the deck. I prefer to have the main cabin at the foot of the companionway and the galley immediately forward of it; the slightly greater motion of this location is, in my view, much more than counterbalanced by the freedom of the galley worker from interference and the freedom of the rest of the crew to move between deck and cabin without slowing up meal preparation or putting a foot in the soup.

Water ballast—Water ballast has some intriguing properties. It is omnipresent, free, and easily moved by pumping. The fact that a pound of water weighs nothing in water but just as much as a pound of lead in air suggested to me a water-filled bilge keel scheme that I patented (long ago expired). Using this scheme, I designed one boat (see figure 15-9). In this design the lee keel provides lateral plane as well as buoyancy tending to right the boat, whereas the weather keel when out of water has a tremendous righting effect due to its weight of water and its extension out beyond the hull limit. The stability of this boat was most interesting—very easy and sensitive when upright but building up stability rapidly with only a small increase in heel. Although only 19′ long, this little boat stood up to squally weather in a most remarkable way and was a very smart sailer. The bilge keels had some problems but I feel these could have been corrected.

Water ballast is now being used in conventional boats in the BOC Single Handed Around the World Race. On long runs, this must surely be helpful, but there are some factors that should be considered. To do the most good the tanks should be located at the farthest extended portion of the heeled hull. From a safety standpoint, the ballast should not be so great that the vessel will capsize if caught aback, thus suddenly placing the ballast to leeward; this may not happen often, but once would be enough. If this latter condition was met, the ballast could be shifted by gravity just prior to coming about without fear of capsize.

Working sailing craft: Even before the gross increase in oil prices in 1973 there was a growing interest in sailing craft built not for pleasure but for profit, and in the application of sails as auxiliary thrust for powered vessels. When the price of oil rose from $3 to $20 per barrel this interest in wind power was greatly accelerated; the recent decline in oil prices has diminished, but by no means destroyed, this interest. It is not possible in this volume to completely cover the subject, but the major uses of sail in working craft will be mentioned below and briefly discussed.

Safety of passengers and crew is especially important on sailing craft because of the added potential for accident and injury. The vulnerability to capsizing in sudden squalls conferred on sailing craft by the sails, and the constant possibility of injury as a result of working around and in complicated rigging, which is often under great stress, are hazards special to sailing craft. There is no way that man has devised to eliminate these hazards, and indeed their presence is part of the appeal of going to sea under sail. But the designer should help the owner and skipper minimize the accident potential, not only by complying in good faith with the pertinent regulations but by incorporating in the design his own knowledge and caring.

This section of the sailing craft chapter should not be studied alone but must be considered supplementary to chapters 16, "Commercial Craft," and chapter 17, "Institutional Craft."

Charter boats—There is an increasing number of fleets of boats being built up for either bareboat or captained charter. These are yachts, and what applies in the section on sailing yachts would apply here, but with a few changes. The important new element is that the boats will be operated by nonowners. Modern sailboats can be quite complex, and in some ways delicate, artifacts, so the wise charter boat owner

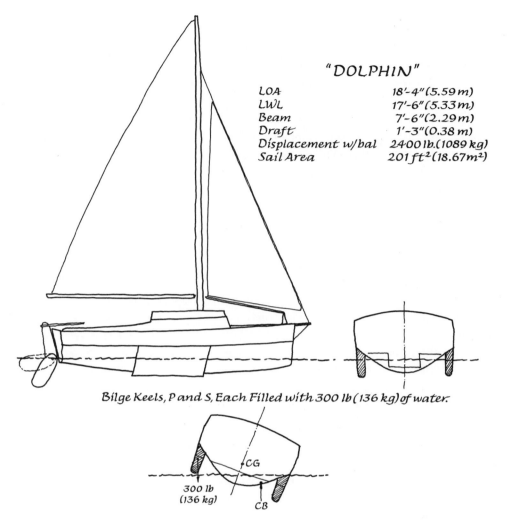

"DOLPHIN"

LOA	18'-4" (5.59 m)
LWL	17'-6" (5.33 m)
Beam	7'-6" (2.29 m)
Draft	1'-3" (0.38 m)
Displacement w/bal	2400 lb. (1089 kg)
Sail Area	201 ft² (18.67 m²)

Bilge Keels, P and S, Each Filled with 300 lb (136 kg) of water.

300 lb
(136 kg)

CG

CB

Fig. 15-9. *Dolphin* and her water-filled bilge keels

keeps this new element in mind in purchasing and outfitting his fleet. Accordingly, the boats should be (1) as foolproof as they can possibly be, with strong gear and no tricky stuff, (2) modestly rigged, (3) well behaved under sail and power, (4) comfortable and attractive—whatever is provided in the way of furnishings and equipment should be of good quality but simple—and (5) suitable for the sailing conditions and grounds in which they will be used (shoal draft for the Chesapeake, modestly rigged for San Francisco Bay).

Passenger-carrying—The range in size of vessels carrying passengers for hire is tremendous, all the way from a 20' (6 m) catboat carrying 6 or fewer passengers on half day trips, to (most recently) a world-ranging 440' (134 m) "schooner" fitted for 160 passengers and 80 crew members (see figure 15-10). But all U.S. vessels carrying more than 6 passengers have one thing in common—to ensure the safety of the passengers they must meet exacting standards set by the Congress and administered by the U.S. Coast Guard. (The definition of "passenger" has been interpreted very broadly in the courts. If one of your guests contributes a couple of six-packs for a sail on your personal yacht and the voyage gets into court for any reason you may be considered to have been carrying a "passenger for hire.") The USCG regulations defining these standards deal with the following: stability; subdivision, that is, dividing the hull into a number of watertight compartments such that any one of them may be flooded by an accident without mortally wounding the vessel; fire prevention and protection; structural strength; passenger and crew accommodations; lifesaving equipment and methods for the passengers and crew; manning to ensure the vessel is in good hands at all times.

The first step anyone should take before becoming involved in passenger-carrying craft is to study thoroughly the regulations pertaining to that craft, including international rules and rules applying where the vessel will be registered and where it will operate. When I design such a craft, I purchase a copy of the *Code of Federal Regulations,* (CFR), Chapter I of Title 46, Subchapter T (for vessels under 100 gross tons and carrying over six passengers) or Subchapter H (for passenger-carrying craft of 100 gross tons or more) depending on which applies to the proposed vessel. Untangling the regulations is a job in itself if one doesn't work with them all the time, so I read the applicable subchapter and appropriate references practically line by line, and highlight those that apply to the new design.

In sketching a passenger-carrying sailing craft, the following points might be kept in mind:

1. The criterion of success of a passenger-carrying vessel, and other sailing craft such as research and school ships, is whether it makes a profit. After the vessel is sketched and a projected annual schedule drawn up, to ascertain its profitability all the information can be run through the economic modeling suggested in the next chapter. (A notable variation to this concept of profitability is *Clearwater,* which has never charged an individual for boarding it, although it does charter itself to school districts. Nevertheless she must work within a budget. Other historic craft and replicas, while not as free as *Clearwater,* are also usually not-for-profit operations.)

2. Crew size on overnighters will range between 15% and 50% of the passenger capacity, the number varying with the elegance of the enterprise, the complexity of the rig, the length of trips, etc. The lower percentages apply to such high density, simple craft as the Maine coast passenger schooners, while the higher percentages apply to luxurious full-service cruise vessels. Roughly a third of the crew will be in the steward's department, and two-thirds will be ship's crew and passenger service people; on smaller craft these last two groups are often combined. A safe axiom is that the crew should be large enough to handle all the necessary functions on the craft; there should be no dependence on passenger participation unless it is clearly

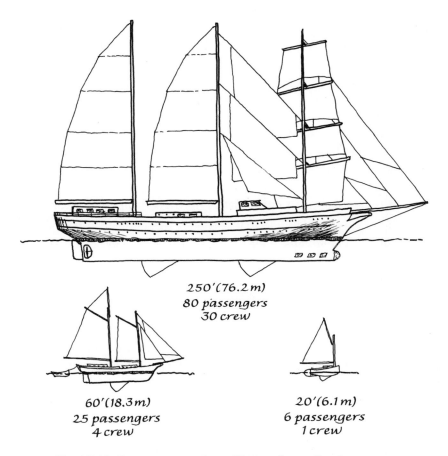

250′ (76.2 m)
80 passengers
30 crew

60′ (18.3 m)
25 passengers
4 crew

20′ (6.1 m)
6 passengers
1 crew

Fig. 15-10. Passenger-carrying sailing craft, small to large

stated and fully understood that the passengers must help work the vessel, as on a school ship.

3. As with yachts, it is important to have places for the passengers to be when not in their berths. I recently sailed on two fishing schooner types in the 100′ (30.5 m) range, each with 25 to 30 people aboard (passengers and crew). On one there were hardly any comfortable places to sit, lie down, or stand, while on the other there were enough such spots for twice our number; the latter would have been much more pleasant to spend a week on than the former. So provide reasonably comfortable daytime accommodations for good weather, for bad weather (with the help of an awning, even a week of Maine fog can be made bearable), and during mealtimes and evenings. Obviously of course, a different approach will suffice in the tropics and subtropics than in northern waters, but there must be accommodation for all expected weather conditions.

4. To make a 7′ × 8′ (2.1 m × 2.4 m) stateroom acceptable to a couple coming aboard from a 10- or 20-room house may not be an easy task. A few suggestions

that may help: keep it simple and uncluttered but tastefully decorated; lighten it with white and other light colors; provide plenty of ventilation and natural or artificial light—a number of passengers can be expected to suffer from claustrophobia and/or be unfamiliar with boats; have a wash basin with running water, including hot if possible, in each cabin; reassure the unfamiliar passenger with generous and well-marked escape routes; provide *reliable,* simple, and easily accessible toilets (surely one of the most embarrassing things a shy person must do is report to the skipper that he or she was the cause of the breakdown of the head).

5. Have berths oriented fore and aft unless all sleeping will be done at anchor. Sitting at table is also better when facing athwartships.

6. Allow for as much participation in the working of the ship by the passengers as they may wish to do. An entirely mechanized sailing craft (it is possible) seems a most unappetizing vehicle for a taste of sailing at sea. Have some sails the passengers can set and lines they can haul, and offer the possibility of observing the helmsman as well as of steering, navigating, etc. To make these activities accessible to the passengers requires that space be allowed for them where the activity is carried out; for instance, provide a large wheelhouse with a settee for observers.

Oceanographic vessels—Sailing craft are very well suited to teaching and carrying out oceanographic work. They can hold approximate station very comfortably and economically by jogging under shortened sail, and can function at the very low speeds required of some oceanographic activities. The extensive use of sail can also significantly extend the endurance of a research vessel.

At one time oceanographic craft were considered by U.S. regulations to be carrying passengers for hire and were therefore required to meet very stringent standards. These standards were so restrictive that it became economically almost impossible to carry out oceanographic research. So the regulation was relaxed; any vessel that engaged *only* and *totally* in oceanography or oceanographic teaching is now (1987) uninspected, that is, it is in the same category as a fishing craft.

An oceanographic vessel really has three crews: the ship's crew that operates the vessel; the scientific crew that takes care of and deploys the scientific instrumentation; and the scientists, who are transient, coming aboard only to carry out specific projects over a limited period of time. Scientists have a reputation for demanding pretty lavish accommodations by comparison with the permanent crew. The scientists, including their assistants and juniors, in a well-designed vessel should about equal in number the permanent (ship's plus scientific) crew.

Special considerations for research vessels include providing assorted booms, derricks, and gantries, etc., for handling sometimes heavy and awkward scientific equipment over the side. These considerations must be met without interference from the sailing rig.

Oceanographic vessels are exempt from the Jones Act and therefore may be built in foreign shipyards for domestic U.S. operation.

Before beginning to sketch your sailing oceanographic vessel, see the comments on passenger craft above (except for regulatory provisions) and on institutional craft in chapter 16.

School ships—These are training and education vessels, designed for introducing people to life at sea and the sailing of large vessels and often also including a general educational curriculum designed to mesh with shoreside institutions. The official U.S. Coast Guard definition of a sailing school vessel is, ". . . a vessel of less than 500 gross tons, carrying six or more individuals who are sailing school students or sailing school instructors, principally equipped for propulsion by sail even if the vessel has an auxiliary means of propulsion, and owned or demise chartered and operated by a qualified organization during such times as the vessel is operated exclusively for the purposes of sailing instruction." A vessel meeting these conditions is subject to the U.S. Coast Guard regulations contained in 46 CFR Part 169.

In sketching a school ship, the following factors should be kept in mind:

1. A school ship is an educational institution. Unlike the shore-based kind with areas specifically set aside for classrooms, everything on a school ship is a classroom. This must be considered when laying out the bridge, engine room, galley, and other working areas so that there is ample room for students to be instructed and to observe. In addition there should be space that can be used as a classroom in a more conventional teaching situation.

2. As far as working the ship is concerned, the students are cadet seamen; therefore, the vessel should be designed to have plenty of work for them, so go easy on fancy winches and other laborsaving devices.

3. The persons aboard will consist of the students, instructors (one for each 10 to 15 students), and the ship's crew (the minimums are set by the Coast Guard).

Like oceanographic vessels, school ships are exempt from the Jones Act and therefore may be built abroad for domestic U.S. operation.

Freight carriers—Some 150 years ago, when railroads were still a novelty and highways were at best hard-packed ground, carriage of pretty nearly everything—passengers, mail, freight of all kinds—was in sailing craft. In some developing countries (generally in tropical and subtropical regions), freight is still carried in sail. But even there the diesel engine is taking over, the advantages of regular scheduled service overcoming the relatively high cost of owning and operating such craft. If present trends continue, carrying freight in sail will largely have disappeared by the turn of the century.

Nevertheless, there are places where commercial sail can remain as a viable means of carrying freight. Generally speaking, trade winds, such as in the Windward and Leeward islands of the Caribbean, offer a steady source of wind power suitable for scheduled routing of sailing craft. And in the Republic of Maldives, in the Indian Ocean southwest of India, the north-south orientation of the archipelago allows the nearly continuous use of the southwest and northeast monsoons by interisland sailing craft. One can easily envision large sailing catamarans plying these routes, carrying passengers and light freight safely and swiftly, and at reasonable cost.

There have been three attempts in recent years to inaugurate sailing freight service in the North Atlantic basin; all are at or near failure. The Maine-built schooner *John Leavitt* was lost on her December 1979 maiden voyage, departing Quincy, Massachusetts, bound for Haiti. And services across Long Island Sound, Connecticut, to Port Jefferson, Long Island, and from Great Britain to the Bahamas, have proven uneconomical. Quite likely all three were, to varying degrees, romantically motivated, but there must be more than romance in a successful commercial venture.

Here are some thoughts on the design of sailing freight vessels:

1. Make up your mind whether this is a commercial venture or a romantic desire to go back to the past. The comments following are based on the venture being a commercial operation, with financial profit or some other social gain being the measure of success.

2. Select a route which (1) has a need for the service, and (2) has a wind force and direction spectrum that ensures effective use of a sailing craft. (However, it should be pointed out that judicious use of the engine can change a too-light following true wind to an effective apparent beam wind.) To satisfy requirement (1), do a market analysis of the proposed route just as you would for any business venture to determine the traffic load, types of cargo, rates which can be charged, etc. For requirement (2), on paper "sail" the route in the various weather seasons to be expected, and determine the percentage of time during which sail power alone will provide the minimum acceptable ship speed. If an excessive amount of time will be spent at 2 to 3 knots or less, then a sail-assisted or all diesel vessel should be studied.

3. Go modern. The traditional coasting schooner or trading barkentine, with its labor intensive operation, functional inefficiencies, and high cost of construction and maintenance, cannot be expected to compete with a modern wood, steel, aluminum, or ferro-cement hull, aluminum spars, leg-o'-mutton sails, winches, lightweight diesels for propulsion and auxiliaries, etc.

4. Assure yourself that suitable officers and crews are available at wages that the operation can afford. A program of training may be necessary before the vessel is launched.

Vessel restoration—Many motivations lead to restoring an old vessel; one is to obtain its documentation which sometimes carries with it useful grandfathering. This is an area more pertinent to the marine conservationist and archeologist than to the naval architect. Nevertheless in restoring an old hulk it is often necessary to redraw the rig and its details, and to lay out an arrangement commensurate with its new life, all of which the naval architect should be involved with. The main task is to learn what the vessel looked like and how it operated in its previous incarnation. In designing *Clearwater,* my starting point was the Smithsonian Institution in Washington, D.C., (it was my good luck that Howard Chapelle was Curator of Transportation there at the time), but other museums, models, books, photographs of the period, paintings, even place mats, can be researched for information. If the restored vessel is to be put into passenger use, the pertinent Coast Guard regulations should be referred to from the start.

Reproduction of old and historic craft—This has become a rather popular effort, usually carried out by foundations or nonprofit organizations. Although motivated by the best of intentions (clean up the environment, recreate local history, etc.) and fueled by emotional appeals for support, these projects are serious business and hasty or quixotic decisions in bringing them to fruition can limit the desired benefits. Reproductions or replicas of old-time craft will differ from the originals in some important ways.

1. The original vessels carried skilled and usually large crews. These men knew the vessels intimately and could cope with any situation that arose.

2. Losses of vessels were expected, and accepted at a much higher rate than present-day society would agree to, especially high performance vessels like blockade runners, warships, and mail packets.

3. The originals were loaded with fail-safe devices; sails, standing rigging, spars, etc. would carry away before the hull was endangered. Modern sail fabrics, wire rope, and synthetic line, all several times as strong as the old materials, don't give way and are implicated in many accidents befalling replicas.

4. In the old days, there was little knowledge of the physical factors important in naval architecture. Many vessels, handsome at launching, led short and tragic lives. (The under-ballasted and over-gunned Swedish warship *Vasa* which rolled down and sank after sailing only a couple of kilometers is the classic example.)

If you become involved in such a project, you can do much to steer it on a successful course. Your entrance should be early on so that from the start you can provide the rational and realistic balance to the commendable but often uninformed enthusiasm that sparks such a project. Your contribution may include some or all of the following:

1. While sharing in the enthusiasm, which can be very exhilarating, hold a part of yourself separate, able to temper the general euphoria by being the devil's advocate and viewing the present and future of the project in real terms.

2. You will probably not be able to influence to any degree the overall organization, but you can provide a valuable antidote for romantic three-beer imaginings by always having ready at hand the realities of the cost of building and operating the vessel. Nothing will bring wishful thinking down to terra firma faster than some authoritative cost estimates. As the project takes shape, apply the cost estimating procedures outlined in chapter 13. For both construction and operation costs of the vessel, start by assuming the whole operation will be done commercially; then subtract those elements that will reduce the cost such as volunteer labor (assume not over half the productivity per man/hour of full time paid labor, and a fluctuating supply of volunteers), contributions by manufacturers of all or part of the cost of their products used on the vessel, free rent of shop space, etc.

3. To be useful, these vessels will all carry passengers, and whether or not they pay a fare the U.S. Coast Guard will consider them to be for hire. Therefore, from the very start, familiarize yourself with the pertinent Coast Guard regulations and assure yourself that your vessel will conform to them. (Beware of a person who tells you he has an "in" with the Coast Guard and it will be duck soup for him to get the vessel certified for carrying passengers; it won't work.) The fact is that a true replica, following the original in every detail of design, construction, and rig, will usually not pass the Coast Guard review. The best course in my opinion is to make minor alterations from the original basic design, such as outside ballast, slightly smaller rig, an increase in freeboard amidships, so that the resulting vessel will pass the Coast Guard criteria but would not look out of place if sailing in its original venue.

If you follow the steps outlined above, and have a good group to work with on the project, the vessel will be a success and a pleasure to all who are associated with it or use it. This combination worked very well with the Hudson River sloop replica *Clearwater,* and after 20 years she is still successfully giving thousands of people a glimpse of what the Hudson River was like 150 years ago, teaching on site lessons in marine biology and care of the environment, and providing many people with their first experience crewing or riding on a sailing craft.

Sail assist for motor vessels (figures 15-11 and 15-12)—At the time of high oil prices there was a good deal of interest and some experimentation with using sails on work vessels to provide motive force in place of some of the installed diesel power. In the United States, Japan, and Greece sail-assist rigs were tried on a tugboat, an oil rig, and various tankers and freighters. (If some of the rigs seem small, remember that whether provided by sail or engine the horsepower per ton for large vessels, operating at speed-length ratios of .6 or so, is a fraction of a horsepower per ton of displacement, while the ordinary sailing yacht has installed about 3 to 5 horsepower per ton.) The present low price of oil has reduced the motivation for sail assist but it is still alive and well; the knowledge gained by present efforts will surely become valuable at some time in the future.

In working with sail-assist design, the following comments may be useful:

1. Sail assist may be defined as the addition of sail to augment mechanical power in a vessel in which the propulsion engines will run all the time regardless of whether or not the sails are working.

2. The greater the work involved in setting and trimming the sails, the less the sails will be used; the crew of a vessel that has operated successfully without sails is hardly likely to be enthusiastic about the extra work involved in setting and trimming the sails. Ergo, setting and taking in of the sails, and adjusting the sheets, should be mechanized and controlled from a central station, presumably the bridge.

3. A spectrum of sail use and benefits for a typical voyage, by month if necessary to reflect seasonal weather variations, can be worked out on the basis of the following information:

Fig. 15-11. A sail-assisted catamaran as research vessel, pilot boat, or fisherman

Fig. 15-12. Sail-assisted tanker with wing sails

a. Weather data for the intended route, which can be taken from the appropriate *Sailing Directions,* available from the U.S. Government Printing Office.

b. The minimum speed the vessel can be allowed to make. When necessary, power will be used to maintain the minimum allowable speed, with sails set whenever the apparent wind makes their use practical. The higher the required threshold speed, the less advantageous the sails will be.

c. Using available weather data, calculate the amount of engine power that can be replaced by sail power, at each of perhaps 20 or 30 stations on the vessel's route.

d. Estimate the added cost of installing and maintaining the rig, and the savings in fuel and engine maintenance.

e. If the machinery savings exceed the rig costs, then sail assist should be seriously considered.

Frequently displacement type power yachts are fitted with a small rig. While the purpose is often to provide an ex-sailor with some canvas to cope with for old time's sake, these rigs can often ease rolling for increased comfort, and with a fresh breeze on the quarter can allow significant throttling back on the engine without loss of speed. This is a pleasing and helpful addition to many power craft.

Until oil becomes very expensive, sail assist will be attractive only when fairly long trips are to be made in average weather conditions that encourage their use. An inshore fishing boat, for instance, with many changes of course and speed and short steaming times, will not put up with the nuisance of sails, especially if the rigging conflicts with the complicated tophamper characteristic of fishing vessels. On the other hand a distant-water fishing vessel or one that lies to for extended periods waiting for suitable fishing conditions, may benefit materially from the addition of some sail area. Each application is a separate and unique problem and should be judged on its own merits.

Other potential uses of sail power—One use for sail assist with considerable appeal is for vessels that must lie to for long periods of time. Sails would ease the motion appreciably, and would allow some control over position. Vessels that might benefit from sails include pilot vessels, weather vessels, and picket boats.

Sail power for pure sailing craft and as auxiliary to motor vessels is alive and well, and interest in it seems to be increasing. It is unlikely that we will see any diminution of that interest in the foreseeable future.

16. Commercial Craft

COMMERCIAL craft differ from all others in that they must make money; their success is measured solely in the amount of profit they return to the owners. A well-conceived commercial vessel when it is actually working—a trawler with its nets fishing on the bottom, a towboat with a tow, an excursion vessel with a capacity trip—can be a financial asset; but whenever that well-conceived and well-built vessel is not working, it is a very expensive liability. It is also probably axiomatic that, while bad management can make even the best designed and built vessel a failure, the very best management cannot make a poor vessel a success.

The vessel is usually the most important single expense in any maritime operation. Also, unlike shore-based structures, once a vessel is built it is usually impossible to make meaningful changes to it at reasonable cost. So the responsibility for the success of a commercial marine venture rests heavily with the naval architectural phase, which begins with you. The need to be profitable places heavy constraints on the owner/conceiver, the naval architect, the builder, and the skipper. To help ensure success, a commercial vessel must be designed not as a separate independent entity, but as a major element of a complete operational system—the entire enterprise of which it is a part. The designer must therefore familiarize himself with that system and do all he can to fit the vessel into it most effectively.

The concern here is with the owner/conceiver, who must provide the other members of the team with appropriate material to work with within their sector; it's all a matter of communication among the cast—owner, operator, builder, customer. The ultimate test of the conceiver's planning and his ability to communicate his concept accurately with words and sketches is whether the vessel is profitable in its intended use.

General comments on commercial craft: The following points should be kept in mind when beginning a sketch design for a commercial craft.

1. The size of a commercial craft is often described in terms of displacement or of gross tons, or even, mirabile dictu, "weight"; these terms are imprecise and can be misleading unless precisely defined. "Displacement," the weight of the water the vessel actually displaces, is a real and important parameter but is variable because vessels float at different waterlines depending upon their state of loading, and each waterline represents a unique displacement. This applies even to noncargo

vessels such as towboats where the fuel capacity is a fairly large proportion of displacement. The most extreme instance of displacement variability is the large tanker, for which the loaded displacement may be six or eight times her light displacement. Gross tonnage is a measure of the internal volume of a vessel for tax and regulatory purposes, has nothing to do with the displacement, and has enough variables within it to make it useless as an engineering quantity.

The problem of defining the size of a commercial vessel is largely resolved by using cubic number, defined as LWL × beam (maximum) × depth amidships. Depth is measured vertically from the top of the main deck (the weather deck) to the rabbet line (where the plating or planking meets the keel). See chapter 3 for more on the cubic number.

2. The need for weatherliness varies with the type of vessel, being most important for fishing vessels, on which the crew works on deck almost continuously, and perhaps least for tankers, which button up securely in bad weather.

Weatherliness in the rolling mode is almost entirely a function of transverse stability, measured by the metacentric height, or GM, (see chapter 6) which should exceed 1.5' (.46 m) in the normal operating condition of loading. Below 1.5' (.46 m) there begins to be a risk of losing stability through changes in loading, cargo or water weight on deck, or icing. For an acceptable upper limit, if the GM is greater than (beam/20)², but not less than 1.5' (.46 m), the vessel's rolling can be uncomfortably quick and may even contribute to the loss of rigidly secured equipment high up in the rigging due to large accelerations at the end of each roll. I once calculated the GM of an 80,000-ton tanker in ballast to be 26' (7.9 m). The beam of 100' (30.5 m) was great enough for the vessel to be comfortable even way up on the bridge. Apparently, the motions were so slowed down by the size of the vessel that, even though *relatively* severe, they were quite comfortable for the crew. If compatible with other vessel requirements, a high freeboard (to the main deck) is preferable to a low one as it will keep the decks from becoming awash and will improve stability at the higher angles of heel.

Weatherliness in the fore-and-aft mode means that the vessel does not pound or easily take green water over the bow when steaming into a head sea, and does not broach or be swept by overtaking seas when running with the seas. Even if no one is required to be working on deck, this type of weatherliness is important. (The Great Lakes ore carrier *Edmund Fitzgerald* while running before a heavy sea, apparently scended down into the back of a sea and just kept on going down until she hit the bottom. There was, however, some question about the state of her hatches and whether she had already taken significant amounts of water into her hull.) Two of the great advantages of the stern trawler are that the crew is sheltered by the raised deck forward and the work area is located where motion is least. Side trawlers must haul back their nets when lying beam to the wind and sea, and even on a quiet day take seas over the hauling rail to weather.

These stability comments do not apply to catamarans, which have a very high GM due to the great transverse stability. As a result they sometimes exhibit unusual motions, such as a very noticeable corkscrewing, which some people find disconcerting. My own experience, though, has been that a catamaran is, in the words of one user, "a fantastic work platform," able to ride comfortably when other, larger craft are rolling their scuppers under.

3. Crew safety is of tremendous importance. Commercial fishing is the most hazardous occupation in the United States, seven times worse than the industrial average and twice as dangerous as coal mining. Bearing in mind that the fisherman is expected to continue working on deck as long as the vessel can fish, the vessel motion, the frequently slippery decks, the massive machinery, the great amount of running rigging, and the complexity of gear on a fishing vessel create an environment full of risk. Anything that can be done to reduce the risks will pay off in fewer injuries and deaths. For instance, if the trawl winches are located on the bridge deck instead of the main deck, the warps can lead above head height directly to the trawl blocks, clearing all this hazardous mess from under the feet of the crew. Trawl doors can be stored in recesses outside the bulwarks instead of inside as is the custom, hydraulic cranes can take over many hoisting and moving jobs in a safer manner than the traditional tackles, and hydraulic control from the bridge of all machinery reduces the need for the crew to be close to the machinery. A major cause for single loss of life at sea is toppling over the rail while answering the call of nature; this can be corrected by having a toilet room accessible directly from the deck; make it large enough—a man in oilskins can be pretty bulky and awkward.

Sinking is always a possibility at sea. Every hatch in the main deck that will ever be opened at sea (are there any that are not?) should have an adequate coaming, and should be hinged, openable from below, and fitted with a device to hold it in open position; an exception would be the bunker plates on a fishing vessel which should, however, be fitted with Bristol funnels when opened to receive fish. It is amazing how many vessels are three-quarters sunk before the crew realizes there is critical flooding; each compartment in a vessel should therefore be fitted with two independent bilge-water-level warning devices, which cost very few bucks.

Subjective aspects of the crew's welfare should be considered on deck and below in order to reduce tiredness and distractions, and to increase alertness. Comfortable, clean, pleasant quarters should be provided; noise should be kept at acceptable levels or earmuffs worn; and illumination, especially on deck, should be carefully designed to light the work station brightly and evenly but without glare. Environmental control should include ample means for supplying fresh air and exhausting foul, and temperature control in the form of heaters and air-conditioning.

4. All commercial craft, even uninspected ones, are governed by rules from the classification societies, from the U.S. Coast Guard, and from insurance companies. Be meticulous in following all regulations that pertain to your craft. These will not

only improve the safety, efficiency, and comfort of the vessel, but may even result in reduced cost of insurance.

5. Since World War II there has been a veritable explosion of different kinds of vessels for commercial applications. In addition to the conventional displacement monohull, the following deserve comment:

a. Planing monohull (maximum LOA about 100′ [30.5 m])—high speed passenger, oil rig crew boats, offshore lobstering.

b. Catamaran (twin hull)—car and/or passenger ferries, fishing, research.

c. Surface effect ship (supported by air trapped by a circumferential skirt; the Hovercraft is an example)—high speed passenger and vehicle ferries.

d. Hydrofoil craft (supported by submerged wings)—high speed passenger.

e. Submarines—underwater sightseeing, tankers.

f. SWATH (Small Water plane Area Twin Hull, catamarans with small water plane area to reduce motion)—passengers, research.

Types of commercial craft: There is a myriad of different types of commercial craft, but they can usefully be collected into the few categories discussed below:

Fishing vessels—The range is huge, from 10′ (3 m) dugout canoes to 10,000-ton factory trawlers, using many types of gear, from simple hook and line to huge electronically monitored midwater trawls (see figure 16-1).

To digress, my favorite fishing gear is teacups. In Hong Kong there is a fishery that uses teacups tied at intervals to a line and lowered to the bottom. Octupi find these attractive homes and back into them. By the time they realize their home is moving, they have arrived at their destination—the fisherman's boat.

Fishing vessels differ from other commercial craft in one extremely important way: the crew must be working all the time, usually around dangerous machinery, often out on deck, and frequently under conditions other seamen would button up in or shun completely. These hazardous and arduous working conditions place a heavy responsibility upon the entire designing and building team to ensure maximum fishing time with minimum danger to the crew.

Towing vessels—These may be classified as oceangoing tugs, harbor tugs, and river towboats, each of which has its own peculiar requirements (see figure 16-2). Oceangoing towboats can be again classified into three groups: those designed for towing barges astern on hawsers, those intended for rigid integration into the barge's stern as sort of an attachable engine room, and those built for salvage work requiring not only great power, on the order of 4,000 to 5,000 horsepower, but also a wide variety of other capabilities necessary for salvaging grounded or sinking vessels and hawser-towing them to a safe port. Harbor tugs are the fussy nursemaids clustered about freighters and tankers being docked and undocked, or towing, usually alongside, car barges, lighters, and other unpowered harbor craft; their requirements are great maneuverability and strength, and rounded sides in plan view to facilitate changing direction when jammed against the side of a vessel. River towboats, actually push boats, are used on all inland waterways in the United States; typically a

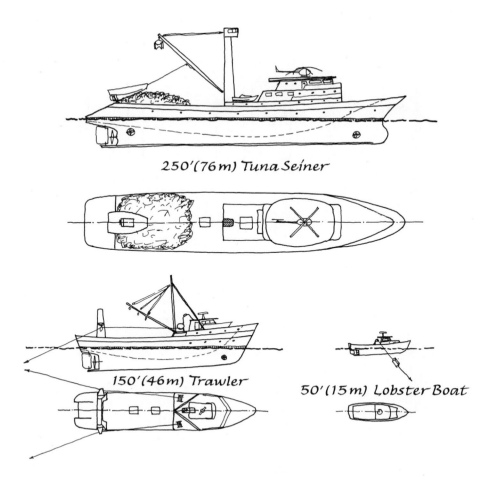

Fig. 16-1. Types of fishing vessels

6,000-SHP towboat will push 50,000 tons of cargo in a raft of barges. Square in plan view and cross section, these shoal draft vessels are usually fitted with nozzles around the propellers to increase towing power and to minimize the extent to which the stern is sucked down against the bottom of very shoal channels (thanks to Mr. Bernoulli's law). Towboats exist solely to apply as much towing power as they efficiently can to the towed objects; this calls for large diameter, slow-turning propellers and makes nozzles very desirable.

Passenger craft (figure 16-3)—From the 25' (7.6 m) yacht club launch delivering three or four yachtsmen to their sloop to the 850' (259 m) cruise ship sailing around the world with 2,700 passengers and 1,000 crew, the definitive phrase is *passenger safety*. Regulations providing for passenger safety are contained in codes prepared by many national agencies (in the United States it's the Coast Guard) and by the IMO (International Maritime Organization), an agency of the United Nations. In addition, many nongovernmental agencies are involved in passenger safety in-

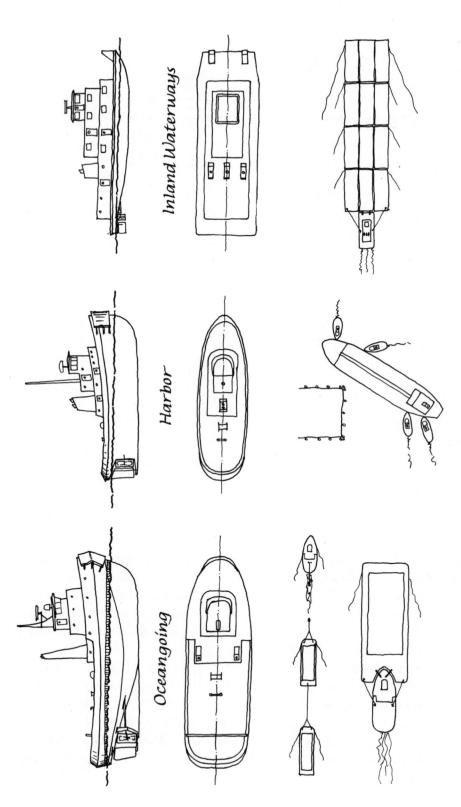

Fig. 16-2. Three classes of towboats: oceangoing, harbor, inland waterways

cluding, in the United States: American Bureau of Shipping (ABS), American Boat and Yacht Council (ABYC), and National Fire Protection Association (NFPA).

Before attempting any planning for a vessel to carry passengers for hire, consult the Coast Guard regulations in Chapter I of Title 46, *Code of Federal Regulations,* Subchapter T, Parts 175 to 187 (governing small passenger vessels carrying more than 6 persons and of less than 100 gross tons), and Subchapter H, Parts 70 to 80 (all other passenger vessels), and numerous other parts by reference. These regulations are very good in substance, but are a maze of cross-references, differing thresholds, bureaucratic and legal lingo, and a huge amount of technical information. As previously mentioned, my practice is, when starting on the design of a passenger craft, to buy the appropriate volumes (available from the U.S. Government Printing Office), read them carefully and thoroughly, and highlight those portions that will or may apply to the new design. I refer to them continuously throughout the design phase.

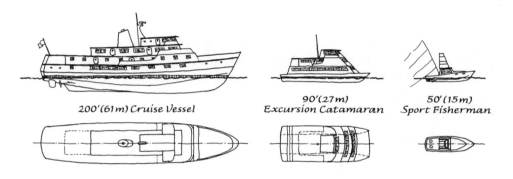

Fig. 16-3. Passenger vessels

In sketching passenger vessels, the following comments may be useful, subject of course to the Coast Guard regulations:

1. The point of least motion on the vessel is about $4/7$ aft from the forward end of the waterline, on the centerline, and at waterline level. Locate those areas most motion-critical as near this point as possible. Don't, for instance, locate a dining room in the very bow on the second deck, no matter how scenic a spot it is; locate it on or below the main deck well aft.

2. Locating the dining hall aft also allows the galley to be aft; galley smells, sound, and heat can be vented out over the stern away from the passengers.

3. If possible, locate the engine room under a working part of the vessel (galley, bridge, crew's quarters) to minimize the sound level in the passengers' areas, and plan the exhaust system so that fumes and sound do not impinge on the passengers.

4. Consider the weather conditions in which the vessel will operate in relation to the passengers. Will all the passengers have reasonable shelter from rain or cold spray? Is there a variety of comfortable seating on longer trips, say over two hours? Is there a facility available for the seriously seasick, injured, or stricken person? Can the toilet rooms be cleaned easily and quickly?

5. On vessels cruising over a period of days, make sure that there is adequate stowage space for supplies, for trash (recently, the impression of elegance given by a small cruise vessel in the Caribbean was spoiled for me by an untidy stack of trash bags, cardboard boxes, and junk on an after deck), and for sewage.

6. Give thought to the catamaran for passenger vessels. The large rectangular deck and the extremely good stability allow multideck arrangement planning in almost shoreside fashion on even a small vessel. Above about 50′ (15.2 m) LOA, it is possible to have full headroom in the hulls below the main deck for crew quarters, machinery spaces, etc. An unsinkable catamaran is possible by filling the hulls with foam to above the water plane. The advantages of the catamaran make it an especially good subject for inventive envelope sketching.

7. Appearance is of considerable importance to prospective passengers. Whereas not long ago any vessel that was neat and clean and offered adequate accommodations was acceptable, the clientele are becoming more sophisticated. If you are planning a Mississippi riverboat it must look like one, with twin stacks, working paddle wheels, and the curves and decorations that are authentic; the imitation paddle wheel is properly on its way out.

Getting afloat as passengers on large and small craft, on rivers, lakes, bays, and the ocean, is a rapidly growing recreation. Cruise vessels, party fishing boats (in some places the total catch landings from these rival the commercial fishery landings), excursion boats, whale watching, dinner vessels, sightseeing, long and short run ferries, all are being patronized more than ever. With careful planning of the vessel and its operations, passenger service offers an intriguing investment of one's time and money.

Offshore oil fleet—The offshore oil industry is relatively new; the first offshore well was drilled, using land type drilling gear, off the Louisiana coast in 1933. As more distant and deeper undersea fields were discovered, offshore drilling rigs became larger and more complex. In 1985 there were approximately 770 floating offshore drill rigs in existence worldwide, with the most advanced of them able to operate in 6,000′ (1,829 m) of water and drill 30,000′ (9,144 m) into the crust.

Several highly specialized types of offshore vessels are beyond the scope of this volume, such as: *jack-up drilling rigs,* pontoon or barge mounted oil well drilling towers that are towed to location and the hulls jacked up clear of the water on three or four legs; *semisubmersible drilling rigs,* pontoon craft moved by tow or under their own power to the drilling location where they are moored or submerged to sit on the bottom for drilling up to 24 wells from one rig; *drill ships,* which are ship-shaped vessels fitted with a drilling tower for carrying out exploratory drilling; *heavy-lift vessels,* used to transport entire rigs all over the world and to transport and lift into place the components, sometimes weighing several thousand tons, of fixed offshore rigs; *pipe-laying vessels* for welding together pipe sections and launching the pipe to the sea bottom from offshore oil fields to the shore.

Supporting these is a fleet of more conventional small craft, in some of which two or more functions are combined: *supply boats* for carrying fuel, drilling mud, and other supplies from the base port to the drill rig; *crew boats,* which are smaller than the supply vessels and faster (up to 25 knots), for bringing out fresh crews and taking ashore the off-duty crew; *anchoring vessels,* used to handle the many heavy anchors, and associated chain and cable, required to hold a floating rig on station (a semisubmersible rig may have eight 45,000 lb (20,420 kg) anchors, each with a rode made up of 2,000' (610 m) of 3½" (8.9 cm) chain and 8,000' (2,440 m) of 2½" (6.4 cm) wire rope); and *seismic vessels* for exploring for oil deep in the earth's crust. The structure of the crust is determined by recording echoes of sound bursts produced from a long 1.1 mi (2 km) or more array by many spark-induced noise makers.

The offshore industry is highly technical, has totally unique requirements, and is in a constant state of development and growth. For these reasons it is a field for specialists; if the reader is interested in pursuing it further, he is referred to his local library or to one of the volumes listed in the Bibliography.

Special purpose craft—The world rediscovered the oceans following World War II. Together with space, the oceans became a new and exciting frontier, and large high tech companies sought to operate in watery space in the same way they did in interplanetary space; one of the lures was an apparently unlimited supply of mineral nodules on the bottom containing high concentrations of valuable metals. Many of these companies retreated to dry land when faced with the realities of the hostile marine environment: tremendous pressures, a highly corrosive medium, the need to carry on most of their work from the constantly moving ocean surface in frequently foul meteorological conditions, the cost of building and especially maintaining the equipment, and on top of it all the fact that "mining" the nodules turned out not to be cost-effective.

Nevertheless, today there is a tremendous amount of innovative activity on and in the oceans of the world. The offshore oil industry is one of the largest marine industries in terms of investment, technical and managerial complexity, and impact on our everyday lives. But there are also many new kinds of vessels that come within the general purview of this book. Among them are dredges and tankers.

Dredges are used to deepen bodies of water and to maintain the dredged depths, and for extracting sand for construction use. There are three types of dredgers: a clamshell dredge, in which a clamshell (sometimes simply a crawler crane with bucket mounted on a barge) digs up bottom and dumps it into a barge alongside for disposal at sea; a ladder dredge, in which buckets, attached to an endless chain mounted on a pivoted arm the end of which is lowered to the bottom, dig out the bottom and haul it to the deck of the dredge for disposal; and a hydraulic dredge, in which the bottom is loosened by a rotating cutter (able to cut into coral), by a scoop, or by water jets, and pumped into the dredge's holds or into a barge, or pumped through pipes for disposal ashore as fill. Holding the dredge in the proper position is obviously a major necessity if the dredged bottom is to be cleanly and uniformly level; this may be done dynamically by operating the vessel's propeller and lateral thrusters located at bow and stern, or by "spuds," vertical beams located at bow and stern and dropped down to embed in the bottom, in conjunction with a pair of anchors off the bows to provide the dredge with a panning motion.

Tankers come in all sizes and are used for hauling all types of liquids: crude oil, refinery products, wine, orange juice, fluidized cement, water, liquefied natural gas. Probably the type of widest interest is the small petroleum product tankers for harbor and inshore coastal work, ranging up to 500 or so deadweight (cargo weight) tons. These are essentially rectangular tanks with shaped bow and stern added for buoyancy and hydrodynamic reasons and for the engine room. For simplicity of construction the engine room, bridge, and crew quarters are located in the stern; any superstructure on the main deck must be watertight because tankers are often awash when in a seaway. A major problem with tankers is how to maintain enough hull and propeller submergence for steaming and maneuvering after discharging cargo. This is usually accomplished by adding seawater ballast, either in separate ballast tanks or in cargo tanks that are dewatered before reloading with petroleum product.

Design steps: Figure 16-4 is a block diagram to complement the design spiral as a road map or game plan in developing a sketch of a commercial craft. The element in commercial craft that is missing from the other types of craft is profitability; it is essential that estimated building and operating costs be compared with expected revenues to evaluate the financial viability of the enterprise. A sound rule in vessel economics estimating is to be generous on costs and liabilities and conservative on revenues.

There may be a tendency to skip over parts of this game plan on the basis that you know it all already, especially if you are familiar with the industry in which the vessel is to operate. I urge the reader not to shortcut the exercise described here, but to take each step in order from beginning to end. If you already know the answer to a particular step, it will take only a second or two to resolve it and move on to the next one. If you can't do it that quickly, then it was well worthwhile having tackled it, since by doing so you will have expanded your knowledge of the industry.

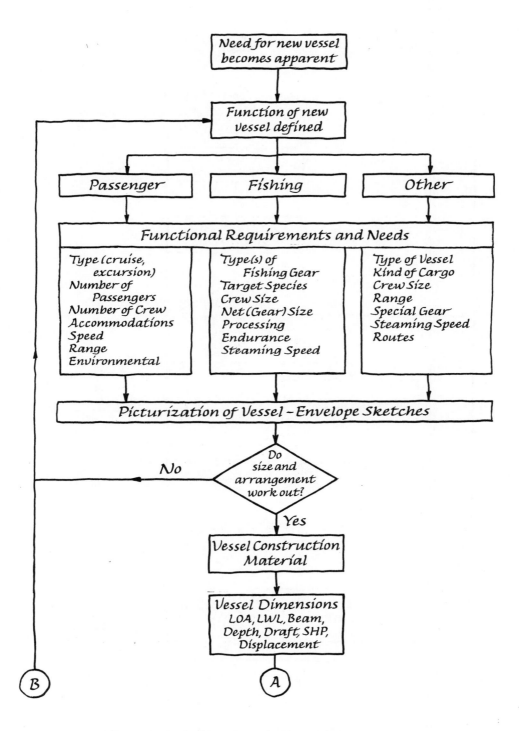

Fig. 16-4. Block diagram—preliminary design process for
commercial craft *(continued on next page)*

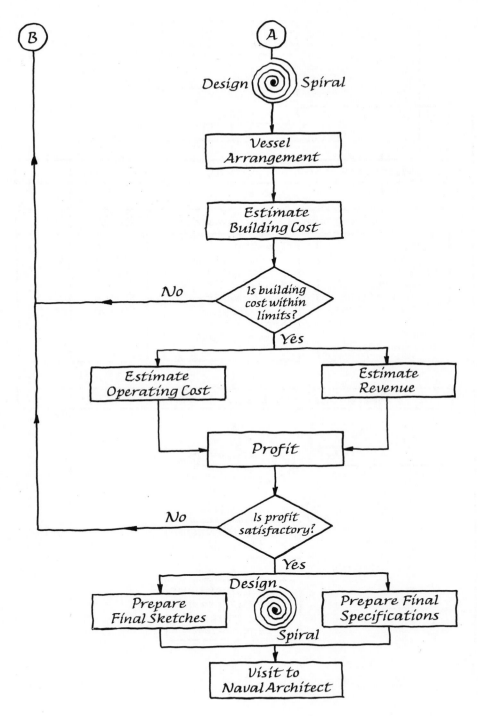

Fig. 16-4. *(continued)*

There is a special quality about designing commercial vessels that I particularly like. The more successful operators are first-class people, good businessmen, very hardworking and diligent, and extremely knowledgeable about the sea and their vessels. While the conservatism that is a hallmark of the working seaman sometimes inhibits his appreciation of an innovative idea, once he recognizes the value he goes for it full bore. Of all the groups of people for whom this volume is written, it is the commercial boatmen I would most like to see benefit from it.

17. Institutional Craft

INSTITUTIONAL craft are defined here as those that are not for pleasure and not for profit. This includes government craft of all types, vessels owned and operated by research and educational institutions, and in fact any craft operated by not-for-profit organizations. There is some overlap with commercial or pleasure types of vessels—for instance, municipal fare-charging ferries, a pilot boat operated by a proprietary company of pilots, the presidential yacht—and when this overlap occurs the vessel should be considered as a commercial or pleasure craft.

Out-and-out military craft are not covered in this book. They are a distinct class requiring a specialized knowledge I do not have. However, Coast Guard vessels are covered because, although the Coast Guard is part of the military in wartime, its primary functions are nonmilitary.

Institutional craft include oceanographic and fisheries research vessels; publicly operated ferries; pilot boats; fire boats; police boats; oil spill recovery vessels; Army Corps of Engineers dredges; Coast and Geodetic Survey vessels; Coast Guard craft such as high endurance cutters, patrol boats, surf boats, buoy tenders, and ice breakers (figures 17-1, 17-2, 17-3).

Fig. 17-1. Coast Guard buoy tender breaking ice

In fact, the diversity of kinds of vessels is if anything greater among institutional craft than commercial craft.

Design philosophy: The foundation of any vessel design is that the vessel must satisfactorily perform its function; the first purpose of any vessel is to do its job well. Institutional craft have another role that must also be considered; it projects a public expression or image of that institution. Governmental bodies, academic institutions, research organizations, all endeavor to give an impression of permanence, excellence, and high duty. Their vessels, as visible extensions of the parent body, can be very important in creating those impressions. Since it sometimes costs money to do this, the designer/planner should clarify the wishes of the institution on this point.

Function in design: Institutional craft are generally very specialized. For that reason it is well for the design/planner to acquaint himself with the functions the vessel will perform and how it will perform them. The only way I know to achieve this knowledge to a meaningful degree is to spend time in the field studying a vessel at work. A few days on a dredge or a pilot boat, observing it in action, discussing all aspects of the vessel and its operation with the crew, and thoroughly familiarizing oneself with the arrangement and operating characteristics of the vessel will give insights that no amount of reading, thinking, or conversation can provide. Even if

Fig. 17-2. Catamaran research vessel lowering a corer in a seaway

Fig. 17-3. Pilot boarding a large vessel

your day-to-day work is intimately associated with the target operation, a field trip will give a valuable fresh slant on it. Very small variations in hull design, arrangement, and machinery and gear selection can have significant effects on the success of the vessel; personal hands-on experience will help ensure that these variations are in the positive, not negative, direction.

It is generally unwise to try to combine more than one function in a single vessel. A fire boat should be a fire boat, a ferry, a ferry. While it may be technically possible to combine two functions in one vessel, it should not be done; the pursuit of each function will be inhibited by the presence of another.

A case history will illustrate the importance of the two points made above. A state with an extensive coast and important fisheries finally decided to have an 80′ (24 m) research vessel designed and built. But they made two serious errors. First, they tried to save money by incorporating two functions—fisheries research and fishery law enforcement—in the one vessel. Secondly, a cumbersome and impractical bidding system resulted in the purchase of a stock vessel. The upshot of it was that the vessel had serious design deficiencies, and was not suitable to perform either function adequately. After a few years the vessel was sold at a large loss. The state agency still has no coastal class research vessel or enforcement vessel.

Cost: Generally speaking, institutional watercraft will cost more than commercial craft of similar type. It is difficult to quantify this statement because there are so many differences between these two categories and so much variability within each one. Also there is an increasing trend to use commercial craft as a basic platform for specialized institutional vessels. For instance, for fisheries research European countries tend to start with a trawler and alter it to fulfill the research function, whereas in the United States we tend to design a research vessel and incorporate in it the facilities necessary for fisheries research; very likely the first approach is less costly and as good as or better for applied research whereas the U.S. approach is best for basic and general research.

Table 17-1 gives off-the-cuff estimates of the increments to be added to commercial vessel costs to estimate the price of institutional vessels having the same cubic number. These relate to the complete vessel exclusive of highly specialized equipment such as armament, research instrumentation, etc.

Each institutional craft is unique. For that reason it does not seem helpful to incorporate in this chapter comments on specific types, comments that might well be wrong in a particular instance. However, in general, when beginning the sketch design of an institutional vessel, the following steps are suggested.

1. Assess as well as you can the temper of the institution. Are they looking for a purely functional vessel, or will they want it embellished a bit to better project their image?

Table 17-1
Estimated Construction Cost Surcharge, Institutional over Commercial Vessels
(Total Vessel Cost = Commercial Cost + Surcharge)

	Percentage
U.S. military craft (for comparison only)	150 to 200
U.S. Coast Guard craft	90 to 100
Other U.S. government craft (except military)	50 to 80
Oceanographic research vessels	40 to 50
Fisheries research vessels	25 to 40
Oil spill recovery vessels	20 to 30
Fire and police boats	20 to 30
Pilot boats	10 to 30

2. Determine as accurately as possible the functions for which the vessel will be built, not only for now but for the decade or two ahead. If possible, translate the function into a typical operating schedule.

3. Spend several days on a similar vessel, learning all you can about what the crew think of it, and what they would suggest as improvements, as well as observing the vessel yourself—arrangement, machinery, hull design, etc.

4. Make great numbers of envelope sketches (don't hesitate to go several times around the design spiral!), concentrating on the arrangement for every deck. In your imagination carry out each of the functions of the vessel, placing the crew and equipment where it will be most advantageously employed.

5. Determine the overall dimensions (from your envelope sketches), main and auxiliary powering needs, displacement, and construction cost. This step will be essentially the same as for commercial craft, with a building cost surcharge from table 17-1.

6. Create your sketch design.

7. Submit the design package (sketches, specifications, recommendations, etc.) for comment to the captain and crew, the vessel shore support personnel, and the administration.

8. If the design is not acceptable for some reason, go back to the appropriate step above and run through the exercise again from that point.

The highly specialized nature of institutional craft makes planning all the more important. As the conceptual designer, you can make a major impact on seeing that the eventual vessel is a success from all points of view. Using the procedure suggested above, your final sketch and associated material will very likely be translated into the finished vessel with few changes. This is a challenging opportunity to make a major contribution to your institution.

PART III

IMPLEMENTATION

18. Specifications

Spec′ i·fi·ca′tion. A statement
containing a minute description or
enumeration of particulars, as of
details of a contract, details of
construction not shown in an
architect's drawings, etc.; also, any
item of such a statement.

—Webster's

THE specifications to go with the conceptual sketch of your vessel will be
rather brief and simple (see chapter 8), but you should recognize a proper
set of specifications for the final design and insist that your naval architect
provide them.

The design of a vessel, as expressed in plans, specifications, and other material,
is a medium of communication. The purpose of all your drawing and writing is to
communicate your design concept to someone else as clearly, precisely, and
reproducibly as possible. Only if this communication is effectively and completely
done will the resulting vessel accurately mirror the creative force within you from
which the design concept grew. Mumbling an idea to another person so that he only
understands half of it is to waste the idea. By the same token, if the design is
"mumbled" on paper it will be very unclearly understood by all who must use it. So
don't mumble.

This is particularly true of the specifications. Just as many ideas cannot be
precisely expressed except by a drawing—for instance the construction plan, or the
curves of form—so others can only be accurately communicated by the written
word, such as the size, type, material, and figure number of a gate valve. A proper
design includes a mixture of plans and text.

It is very easy for a naval architect to prepare a voluminous and handsome set
of plans and specifications for a design while sitting in an office. But when the design
gets down to the people actually doing the work, the pretty pictures and nicely bound
set of specifications lead another life. If a workman must interrupt his work for appreciable periods in order to study voluminous and poorly expressed information in
order to figure out what he is to do, he will tend to spend less and less time examin-

ing the designer's material and instead substitute his memory of what he thinks he saw, sometimes amended by a few ideas of his own. After all, his job is to get things built, not act as file clerk for a pile of papers that keep getting dirty, lost, and superseded. So if the very important builders are to do their best, the design must be presented to them so that they can quickly and effectively interpret it, and have a degree of satisfaction in building to it.

Inadequate information is as bad as too much. To use terms like "suitable material" or "securely fastened" leaves decisions up to the builder that he should not, and perhaps cannot, make. Therefore, in all important applications, the specifications should fully and completely define the materials, the hardware, and the method of putting it all together.

A special effort is required to ensure that the workmen will use specifications whenever necessary but, unlike the awkwardness of large plans, specifications are easily lost, hidden, or borrowed. Some naval architects try to overcome this difficulty by including directly on the plans as much of the specifications as they can. The concept isn't bad, but the result is plans that are so loaded with text that it's difficult for the worker to separate the plans from the text, especially after a couple of weeks of exposure to shop dirt.

One method of encouraging referral to the specification booklet is to put as few specifications on the plans as possible so that the writing on the plans is only that which is required by the particular drawing, such as identification of lines, dimensions, etc. However, *all* the specifications should be covered in a booklet, so that the worker, finding it easier to go by the specifications than to think something up on his own, is inclined to refer to them for just about every task. Not only does he quickly get in the habit of referring to the specifications whenever he looks at the plans, but the lack of a mass of information on the plans makes them much easier to use.

I also do as much as I can to ease the worker's use of the specifications. Of great importance is a complete and extensive index or table of contents; nothing can cool the specification ardor more quickly than having to plow through 100 pages or so looking for the precise place where some item is described. Secondly, the writing must be as simple and concise as possible; after all, the specifications booklet is not the great American novel.

But perhaps the most important requirement for good specifications is completeness and precision. A specification calling for "a suitable valve" is useless; it should be "a $1/2''$ (13 mm) bronze rising stem gate valve, Pucker Figure 203 or equal." Such a specification not only is a great help to the purchasing agent, but the specified valve is then destined from the beginning for a particular use and location, greatly simplifying the stock clerk's task. So be sure the specifications are as specific as possible.

Often, too, I will supplement the specifications with full-scale sketches of such difficult items as the framing around a companionway or the construction where the deck and hull side come together (see figure 2-5). Such sketches help me work the details out properly at the time of designing and are of great assistance later on to the builders. Similarly, simple freehand schematic sketches such as figure 18-1 will be most helpful to you in planning systems and a great aid for the architect in making detailed plans.

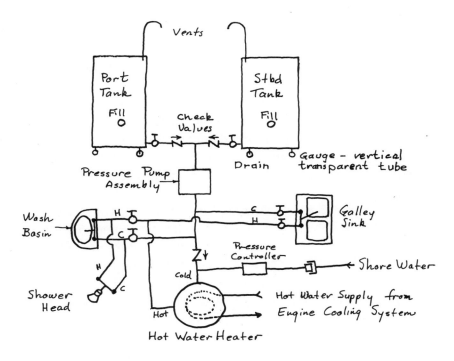

Fig. 18-1. Schematic sketch of fresh water supply system

Writing a full set of specifications can be a long and tedious task; fortunately most of this will be done by someone in the architect's office. However, in preparing your sketch design you should record all specification items to which you have given thought and which are important to you. For instance you must obviously specify the construction material for which your sketch design was prepared. Your specifications may amount to 3 to 6 pages, whereas the final specs may have 50 to 100 or more pages.

A listing of most of the subjects one would expect to find in the final and complete set of specifications prepared by the naval architect follows. This constitutes a convenient checklist to help ensure that all the important elements in your sketch design have been given consideration, and that those of particular interest to you are adequately covered in your own sketches and specifications.

Index: Listing alphabetically each element of the vessel and the page(s) on which it is found.

General: Comments and specifications applying to the entire boat.

  *Particulars—LOA, LWL, beam, draft, depth, displacement, ballast (if sail), sail areas (if sail); may include hull form coefficients, propulsion horsepower, cruising and top speed.

  *Standards—A narrative description of the quality of materials, workmanship, and outfit expected; specifying what regulatory agency standards must be followed.

  *Construction conditions—Shelter, heating, storage of materials, etc.

  *Inspection—Availability of boat and materials for inspection; handling of deficiencies.

  *Materials—General comments on standards of timber, and on materials for fastenings, glues, plastics and reinforcement, joiner hardware, etc.

  *Trials—List of trials to be carried out and who is responsible for what.

  *Delivery—Statement concerning where delivery will be made, and the terms of the transfer of ownership from shipyard to owner; may be in contract instead.

Hull construction: Description of the construction of the hull and superstructure. Care must be taken that it be coordinated with other sections; for instance, that engine bed construction is covered either here or under "machinery." (The construction material will dictate what specific elements are included in this section; given below are general categories of structural elements.)

  *Backbone—The "spine" of the boat, along the centerline extending from the stemhead to the deck at the stern is an important element because it ties the two sides of the vessel together. In a sailboat it is the chief resister of the heavy loads on stays, and is the part that is most often in contact with terra firma, either from running aground or being slipped. Connection of the sides to the backbone is especially important.

  *Centerboard and trunk—A wooden trunk may be a source of weakness and leaking so should be well tied into the keel and the side structure. Covered should be such elements as centerboard sectional shape, pin details, and pendant arrangement.

  *Ballast keel—Material, finished weight, and bolting method.

  *Framing—Materials and methods of attachment of floors, frames, bilge stringer, sheer clamp and shelf, coring material and lay-ups (FRP), longitudinal or transverse (steel), etc.

  *Skin—Planking or plating; materials, thickness, attachment to framing, coring material(s), and lay-up schedule (FRP). The transom may need special attention.

  *Engine foundation—Materials and dimensions of engine stringers, beds, brackets, etc. Identify special features to be observed in installation. (The engine foundation has the functions of transmitting the thrust of the propulsion engine to the hull in ahead or reverse, of supporting the weight of the engine and accessories, and of damping out undesirable vibrations.)

*Bulkheads—Identify watertight and nonwatertight bulkheads. For each, specify the material, stiffening, attachment to hull and deck, limbers if necessary.

*Deck framing—Size, spacing, material, how fastened; blocking or stiffening for deck fittings.

*Deck—Thickness, material, fastening to framing and to hull, sheathing (no-skid?).

*Deck structures—Materials, sizes, and fastenings of vertical and horizontal surfaces. Fastening of structures to deck is especially important to resist being torn off by boarding seas. Specify windows, doors, hardware.

*Cockpit—Materials, sizes, fastenings of framing and of surfaces; sheathing if any (no-skid?); hatch construction and hardware; drainage and gasketing; scupper construction and terminations.

*Steering gear (May have section of its own if complex.)—Historically, rudder assemblies and steering gears have a consistent record of failure; it is much better to over-design than to try to save weight or cost here. Rudder stock material, size, bearings, port; rudder blade material, method of fastening to stock. Specify manufacturer, size, etc. of steering mechanism (tiller, cable, worm gear, hydraulic), steering wheel, emergency steering system.

*Exterior joiner work—Hatch covers, moldings, trim, handrails, etc.; materials, level of finish, matching of colors, types of joints, bedding, fastenings. Specify precisely all joiner hardware.

*Ventilation (May have its own section if complex.)—Specify internal ventilation paths, fans, ducts, etc. (No internal space, however small, should have less than two openings into it.) Describe all deck ventilation fixtures and means of excluding water. Ensure adequate aspiration air to engine(s) as well as engine room ventilation. Specify any fans and locations. (An excellent place to use a schematic sketch as a starter.)

Interior joiner work: Covers all the interior furnishings and associated hardware, including housings for purchased items like stoves.

*General—Give guidelines for general nature of interior—painted versus waxed/varnished surfaces, species of wood to be used, type and finish of partitions, general details of hardware. The tone set by these comments assists the joiner and finishing crews to achieve the desired atmosphere at acceptable cost.

*Overall specifics—Doors (solid paneled, or cored flush); berth bottoms, fronts, risers; drawer construction, face material, pulls, lock; sole (floor) material, thickness, scuttles for access to bilge; shelf bottoms and faces, brush-out holes; ladder material and construction; bulkhead moldings; facia (covering deck edge); specifications for all hinges, latches, locksets, and other joiner hardware.

* Compartment details—Starting with the forepeak, describe each compartment in detail, covering those items such as the main cabin table or the galley icebox, which have not been previously covered. To do this, with the help of the sketches previously made mentally put yourself in each compartment, installing and/or using whatever is there, making sure no element has been overlooked. A typical list of compartments treated in this way, from a 48′ (14.6 m) yawl, is: forepeak; forward cabin (two berths); toilet room (to port); hanging lockers (to starboard); main cabin (two fixed and two extension berths, chart table, hanging lockers); galley (to port); sea berth (to starboard); engine compartment (under cockpit); lazarette.

Plumbing: Covers all plumbing associated with fresh water supply system, sewage and gray water disposal, bilge pumping, deck washdown, fire hydrants.

* General—General specifications for materials, plus standards to be followed, through-hull fittings.
* Water tanks—Material, size, locations, fill systems, vents, hardware such as level gauges, etc. Supporting and securing the tanks from movement in the worst case is important.
* Water supply system—Type of pressure system (if any), backup hand pumps, hot water tank, shore connection, faucets (spring-loaded?), sink, washbasins, shower, drains/sumps; water maker if used.
* Sewage system—Specify general type (holding tank, treatment, incineration); toilets; pump-out arrangement; holding tank size, material, location, fittings.
* Bilge drainage—Pump(s) specified, compartments pumped, limbering throughout described, discharge, manifold, foot valves, bilge level warning devices.
* Fire system—Pump(s) specified (combined with bilge pump?), intake size and location, hydrant location(s), fire hose and nozzle.

Electrical: Includes all electrical systems in the vessel except independent system(s) associated entirely with prime movers, such as starting and electrical instruments. (This is another place where I find an early schematic is almost a necessity).

* General—This should state quite precisely which standards (USCG, ABS, Underwriters Laboratory, National Fire Protection Association) are to be followed in the installation. If there are additional requirements beyond these, they should be clearly stated here. It helps to give a general description of the systems (voltages, frequencies, etc.) and a general outline of the regular and emergency systems.
* Generator—Specify the particular generator/prime mover assembly that will be used. In this section the electrical characteristics of the generator

are of importance; installation of the prime mover will be covered in "Machinery."

*Shore power—Specify the fittings, amperage, length of cable.

*Batteries—Specify the size, number, and capacity of batteries, where they will be located, and the nature of their containment. Allow for venting of the hydrogen gas. Describe how the batteries will be charged (generator, main engine alternator, shore power through a converter).

*Circuits—List the circuits, and the catalog number and location of each fixture in each circuit. Except for the separate engine electrical systems, every electrical fixture on the vessel must be included in one of these circuits.

*Switch panel(s)—Specify the main and day panels and their locations. Itemize the circuit breakers or fuses for the circuits, main switches, and instruments. Describe how the switches will be shielded to protect them and the user.

*Wiring—Specify what cables are to be used, and how they will be installed and protected from damage. Stipulate that each circuit should be marked at frequent intervals.

*Electronics—Identify what electronic communications, navigation, and monitoring instruments will be installed, how they will be installed, and where.

*Grounding—Specify the grounding systems, including metal mass, materials of different potential, lightning, and protection against external stray currents.

Machinery: Includes installation of all prime movers and their accessories. (Electrical side of generator/prime mover is covered under *Electrical* and refrigeration system side of refrigeration/prime mover would be covered in a separate section.) A sketch like figure 18-2 is a great help.

*Propulsion system—Specify main engine(s) with all options, including reverse/reduction gear, power takeoff, type of cooling; include attachment to foundations. Specify propeller and tail shaft size, material, bearings, stuffing box, stern bearing, and propeller size, material, type, with or without a nozzle. Describe engine subsystems: exhaust with muffler, cooling, electrical, monitoring, controls.

*Auxiliary system(s)—Same as above except for shaft assembly.

*Thrusters, if any—Locations, size, power source.

*Fuel system—Specify size, capacity, location, and material of fuel tanks (storage and day), and all their fittings (fill, feed, return, vent, level gauge). Stipulate tests to be made on tanks, and how they will be supported and restrained from motion. Describe how tanks will be removed for repair or replacement. Describe fuel lines to prime movers, including size and material of lines, valving, manifolds, cross-connections, filters, flexible sections.

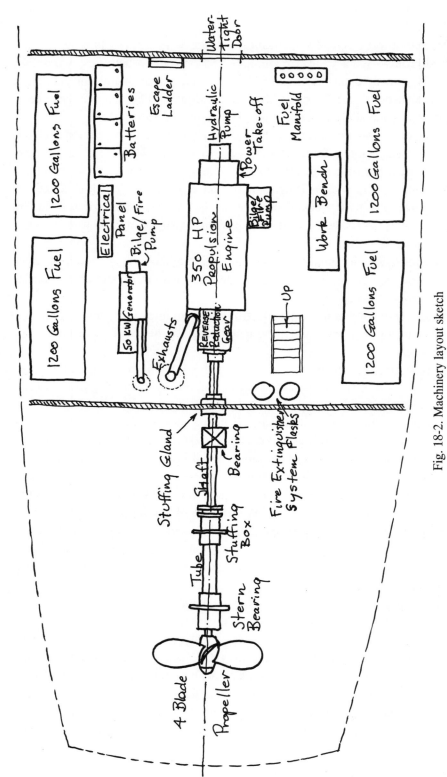

Fig. 18-2. Machinery layout sketch

*Bridge controls—Specify bridge engine controls for all prime movers and their locations.

Rigging: Every vessel has some rigging, usually enough to qualify for its own section in the specifications. Since there are as yet no regulatory standards applying to most rigging, as there are for electrical systems for instance, it is necessary to be very precise in specifying every aspect of spars, standing rigging, running rigging, and rigging fittings and equipment. "Just as good" won't do. Of all systems on a vessel, rigging is perhaps the only one in which a small failure can demolish it in seconds before corrective action can be taken. A rigging system should be carefully designed in all its parts, and as carefully drawn and specified.

Equipment: Includes individual items that are not otherwise included in previously covered subsystems. For instance: mooring system elements such as cleats and bollards, anchors, rodes, windlass, stowage; boarding ladders; heating system; canvas work such as dodgers, covers, awning; compass(es) and mounts; fire extinguishers, portable and fixed; trash stowage and disposal; life rails including stanchions, gates, caps; lifesaving equipment including life jackets, throwing gear, life raft(s) and life boat(s), survival suits, EPIRBs; galley range including fuel supply and exhaust stack; galley refrigeration; upholstery; miscellaneous equipment and supplies not otherwise covered. Some of these may deserve their own subsection.

Painting and finishing: Describes the preparation of all the surfaces, final finishing, and preservation measures. Should specify in detail what products will be used and how.

Depending upon the use of the vessel, other sections may be required in the specifications, such as: refrigeration and air-conditioning, lifesaving, and fishhold.

This fairly complete list covers what the naval architect will include in the specifications, not what you will provide with your sketch design. However, you undoubtedly will have certain special desires based on your experience or your tastes, and these should be clearly stated in a set of brief specifications you prepare for the naval architect. You will want to include at a minimum the general level of construction and finish you wish, the building materials, the joiner finishes (ranging from all painted to exotic hand-rubbed woods), and special items of equipment with which you have been particularly happy (or unhappy) in the past. To be of greatest utility, your specifications should be a useful guide to your naval architect, not an encyclopedia.

19. A Visit to the Naval Architect

WHEN you have been around the design spiral for the last time and there is just nothing more you can think to do to improve your sketch design, it is time to pay a visit to your naval architect. This starts a process that will end when your new vessel is ready to start on its first trip.

Figure 19-1 is a diagram illustrating in simple terms the steps and relationships involved in taking your original vessel concept through to operation. The concept begins with you, progresses through an involvement with a naval architect and a builder, and ends up with you when you operate the vessel. Your responsibility for the success of the vessel is very heavy, and it might be said that if the vessel is not a success the fault lies largely with you.

The block diagram, figure 19-2, lays out in detail the program to follow in getting from the beginning to the end of this process. Unless special circumstances dictate departures from this program, it should be followed through step-by-step for best results. The remarks below will help you do this.

Naval architect selection process: The fact that naval architecture is partly art, and partly science, suggests the same care be taken in choosing your naval architect as you would take in choosing your doctor or lawyer. For a straight engineering problem, like designing a bridge, it is possible to get along with even the most unpleasant professional as long as he is competent. This is not so of naval architecture. The client (you), the naval architect, and the builder are the three legs of a stool upon which the success of the vessel depends. If any one leg is too long or too short or is weak, the stool is insecure and the success of the stool (*your* vessel) is at risk. It is up to you, as the originator of the project and the payer of bills, to make sure that the other two legs of the stool are not only competent professionally but have temperaments and outlooks that are compatible with each others' and with yours. Therefore choose your architect with care; it is one of the most important decisions you will make in this whole process.

As a basis for making the selection you probably have a good deal of information about contemporary naval architects gleaned during research in preparation of the sketch design; you may already have picked one and had conversations with him or her. If not, however, the work of some architects must have appealed to you more than that of others and from those you can pick a short list of three or four who are of definite interest. (A good way of doing this is to list on cards all the architects whom you have come across, rearrange the cards in descending order of appeal, and take the top three.) To these top candidates write a letter explaining who you are, what you have done, why you are doing it, that you are looking for a naval architect to complete the design, and that he is one of three candidates for the job. If the recipient is interested in the job, ask for an interview with him. Naval architects receive a lot of the scattergun type of inquiries that are generally not worth responding to, so write each letter individually to show that you are truly interested in *his* designing style, and wish to seriously explore the possibility of working with *him.*

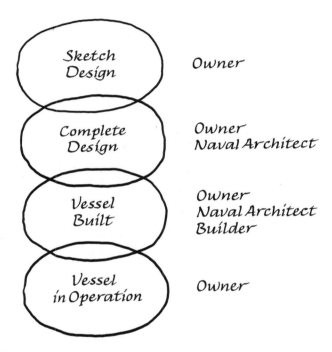

Fig. 19-1. The four steps from concept to commissioning,
and where responsibilities lie

On the basis of the architects' responses and your interviews with them, select the one to whom you react most positively; if you can't seem to be enthusiastic about any of them, try the next three or four. But don't settle for one about whom you have lingering doubts of either his professional competence or his personal style; resolve these doubts or look some more.

The question of fees should not influence the selection of a naval architect, and should therefore be one of the last things discussed. Five years after launching a $200,000 yacht or a $500,000 fishing vessel, the dollar difference between $5,000 for a quickie design and $20,000 for a real design will have been long forgotten;

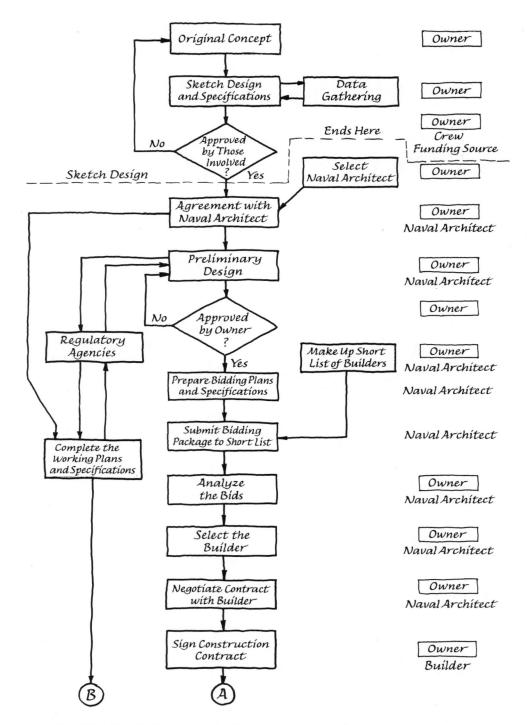

Fig. 19-2. Block diagram—vessel procurement procedure from conception to commissioning *(continued on next page)*

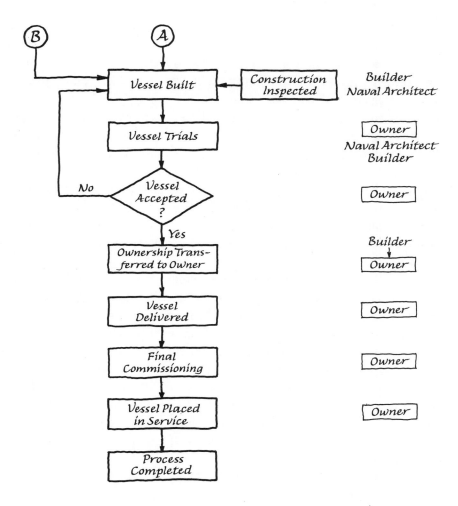

This flow chart describes a procedure for designing and building a privately owned vessel up to perhaps 200'(60m) LOA for which a naval architect's office prepares all the plans. For large vessels the shipyard often prepares many of the working plans based on guidance plans prepared by the naval architect's office. Other variations may occur in the procedure; the reader should familiarize himself with the circumstances applying to the specific vessel he is sketching.

Fig. 19-2. (continued)

what will be with you still and forever is whether or not the vessel is a good one that fulfills your expectations.

For a complete original design, I charge a percentage of the estimated value of the finished vessel: 10% for sailing yachts, 8% for power yachts, 4% to 6% for commercial craft; if periodic inspection (averaging about every two weeks) is desired during construction, an additional 2% plus travel is charged. If the design is one from my files that has already been built to, the charge is half the original fee; this includes minor revisions to the design to suit the new client's needs.

Many architects charge an open-ended fee, based not on what they estimate the cost of the vessel to be but on what the final billing for the vessel is. This approach hardly encourages designing an economical vessel; for this reason, and because the client is entitled to the most honest and realistic cost estimate, I calculate the estimated cost of the vessel and fix the design fee before asking the client to sign a contract.

You may wish to explore with the architect the possibility of completing the design on an hourly basis. Whether this is a good idea depends largely on how much work you have done and how good it is. If you are concerned about possible excesses in an open-ended fee agreement, it may be possible to set a cap beyond which you will not go without reexamining the project. The hourly basis has the advantage that either party may bow out at any time without contractual problems.

Who owns the final design? In the traditional situation, where the architect creates the entire design for his client, the rights to the design remain with the architect; in effect he licenses the construction of each boat from that design. (The architect may, of course, sell his rights to the design to the builder or anyone else if he wishes.)

In the situation outlined in this book, it may be argued that the client has already completed an appreciable part of the design, and some rights to the final design should accrue to him. This would be especially so if the architect completed the design on an hourly basis, in which case he may be considered to be a temporary employee of his client, who might then retain all rights to the design. This question of the ownership of the design should be clearly defined before the design contract is signed so that there are no surprises down the line. (In my experience, all serious problems between contracting parties stem from surprises resulting from situations and circumstances not being clearly understood and provided for before they arose.)

One way this may be settled is to have the client retain rights to the sketch design he has prepared, the architect to retain rights to the completed design. If the client has an interest in having all the rights, he may be able to purchase them for an additional fee, but the architect may well wish to retain in his files copies of all the material for reference use in future designs.

Have a written agreement with your architect setting forth the conditions under which the design will be completed. This need not be a formal, legal-style contract— a letter will do—but it should include all the terms and should be endorsed by both parties. One term I always include is that in the event of an irreconcilable difference of opinion the difficulty will be resolved by binding arbitration; this eliminates high lawyer's fees and drawn out litigation.

Final design preparation: You should expect to work closely with your naval architect, but at his initiative, not yours. Being constantly on his case and peering over his shoulder will do neither you nor him any good, nor will it help the design. After you have given him your sketch design and all backup data and calculations, it is best to leave him alone while he absorbs it, checks the calculations and sketches, and perhaps generates a few ideas of his own. Once he has familiarized himself with your wishes and your expression of them in the plans and specifications you have given him, he will no doubt want to get together with you for a discussion during which any outstanding questions and suggestions can be resolved.

During these discussions the personalities of both parties will meet head on, and the ability to work together will receive its final test. You are naturally enough pretty sure of the correctness of your sketch design and will resist any changes to it. The architect on the other hand has views based on his own experience and professional knowledge; he may also unconsciously resist "amateur" ideas. My procedure, developed from many such discussions, goes like this: I analyze my client's suggestions as objectively as I possibly can. If I have a question about one, I express my doubts to the client, explaining my views in detail. How vociferously I press my case depends on the seriousness of my concern. If the client still insists on his way of doing it, I will do it that way with the clear understanding that he made the final decision. In extreme cases I say flat out that the idea will not work or is hazardous and cannot be incorporated; if the client still insists I refuse to continue with the design.

The purpose of these client/architect discussions is to have a total meeting of minds, so each understands the other and together they make all the major decisions. Once the architect begins serious design work, any major changes not only slow the work down, but frustrate the architect and in fact tend to reduce the quality of the final vessel. Following the initial discussion, it is my practice to prepare a set of preliminary plans and specifications which, after checking by the client and incorporating any changes agreed upon, become the bidding plans used by the builders in preparing quotations. In order that the bidding plans can also be considered final plans so that no further important changes need be made, during their preparation I send frequent prints, sketches, notes, etc. to the client so that he has full opportunity to raise any questions or offer any suggestions.

If approval is required of a regulatory or standards organization, such as the U.S. Coast Guard, American Bureau of Shipping, or your insurance company, they should be apprised from the beginning of what is being done. You may already have been in touch with them during the preparation of the sketch design. The architect in his turn should keep them fully advised as the work progresses so that any questions they raise can be coped with as soon as possible. My experience has been that these agencies, whose function is to protect life and property, are well staffed with sincere and usually competent personnel administering generally sensible regulations. The sooner and more often they are communicated with as the job progresses, the fewer hangups will occur.

The bidding plans, which will be a formalization and refinement of the client's sketch design as amended during the discussion, according to my practice include the following:

> Outboard profile (sail plan), small scale
> Inboard profile, if desirable, small scale
> Construction section(s), large scale
> Arrangement plans for each deck, small scale
> Arrangement section(s) if desirable, small scale
> Full specifications, including schematic diagrams of major subsystems

"Small scale" would be, depending upon the size of the vessel, $1/4''$, $3/8''$, or $1/2''$ to the foot (1:50, 1:30, 1:25). "Large scale" would be, respectively, $1/2''$, $3/4''$, or $1''$ to the foot (1:25, 1:15, 1:12.5).

A preliminary set of lines will have been drawn and all basic calculations carried out on a preliminary level. This material is not included in the package sent to the builders for bidding.

Once the preliminary design has been completed and fully approved by the client, two actions are commenced: the bidding process (see below) and preparation of the working drawings, that is, the plans, details, etc. required by the builder. The drawings should proceed at a rapid pace because, since all major questions have long since been resolved, only minor problems need to be handled. When the working plans are completed the design is essentially finished except for such supplemental sketches as the shipyard may call for as the work progresses in order to do its job better.

Although the design is finished, my responsibilities as an architect are not. Even though my client has not chosen my inspection services during construction, I feel I have an obligation to remain in contact with the construction of the vessel through the trials. If I possibly can, I attend trials in my own interests in order to obtain a quantitative as well as qualitative feel for how the design worked out.

Bidding process: Selecting the builder, the third leg of the stool, is obviously very important. From the tens, perhaps hundreds, of possible builders it is well to make up a "short list" of three or four who will be asked for serious bids; your architect can give you valuable guidance in making this selection because he is as interested as you are in working with a good one. (International bodies such as the World Bank, when making up a short list, advertise widely for candidates who, if they are interested, send in essential information about their yards, their financial position, and the history of the yard, including craft they have built. From this long list of candidates a short list is made up.)

Requests for bids should state how many builders are being asked to bid. When a builder knows he is competing against a large number, he often feels he doesn't have a chance anyway so why make a really sharp bid? The requests should also include a deadline of the day and hour when the bids will be opened; for private construction, this deadline need not be ironclad but will give the bidders an idea of your schedule.

After the bids are received comes the frequently difficult task of choosing the winner. This should of course be done in concert with your architect. Avoid the error of accepting the lowest bid merely because it is the lowest; sometimes a really low bid indicates either a poorly prepared bid or an indication of financial desperation on the part of the shipyard. Once the builder is selected, contract negotiations are carried out.

Contract negotiations: Before the contract between the owner and the builder for the construction of the boat is signed, there are generally some points that need to be clarified by negotiation. These might include:

Revisions to plans and specifications—Most builders have some pet building practices or methods and prefer to use these when possible. I go along with these unless there is reason not to, and incorporate them in the bidding plans and specifications, which then become contract plans and specifications and are incorporated into the contract.

Change orders—Inevitably during construction there will arise revisions to the plans and specifications; for instance, a different engine is selected. The contract should stipulate that these changes be formalized and recorded in change orders, documents that describe the change in detail (architect), price it out and schedule it (builder), and then accept or reject it (owner). When the change order, which is prepared by the architect, has been endorsed by the owner and the builder, it becomes an addendum to the contract and the price structure is altered accordingly. (Change orders are generally handled by the shipyard, but I have found it worthwhile to do it myself. This gives me an opportunity to integrate the proposed change in the complete vessel system, to protect the interests of the owner, and to require the builder to be very specific about the cost of the change rather than giving a vague telephone quotation.)

Method of payment—There are three common methods of payment for construction of a vessel: fixed price, in which the complete vessel or a precisely defined portion of it is built for a flat price, any additional work being charged for separately; cost plus, in which all direct labor costs have a fixed percentage added on to cover overhead and profit and direct material costs have a percentage added on for handling, taxes, etc.; and cost plus fixed fee, in which the builder charges a fixed fee for his overhead and profit, charges the direct cost of labor, and charges for material as in cost plus. Fixed price is not popular with builders because it locks them into a price that does not provide for cost increases beyond their control. Cost plus is not popular with owners because there is no control over the amount of labor the builder may put on the job and hence the overall cost of the vessel, and even the most conscientious builder finds it difficult to resist moving men onto the cost plus job when work in other departments slacks off, even if they cannot be used efficiently. Cost plus fixed fee, on the other hand, has worked very well for owners, builders, and me (because the architect can be the ham in a legal battle sandwich between owner and builder). This method requires the builder to make an accurate estimate of the cost in order to calculate his overhead and profit with the result that the owner has a pretty firm estimate of what the final cost will be. The only real variable is in the direct labor cost which, if it varies upwards above the estimate, only means that the builder's overhead and/or profit rate is lower and that the owner has a rather mild increment on the billings, while if it varies downwards both owner and builder (with his higher profit percentage) benefit.

Payment schedule—Payment of part of the building cost is usually made at the time of signing the contract, and 5% or 10% is held out pending acceptance of the finished vessel, with the balance spread across the construction period as the owner and builder may agree. A cost plus job is billed on two-week or monthly intervals as the costs are incurred, depending on the preferences of the builder. This also goes for the cost plus fixed fee contract, except that the fixed fee portion is paid at previously established intervals spaced out over the construction period.

Delivery date—This can range from "whenever it's done" to a fixed date with severe financial penalties for each day of overrun. Unless circumstances dictate otherwise, delivery is specified as "on or before" a certain date and there are no penalties for overrun.

Insurance—From the signing of the contract, the vessel should be insured during construction for its total value at any time, with the owner protected to the extent he has paid into the vessel.

Settlement of disputes—These can and do often arise, especially when emotions tend to become high as the contract approaches completion. It therefore is an advantage to agree beforehand on how unresolvable disputes will be handled. The courts are expensive, take a long time, and frequently are lacking in the specialized knowledge required for a fair decision. As mentioned previously, in my own contracts for preparing a design I always include a clause requiring disputes to be settled by arbitration which shall be binding on both parties. This is much less expensive, much quicker, and also fair since both parties have veto power in selection of the arbitrator(s).

Vessel construction: The best advice to the owner is to stay away during construction. (Not, however, to the extent of the reported Nathaniel Herreshoff approach in which a client, having ordered a schooner for six in the owner's party, would be told he would be advised when his schooner was ready to be picked up and he would not be welcome until then. Only then would he know what he had bought.) Do not attempt to be your own "clerk of the works," inspecting construction as it progresses; leave inspection to the professionals, such as your architect or another agent, or to a Lloyd's or ABS inspector. Restrict your visits to the builder to a few, arranged well in advance. You will do better following the job by means of progress reports and photos—and the bills—than by hanging over the shipbuilder's shoulder. With your architect you can develop a projected building schedule that you can compare with the progress reports to establish a realistic delivery date; if things seem to be going too slowly, the inspector can take it up with the shipyard. (One of the great advantages of the cost plus fixed fee payment method is that it is to the shipyard's advantage to get the vessel out of the yard as quickly as possible, thus in effect increasing profit.)

Vessel acceptance and commissioning: At some time the yard will set a date for the vessel's trials. Trials should be carried out on every craft before the final payment is made—even a rowing skiff may have a leak that needs fixing. The conditions for the trials should be clearly stated in the specifications or the construction contract; generally there are machinery trials alongside the wharf to put several hours on the machinery, and trials under way when all the gear is tested in actual use—are the oars the proper length?

Once the trials have been completed and any deficiencies corrected, the last payment is made to the shipyard and to your naval architect if owed, after which the craft is yours, all yours! Following delivery and incorporation of your individual touches, it's time to load on the necessary supplies and cast off for the first trip.

If you have completed the sketch design as described in this volume and completed the vessel procurement process, and are now standing on the deck of your finished vessel, you must surely have a most satisfied feeling. Out of your brain and by your hand came the concept of a vessel that now lies on its mooring, waiting to do your bidding. Getting from one end to the other of this process has stimulated your brain cells and has surely challenged you to overcome discouraging and sometimes seemingly insurmountable problems. Yet you have prevailed, and in the process you have learned a tremendous amount about yourself, and about naval architecture in general and your vessel in particular. Also you have become acquainted with people—your naval architect and the builders of your vessel—whom you can call your friends as well as your colleagues. Over the next few years, as you operate *your* craft and begin to discern the subtle ways in which it could be improved, you may well decide to start the process all over again, hopefully with the same cast of characters.

Appendix I. Addresses

Professional and trade societies:

SNAME—Society of Naval Architects and Marine Engineers, 601 Pavonia Avenue, Jersey City, New Jersey 07306, USA. Telephone: 800-798-2188.

MTS—Marine Technology Society, 2000 Florida Ave. NW, Suite 500, Washington, D.C. 20009, USA. Telephone: 202-462-7557.

American Boat Builders and Repairers Association, P.O. Box 1236, Stamford, Connecticut 06904, USA. Telephone: 203-967-4745.

UNOLS—University-National Oceanographic Laboratory System (coordinates U.S. research vessel fleet), School of Oceanography, University of Washington, Seattle, Washington 98195, USA. Telephone: 206-543-2100.

United States government:

USCG—United States Coast Guard (transportation), 2100 2nd Street SW, Washington, D.C. 20593, USA. Telephone: 202-267-2229.

MARAD—Maritime Administration (transportation), 400 7th Street SW, Washington, D.C. 20590, USA. Telephone: 202-366-5812.

NMFS—National Marine Fisheries Service (commerce), Page Building 2, 3300 Whitehaven Street NW, Washington, D.C. 20235, USA. Telephone: 202-673-5450.

NOAA—National Oceanic and Atmospheric Administration (commerce), Rockville, Maryland 20852, USA. Telephone: 301-443-8910.

NTIS—National Technical Information Service, 5285 Port Royal Road, Springfield, Virginia 22161, USA. Telephone: 703-487-4600.

NTSB—National Transportation Safety Board, 490 L'Enfant Plaza East, SW, Washington, D.C. 20594, USA. Telephone: 202-382-6600.

International agencies:

IMO—International Maritime Organization, 4 Albert Embankment, London SE1 7SR, England.

FAO—Food and Agriculture Organization of the United Nations, via delle Termi di Caracalla, Rome, Italy.

World Bank, 1818 H Street NW, Washington, D.C. 20433, USA. Telephone: 202-477-1234.

IDB—Inter-American Development Bank, 1300 New York Avenue, NW, Washington, D.C. 20577, USA. Telephone: 202-623-1000.

ADB—Asian Development Bank, 2330 Roxas Boulevard, Metro Manila, Philippines. Telephone: 632-711-3851.

ICC—International Chamber of Commerce, 1155 15th Street NW, Washington, D.C. 20005, USA. Telephone: 202-466-2453.

Regulatory agencies:

ABS—American Bureau of Shipping, Two World Trade Center, 106th Floor, New York, New York 10048, USA. Telephone: 212-839-5016.

ABYC—American Boat and Yacht Council, 3069 Solomons Island Road, Edgewater, Maryland 21037, USA. Telephone: 410-956-1050.

Det norske Veritas, Veritasveien 1, 1322 Hovik, Norway. Telephone: +42 2 12 99 00.

Lloyd's, 71 Fenchurch Street, London E.C.3, England.

Bureau Veritas, 31, rue Henri-Rochefort, 75 821 Paris CEDEX 17, France.

Miscellaneous groups and organizations:

US Sailing—Box 209 (Goat Island Marina), Newport, Rhode Island 02840, USA. Telephone: 401-849-5200.

ORC—Offshore Racing Council (IOR Racing Rule), 19 St. James Place, London SW11A 1NN, England. Telephone: 01-629-8701.

BOAT–US (boat owners' association), 880 S. Pickett Street, Alexandria, Virginia 22304, USA. Telephone: 703-823-9550.

Periodicals:

Boating (contemporary U.S. power boating), 1515 Broadway, New York, New York 10036, USA. Telephone: 212-827-4125.

Commercial Fisheries News (New England commercial fishing), Main Street, Stonington, Maine 04681, USA. Telephone: 207-367-2396.

Cruising World (cruising under sail), 524 Thames Street, Newport, Rhode Island 02840, USA. Telephone: 401-847-1588.

Fishing Boat World, 44 Carmelite St, London EC4Y 0BN, England. Telephone: +44 171 353 1085.

Fishing News International (worldwide commercial fishing), EMAP Heighway, Meed House, 21 John St., London WC1N 2BP, England. Telephone: +44 171 5513.

Marine Log (commercial vessels, mostly in the United States), 345 Hudson Street, New York, New York 10014, USA. Telephone: 212-620-7225.

Marine Propulsion International (marine engines and drives, mostly for medium and large vessels), Industrial and Marine Publications, Queensway House, 2 Queensway, Redhill, Surrey RH1 1QS, England. Telephone: Redhill (0737)768611.

Maritime Reporter (U.S. commercial ships and shipping), 118 East 25th Street, New York, New York 10010, USA. Telephone: 212-477-6700.

National Fisherman (U.S. commercial fisheries), 120 Tillson Avenue, Suite 201, Rockland, Maine 04841-0908, USA. Telephone: 207-594-6222.

Practical Sailor (critical reports on yachting products and boats; no advertising), Box 819, Newport, Rhode Island 02840, USA. Telephone: 401-849-7438.

Professional Boatbuilder, P.O. Box 78, Brooklin, Maine 04616, USA. Telephone: 207-359-4651.

Sail (sailing yachts), 275 Washington St., Newton, Massachusetts 02158-1630, USA. Telephone: 617-964-3030.

Sailing World (covers U.S. sailboat racing), 5 John Clarke Road, Newport, Rhode Island 02540-0992, USA. Telephone: 401-847-1588.

Seascape (commentary on old and new ships and shipping, mostly in Europe and the United States), 52-54 Southwark Street, London SE1 1UJ, England. Telephone: 01-403 3771.

Sea History (old vessels), National Maritime Historical Society, 5 John Walsh Boulevard, P.O. Box 68, Peekskill, New York 10566-9934, USA. Telephone: 1-800-221-6647.

Sea Technology (devoted largely to oceanographic research equipment and vessels), Suite 1000, 1117 N. 19th Street, Arlington, Virginia 22209, USA. Telephone: 203-524-3136.

Ship and Boat International (worldwide coverage of small craft to 300′-400′, with emphasis on the United Kingdom), (publication of Royal Institute of Naval Architecture), 10 Belgrave Street, London SW1X 8BQ, England. Telephone: 071 235 4622.

Soundings (sail and power yachting), 35 Pratt Street, Essex, Connecticut 06426-9952, USA. Telephone: 860-767-3200.

Work Boat (small work boats), P.O. Box 1348, Mandeville, Louisiana 70470, USA. Telephone: 804-626-0298.

Work Boat World (small commercial craft), 10 Oxford Street, South Yarra 3141 Australia. Telephone: +61 3 826 8741.

Wooden Boat Magazine (wooden boat building, mostly yachts, mostly in the United States), Naskeag Road, Brooklin, Maine 04616, USA. Telephone: 207-359-5651.

World Fishing (worldwide coverage of commercial fishing), Nortide House, Stone Street, Faversham, Kent ME13 8P6, England. Telephone: 0795 536536.

WorldWide Shipping (covers shipping and ports, mostly U.S. and Western Hemisphere), 77 Moehring Drive, Blauvelt, New York 10913, USA. Telephone: 914-359-1934.

Appendix II. Useful Data

A brief summary of useful data is given below. For information not found here, refer to dictionaries, encyclopedias, engineering texts.

Weights:

Liquids—Weight in lb per U.S. gallon and per ft^3, and specific gravity (= weight of fluid/weight of an equal volume of fresh water)

Alcohol	6.77 lb/gal	50.7 lb/ft^3	(0.81)
Gasoline	6.1	46.3	(0.74)
Oil			
diesel	7.13	53.4	(0.86)
fuel	8.09	60.6	(0.97)
crude	Various		(<1.00)
Water			
fresh, 59°F	8.33	62.4	(1.00)
salt, 59°F	8.56	64.0	(1.026)

(7.48 U.S. gallons = 1 ft^3)

Metals—Weight, lb per ft^3 (kg per m^3)

Aluminum, cast	165 lb/ft^3	(2,643 kg/m^3)
Aluminum, plate/rod	168	(2,691)
Bronze, manganese, cast	475	(7,610)
Bronze, silicon, plate/rod	509	(8,154)
Copper, cast	556	(8,907)
Copper, sheet/plate/rod	552	(8,843)
Iron, cast	450	(7,209)
Lead, cast	712	(11,406)
Monel metal (nickel copper)	556	(8,907)
Stainless steel, cast	501	(8,026)
Stainless steel, plate/rod	492	(7,882)
Steel, cast	493	(7,898)
Steel, plate/rod	489	(7,834)
Titanium, cast	281	(4,500)
Titanium, plate/rod	277	(4,439)

Timber, at 12%-15% moisture content—Weight, lb per ft³ (kg per m³)

Cedar, Northern White	23 lb/ft³	(369 kg/m³)
Cedar, Eastern Red	33	(529)
Fir	34	(545)
Mahogany, Light	31	(497)
Mahogany, Dark	34	(545)
Oak, Red	43	(689)
Oak, White	47	(753)
Pine, White	25	(401)
Pine, Yellow	41	(657)
Spruce, Sitka	28	(449)
Spruce, White	28	(449)
Teak	43	(689)

Miscellaneous—Weight, lb per ft³ (kg per m³)

Concrete	144 lb/ft³	(2,307 kg/m³)
Fiberglass, 60% resin	105	(1,683)
Fish, in RSW or CSW	45 to 50	(721)
Fish, in bulk (no ice)	55	(801)
Fish, iced in bulk*	31	(481)
Fish, iced shelved*	20	(401)
Fish, iced boxed*	23	(352)

*The fish packing rates given here allow for structure in the fishhold and for some ice.

Measurements:

1 U.S. gallon = 231 cubic inches
7.48 U.S. gallons = 1 cubic foot
1 barrel, oil industry = 42 U.S. gallons
1 drum = 55 U.S. gallons
1 bushel = 1.25 cubic feet
1 pound = 16 ounces, = 1 pint of fresh water
1 kilogram = 1 liter of fresh water
1 short ton = 2,000 pounds
1 long ton = 2,240 pounds, = 35 cubic feet of seawater
1 metric ton = 2,204 pounds, = 1,000 kilograms
1 statute mile = 5,280 feet
1 nautical mile = 6,080 feet, = 1 minute of longitude at the equator
1 nautical mile per hour = 1 knot
1 knot = 1.689 feet per second

Measurement conversions:

1 meter = 3.281 feet	1 foot = 0.3048 meters
1 centimeter = 0.394 inches	1 inch = 2.54 centimeters
1 kilometer = 0.540 nautical miles	1 nautical mile = 1.85 kilometers
1 liter = 0.254 U.S. gallons	1 U.S. gallon = 3.79 liters
1 imperial gallon = 1.2 U.S. gallons	1 U.S. gallon = 0.833 imperial gallons

Appendix III. Symbols

BM   Distance from upright center of buoyancy to metacenter, ft (m).

CB   Center of buoyancy.

CE   Center of effort of sail forces.

CG   Center of gravity.

CLR   Center of lateral resistance of underbody, sailing craft.

C_P Prismatic coefficient—the ratio of the displaced volume to the volume of a prism having the same cross-sectional area as the midsection and a length equal to the LWL, which equals displaced volume (midsection area × LWL)

D   **1.** Drag of the fluid on a body in the direction of flow. **2.** The vertical depth from main deck to the rabbet or intersection of the plating with the keel, taken amidships.

DWL   Designed waterline, ft (m).

DWT   Deadweight tons, the weight of cargo plus consumable supplies.

EHP   Effective horsepower—the sum of all resistances to forward motion acting upon a hull, expressed as horsepower.

g   Acceleration due to gravity, 32.2 ft/sec^2 (980.7 cm/sec^2).

GM   Metacentric height, distance from center of gravity to metacenter, ft (m).

GZ   Righting arm, the horizontal distance between the center of gravity and the center of buoyancy. Also abbreviated RA.

HA   Heeling arm; for a sailboat the vertical distance CLR to CE, ft (m).

HF   Heeling force, the force tending to heel a boat, commonly the wind pressure times exposed area, lb or tons (kg or metric tons).

HM   Heeling moment, HA × HF, ft lb or ft tons (meter kgs or meter tons).

I   Moment of inertia, of a shape or body about an axis (specify the axis).

L   **1.** Length, in general. **2.** Vessel length as used in various applications, ft (m). **3.** Lift of a lifting body or foil, lb/ft^2 (kg/m^2).

LCB   Longitudinal position of center of buoyancy, ft (m) aft (or forward) of midsection or percent of LWL aft of forward end.

LCF   Longitudinal position of center of flotation, lying in the plane of flotation, ft (m) aft (or forward) of midsection or percent of LWL aft of forward end.

LCG   Longitudinal center of gravity, ft (m) aft (or forward) of midsection or percent of LWL aft of forward end.

LOA   Length overall of vessel's hull, exclusive of spars, bowsprits, booms, etc., ft (m).

LWL   Length of waterline, ft (m). Also identifies load waterline.

M   **1.** Moment, in general. **2.** Metacenter.

MCT 1″   Moment in ft lb or ft tons (meter kg or meter tons) to change trim 1″ (1 cm).

PC   Propulsion coefficient, EHP (effective horsepower)/SHP (shaft horsepower)

R   Resistance, in general.

RA   Righting arm, the horizontal distance between the center of gravity and the center of buoyancy, ft (m). Also abbreviated GZ.

RF   Righting force, displacement, lb or tons (kg or metric tons).

RM   Righting moment, $RA \times RF$, ft lb or ft tons (meter kg or meter tons).

S   Scale; for instance a ratio of ship to model of 10:1 gives a model scale of 0.1.

SHP   Shaft horsepower, the power actually delivered to the engine's output coupling.

SLR   Speed-length ratio, $V/\sqrt{L_{ft}}$ (which equals $1.81 \times V/\sqrt{L_m}$). (SLR is dimensional and is therefore usable only with the English system. The dimensionless form of SLR is the Froude Number, $F_N, = v/\sqrt{gL}$, where g = the acceleration of gravity in appropriate units.)

V   Ship or model speed, knots.

v   Speed, ft per sec (m per sec).

VCG   Vertical position of center of gravity, usually given in ft (m) above or below a baseline or the DWL.

WS   Wetted surface, ft^2 (m^2).

Δ   (delta) Displacement in lb or tons (kg or metric tons), specify.

∇   (delta inverse) Displacement in ft^3 (m^3).

θ   (theta) Angle of heel or list, degrees.

            Subscripts:

L   Longitudinal

M   Model

S   Ship

T   Transverse

Appendix IV. Planning for Profitability

Anyone involved in drawing up specifications for selecting and purchasing a new fishing vessel faces a complex task. Whether the prospective buyer is a fisherman, vessel owner or investor, it is essential to maximize the chances that the vessel and its operation will be profitable. But just what are the best ways to ensure this success?

Over the past 15 years, my colleagues and I have developed a relatively simple, clear procedure that has proven to be of great use in the preliminary planning process undertaken by all those seeking to buy a new vessel. Naturally, the details, including the figures, will vary from case to case.

Still, the procedure is based on a wide variety of actual experience, some of it our own but most of it that of commercial fishermen. As such, it has shown itself to be valid whether the buyer needs a shrimper for the Indian Ocean or a longliner for Georges Bank.

There are essentially four steps in making certain that the new vessel fits the needs outlined by the owner:

Selecting a fishery—Before making the large capital investment required for a fishing vessel, the owner should satisfy himself that a sufficient fisheries resource (or resources) is (are) available to support the fishing operation at a reasonable level and with consistent income.

Determining a suitable vessel—Having selected the fishery or fisheries, one must identify the characteristics of a suitable vessel.

Acquiring the vessel—Whether you decide on a custom-designed boat, a stock hull or a used vessel, don't negate all your research by compromising too much.

Estimating vessel cost—Prices must be calculated for a completely rigged vessel that is ready to leave on its first trip.

Selecting a fishery: When you have decided to purchase a new vessel, you would do well to consider whether you wish to use the boat in the fishery in which you have been engaged or whether you should base your new venture on another, different fishery. If you are going to pursue the latter course you must consider the fishery in its entirety.

The fishery must be a healthy one at every step—from the resource to the final consumer. The sectors that must be examined are illustrated in Fig. 1a, a block diagram in which the fishery system is broken down into its major subsystems.

While our interest here is primarily in the harvesting subsystem, Fig. 1b, all the other subsystems of the fishery must be reviewed in order to guarantee that your fishing vessel is entering a strong industry that will provide adequate income. Particularly if you are leaning toward targeting on an underutilized species, you should assure yourself that you can deliver your catch into a profitable and stable system.

(Reprinted, with minor editorial changes, from "Careful planning maximizes your chances for profitability," *National Fisherman Yearbook 1983,* by permission of the publisher)

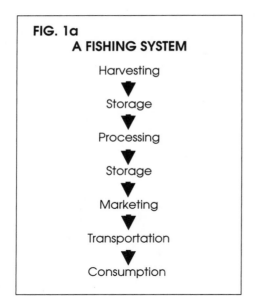

FIG. 1a
A FISHING SYSTEM

Harvesting
▼
Storage
▼
Processing
▼
Storage
▼
Marketing
▼
Transportation
▼
Consumption

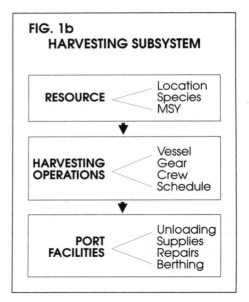

FIG. 1b
HARVESTING SUBSYSTEM

RESOURCE — Location / Species / MSY

HARVESTING OPERATIONS — Vessel / Gear / Crew / Schedule

PORT FACILITIES — Unloading / Supplies / Repairs / Berthing

If one of the subsystems—marketing, for instance—is weak and inadequate, you will very likely find it difficult to sell your catch at steady, healthy prices. Even though you can land a million pounds of something, it will only be worth peanuts if there isn't a well-defined path between the product and the consumer.

Whatever fishery you may be engaged in now, don't let yourself be stuck in it; there may be a better one available to you. Do some snooping among other fisheries. Find out such things as whether the catch rates and/or the prices are fluctuating widely, or whether they show a historical trend downward. There are many sources of information, including other fishermen, fisheries publications, extension services, NMFS (National Marine Fisheries Service) and universities.

Once you have a good supply of information on a fishery, try it out on the fishery analysis form shown in Fig. 2; this asks most of the important questions. If, after running through these questions, you still have doubts about the fishery, you had best discard it from further consideration.

Matching vessel and fishery: In this step, we enter information concerning the target fishery into a simple program for defining the vessel required to work in that fishery.

Carrying out this process requires a good knowledge of the fishery in question. The information used should be as accurate and realistic as possible; personal experience, your own or someone else's, is one of the best sources of such information. If the resource is totally unutilized at present, a visit to a country in which the species has been exploited for some time could be invaluable.

Also refer to the fishing boat and fishing gear series published by the Food and Agriculture Organization of the United Nations.

NMFS experts, Sea Grant Marine Advisory Service agents and the staff biologists at the various fishery management councils can also be good sources. If some of the required information is not readily available, make some assumptions based on your own common sense.

FISHERY ANALYSIS FORM

1. Has the catch rate gone down significantly over the past few years?

    If YES, discard.   If NO, go to #2.

2. Has the landed price held reasonably steady, allowing for inflation?

    If YES, go to #3.   If NO, discard.

3. Are many boats entering the fishery, meaning it will be overcrowded by the time you enter it?

    If YES, discard.   If NO, go to #4.

4. Is there a healthy end market for the resource?

    If YES, go to #5.   If NO, discard.

5. Does a strong, committed industry network extend from the landing place to the consumer?

    If YES, go to #6.   If NO, discard.

6. Include this as a possible fishery.

The basic list of things you'll need to know is:

Type(s) of gear best suited to the fishery

Average distance of the grounds from port

Degree of on-board processing normally carried out and stowage method (bulk, boxed, with or without ice, RSW, CSW, etc.) required to assure high quality at landing

Crew size normally used and schedule of watches (one or two) employed during fishing operations

Average length of trip and/or days of fishing per trip

Average catch rate (in pounds per day)

Average size of main and auxiliary engines

Once this information is collected, it serves as the basis for the calculations shown in Fig. 3, the Fishing Vessel Estimating Form. Tables A and B, and graphs A-F, have been prepared to help in filling out the form.

By the time you have completed the vessel evaluation form (the calculations are very simple and can be done on a hand calculator), you will have established the major characteristics of a vessel that should be suitable for the target fishery. Examine the results to see whether there are any special requirements that are not fulfilled, such as sufficient deck space for carrying fish or lobster pots.

If there are problems such as this, solve them by adjusting the vessel dimensions on the estimating form. This can often be done by holding the Cubic Number ("Cube") constant and changing the proportions of length, beam and depth in order to reach the desired solution; if this is not possible, then the Cube must be altered.

This exercise can be carried out for as many fisheries as desired. After selecting those fisheries in which you would like to operate, you can combine the vessel characteristics for each of them. Then, using the largest values of crew size, machinery space and hold volume, recalculate the characteristics of the combination vessel that will function adequately in all of them.

FIG. 3   FISHING VESSEL ESTIMATING FORM

ITEM NO.	DESCRIPTION	FROM	SAMPLE
1	Shaft h.p., main engine(s)	Select one	300
2	Auxiliary h.p., except winch	Estimate	16
3	Winch h.p., if separately driven	Estimate	—
4	Total h.p.	Items 1 + 2 + 3	316
5	Normal engine room area (sq. ft.)	Graph A	170
6	Crew size	Select	6
7	Number of watches	Select	1
8	Total crew size	Item 6 × item 7	6
9	Average accommodation area per man	Table A	71
10	Nominal accommodation area (sq. ft.)	Item 9 × item 8	426
11	Average catch per day (lbs.)	Estimate	6,000
12	Number of days fishing per trip	Select	5
13	Average catch per trip (lbs.)	Item 12 × item 11	30,000
14	Hold packing density (lbs./cu. ft.)	Table B	20
15	Hold volume (cu. ft.)	Item 13 ÷ item 14	1,500
16	Nominal hold area (cu. ft.)	Graph B	215
17	Total nominal area for vessel (cu. ft.)	Item 16 + 10 + 5	809
18	Cubic number, "Cube" (Cube = L..W.L.. × beam × depth)	Graph C	11,700
19	Displacement (long tons)	Graph D*	100
20	Length on waterline (ft.)	Graph E*	65
21	Length overall (ft.)	Item 20 ÷ .92	70.5
22	Beam (ft.)	L.W.L. ÷ ±3*	20
23	Depth to deck amidships (ft.)	Item 18 ÷ (item 20 × item 22)	9
24	Draft, approx. max. (ft.)	Item 23 × .8	7.2
25	Estimated steaming speed	Graph F*	9.6

*Note: These particular relationships are limited to trawler-type hulls.

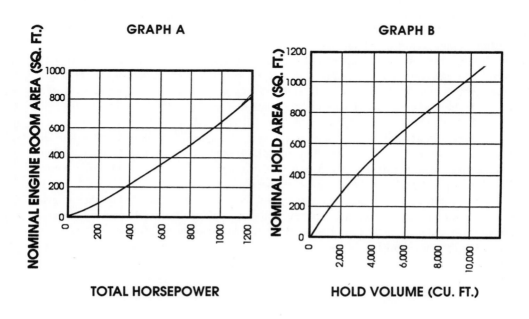

GRAPH A

NOMINAL ENGINE ROOM AREA (SQ. FT.)

TOTAL HORSEPOWER

GRAPH B

NOMINAL HOLD AREA (SQ. FT.)

HOLD VOLUME (CU. FT.)

272   :   Preliminary Design of Boats and Ships

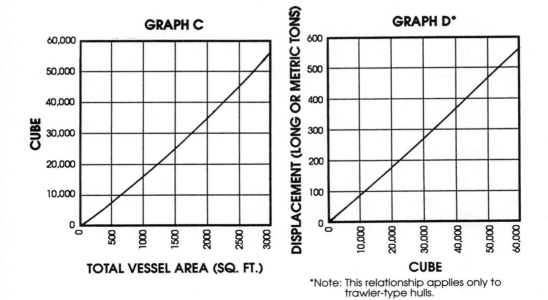

GRAPH C

CUBE vs. TOTAL VESSEL AREA (SQ. FT.)

GRAPH D*

DISPLACEMENT (LONG OR METRIC TONS) vs. CUBE

*Note: This relationship applies only to trawler-type hulls.

GRAPH E*

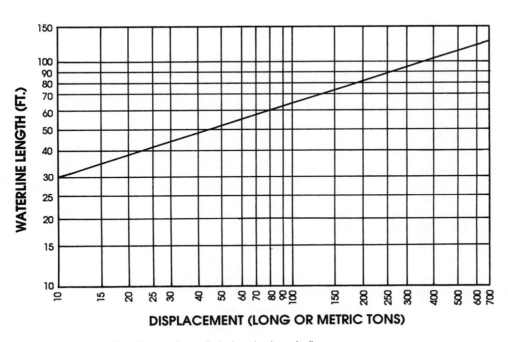

WATERLINE LENGTH (FT.) vs. DISPLACEMENT (LONG OR METRIC TONS)

*Note: This relationship applies only to trawler-type hulls.

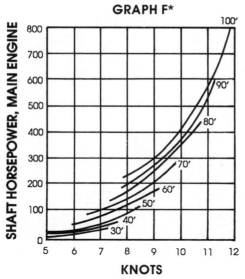

GRAPH F*

SHAFT HORSEPOWER, MAIN ENGINE

KNOTS

*Note: This relationship applies only to trawler-type hulls.

TABLE A
APPROXIMATE ACCOMMODATION AREA PER CREWMAN

TRIP LENGTH	AREA PER CREWMAN
1-2 days	40 sq. ft.
2-4 days	50 sq. ft.
4 or more days	71 sq. ft.

(Double area to give actual accommodation area.)

TABLE B

APPROXIMATE PACKING RATES FOR FISH IN HOLDS
(with allowance for hold fixtures, working space, etc.)

Bulk fish and ice	31 lbs./cu. ft.
Fish iced in boxes	23 lbs./cu. ft.
Fish in RSW or CSW	45 to 50 lbs./cu. ft.

One further step can be fun and very rewarding: make a small sketch of the vessel derived from this estimating process. The vessel should be drawn to a particular scale—a fraction of an inch on the sketch will represent 1′ on the actual vessel. Make the sketch fairly small, so that it will fit on an 8 1/2″ × 11″ or legal-size sheet of paper.

The value of the sketch is that it gives you an actual picture of a fishing vessel that, until now, has existed in your mind only as a collection of numbers and fleeting images. By making several duplicate copies of the sketch before it is completely finished, it is possible to try out various layouts for the gear, deckhouse, engine room, rigging, etc.

In fact, any idea that comes to mind can be tried. The sketch has further use as a check on the estimating process—it serves to make sure everything will fit into the estimated hull dimensions.

Procuring the selected vessel: All the foregoing effort at planning your new vessel is fruitless if the boat finally obtained does not closely match the characteristics identified as necessary for a specific fishery. This identification process has been a rational one, requiring a good deal of hard work and hard thought. To discard the results is to admit that all this effort—the information gathered and the assumptions made—was a mistake.

So, have the courage of your convictions (and your calculations) and match the vessel you buy to the planned vessel as nearly as possible.

The actual purchase of a boat can be carried out along three main paths:

Have a naval architect prepare a design, and have it built as precisely as you want it.

Select a stock vessel offered by one of several shipyards, a boat which, with modifications, can be made acceptably similar to your planned vessel.

Purchase a used vessel with general characteristics like those of your planned vessel. Then modify, refurbish and replace as necessary to put the boat in first-class condition to suit the selected fishery or fisheries.

As a generality, it can be said that these three paths of vessel procurement are listed in descending order of cost and satisfaction.

Vessel cost estimating: To obtain a precise cost for the construction of your boat requires a firm quotation based on actual drawings (plans) of the vessel. However, there is a rather simple procedure for estimating construction costs, one that can be useful in planning for your new vessel. The estimated building cost is made up of four components:

Hull and furnishings = Cube × K, where K is a cost per cubic unit (ranging now from $25 to $35 and up).

Machinery, including electrical and steering systems, and installation = cost of main engine(s) × 2

Electronics = 1.2 × cost of electronic equipment

Fishing gear, both fixed (such as winches and power block) and loose (such as nets) = actual cost of gear

There will also be other costs associated with acquiring and commissioning the vessel. It is essential that these be included when comparing different vessels. The list of ancillary costs includes: delivery, taxes, architect's fee and classification or construction-supervision fee.

It is not so easy to estimate the cost of bringing a used vessel up to reliable condition and modifying it to conform to the new owner's needs. The bill is usually more than the purchaser expects—in fact, it can often be as much as 75% to 85% of the amount needed to build a new vessel.

One last word about planning the purchase of a fishing vessel: When figuring the cost, and especially when comparing several vessels, compute the price of each vessel as of the time it leaves for its first fishing trip. This means the price for a completed boat with all gear aboard and all systems in first class condition.

Also, don't be misled by bare-boat prices, quick bargains or off-the-cuff estimates. Work up total vessel and gear costs using only hard-headed, firm quotations or realistic estimates on everything from the basic hull to the tool kit.

Fishing is an industry with too many uncertainties and surprises to make vessel selection a precise science. But if the procedures presented here are followed, fewer mistakes will be made, and a better and more profitable vessel will result.

Glossary

Acceleration: The rate at which a body changes velocity per unit of time. When acceleration is zero, velocity is constant; when acceleration is positive, velocity is increasing; when negative, velocity is decreasing.

Aspect ratio: A ratio defining the slenderness of a foil such as a keel, rudder, or sail. For a rectangular foil, aspect ratio (AR) is the span (*q.v.*) divided by the chord (*q.v.*). For an irregular shape AR = span^2/area.

Balance, sailboat: The tendency of a sailboat to bear up into the wind (weather helm), bear off the wind (lee helm), or hold a straight course (balanced). It is generally considered best to have a small and constant amount of weather helm.

Ballast: Fixed weight incorporated in a vessel to improve its stability, or removable weight (water, fuel, etc.) to sink the vessel in the water in order to, for instance, completely cover the propeller of an empty tanker.

Beam: **1.** The width of a hull; usually taken at the widest point, but may be taken at the waterline or any other specified location. **2.** A member with supports at the ends and possibly in between for carrying a load; such as a deck beam.

Bilge: **1.** The lowest portion of a vessel's interior, usually below the lowest deck or sole. **2.** The corner where the bottom of a hull turns upwards to become the topsides.

Body plan: The portion of the lines plan showing the sections, that is, the cross-sectional shape at each station (*q.v.*).

Bow: The foremost portion of a vessel's hull. How far aft the bow extends is indeterminate and may range from only the very foremost tip to the forward quarter or third of the vessel.

Buoyancy: That upward force which, acting on a body in a fluid, tends to cause the body to rise. According to Archimedes' Principle, every body all or partially submerged is acted upon by a buoyancy equal to the weight of the fluid displaced by the body.

Buttock: Imaginary vertical plane, parallel to the central plane, used in drawing a vessel's hull so that all portions of it are smooth and fair.

Catamaran: A vessel composed of two separate hulls, connected by beams or a deck so as to act as one. (Not to be confused with the katumarans of India, which are made of 5 or 7 logs lashed together.)

Cavitation: Vapor-filled bubbles formed in water, usually at propeller blade tips, when the negative pressure exceeds the pressure of vaporization of the water. The deeper the propeller, the greater the pressure of vaporization of the water and the less likely is cavitation. (Cavitation is often confused with "ventilation," which occurs when air is drawn down into the propeller from the surface, creating a somewhat similar appearing situation.)

Center of gravity: A point at which all the mass (*q.v.*) of a body may be considered as being concentrated. If the body is hung from any point on its surface, extensions of the hanging line will pass through the center of gravity.

Center of buoyancy: The center of gravity (*q.v.*) of the body of water displaced by a vessel or other partially or completely submerged body.

Center of effort: A point at which all the wind forces on a sail or sails are assumed to act; assumed, somewhat incorrectly but conveniently, to be the center of area (or gravity) of the sail or sails.

Center of flotation: The center of gravity of the plane of flotation, or water plane. When a weight is loaded on a vessel directly above the center of flotation, the hull will sink but will not change trim (*q.v.*).

Center of lateral resistance: The point at which all the water forces of a sailboat making leeway are assumed to act; assumed, incorrectly but conventionally, to be the center of area (or gravity) of the underwater profile of the sailboat.

Chine: A longitudinal corner in a hull between the keel and the deck; usually limited to one or two chines on each side; used to simplify construction of frames and to allow planking or plating with flat sheets of steel, aluminum, or plywood.

Chord: The width of a lifting foil (keel, wing, rudder) measured in the direction of the airflow (*q.v.* span and aspect ratio).

Corrosion: The loss of metal through chemical or electrical action.

Couple: The distance separating two equal and opposing forces, tending to cause the body to rotate.

Cubic number: Length × beam × depth (*q.v.*); an absolute measure of a vessel's size.

Curves of form: A graph that summarizes the fixed geometric characteristics of a vessel for a wide range of conditions of loading and trim. In combination with the center of gravity location, a frequently changing variable, all the static conditions, and many of the dynamic conditions, can be derived.

Deadrise: The rise of a vessel's bottom from the keel to the turn of the bilge; usually given as an angle.

Deck: A horizontal structural surface in a vessel's hull. The main, or weather, deck is of major importance for hull strength as well as for enclosing and protecting the hull interior. The naming or numbering of decks may change from vessel to vessel.

Depth: The vertical distance from the top of the main deck at the side to the rabbet line or intersection of plating with the keel, measured at the midpoint of the LWL.

Diagonal: A fore-and-aft plane intersecting the center plane at less than a right angle used in conjunction with sections, waterlines, and buttocks (*q.v.*) for shaping and fairing the hull in the design stage.

Displacement: The size of the hole in the water occupied by a floating or submerged object, expressed as the weight (pounds or tons) or volume (cubic feet or meters) of the water displaced.

Draft: The vertical distance from the plane of flotation to the deepest part of the hull; may be at any point along the hull. On larger vessels, draft marks (in feet [meters]) are painted at the bow and stern to permit instant determination of the plane of flotation. Maximim draft is the draft to the deepest part of the vessel.

Drag: **1.** The resistance to forward motion of any body with a fluid flowing past it. **2.** The slope of the bottom of the keel on many small craft downwards from the bow to the stern.

Effective horsepower: The actual resistance to forward motion of a vessel, expressed in horsepower. EHP may be thought of as the tension on a towline towing the vessel, and therefore does not include propeller losses, etc.

Fairbody line: A line on the center plane of the lines plan used to simplify the design and fairing of a hull with reverse curves fairing into the keel.

Fluid: A substance capable of flowing, such as a liquid or a gas.

Foil: A form used to extract lift from a fluid flowing around it, such as a wing, a sail, or a keel. In cross-section a foil may be a flat plate, a curved form without thickness (such as a sail), or a form with thickness (such as an airplane wing).

Frame: The transverse strength members of a hull to which the planking or plating is secured (often termed "ribs," especially in small boats).

Friction: The resistance to movement of one material past another. Either or both bodies may be solids or fluids. To a naval architect the friction of greatest interest is the friction of water flowing past the hull or its appendages.

Ghost line: A construction line used by naval architects to precisely define a corner that is eventually to be rounded off, so that the line does not exist in the finished boat.

Grid: The basic construction lines forming a matrix within which a vessel's design is drawn; consists of primary lines (designed waterline, centerline, stations) and secondary lines (waterlines above and below LWL, buttocks, diagonals).

Heave: The vertical movement of a vessel's center of gravity due to passing over waves.

Heel: The tipping of a vessel from the vertical due to the force of the wind on the sails and/or the hull and superstructure.

Horsepower: The unit of power devised by James Watt and still in use. His estimate was that a good horse could lift 550 lb 1 ft in 1 sec (which equals 1 horsepower).

Hull: The basic structure of a boat or ship, including the deck, plating, and bulkheads. Deckhouses are considered superstructure and are not properly part of the hull.

Keel: The main structural member of a hull. It provides the connection between the two sides, and much of the strength against the hull's vertical bending.

Length: The length of a vessel's hull, which is defined in many ways. Refer to chapter 3 for a detailed description of important lengths used in naval architecture.

Lift: The force provided by a lifting surface such as a sail, wing, or keel in a useful direction; usually taken perpendicular to the drag (*q.v.*). A measure of the overall efficiency of a lifting surface is the lift-drag ratio.

Lines: The three-dimensional shape of a boat or ship's hull expressed in three two-dimensional orthographic views (profile, plan, and body plan = side, top, and end views) drawn by the naval architect.

List: The tipping of a vessel from the vertical resulting from distribution of weights to one side or the other.

Mass: The amount of matter in a body. The mass of a body remains constant anywhere in space and at any practical velocity.

Metacenter: The point on a heeled or listing vessel's centerline vertically above the heeled center of buoyancy.

Midsection: Usually the section at the midpoint of the load waterline. May sometimes be the maximum section, which is usually somewhat aft of the midpoint.

Moment: A force times a distance. An 80 lb boy sitting on a seesaw 5′ from the fulcrum (pivot) is exerting an 80 × 5 = 400 ft lb moment downwards on his end, tending to rotate the seesaw. He could be balanced by an equal but opposite moment, say a 100 lb boy 4′ from the fulcrum (which equals 400 ft lb).

Monohull: A boat or vessel with a single hull.

Multihull: A boat or vessel with two, three, or more hulls, including canoes with one or two outriggers.

Pitch: The longitudinal rotational motion of a vessel about a transverse axis (usually close to the LWL and approximately $4/7$ of the LWL from the bow).

Planing: The condition in which some of the weight of a boat is supported by dynamic lift so that the weight is in part supported by the upward water pressure on the bottom resulting from forward motion.

Pounding : Describes the impact on the bottom of a boat or ship when the bow reenters the water after being lifted out by a wave.

Prime mover: A fundamental source of mechanical power, such as an internal combustion engine, steam engine, gas turbine; does not include electric or hydraulic motors.

Resistance: In naval architecure is usually understood to be the resistance to passage of a hull through the water caused by the viscous friction of the water, by wave-making, and by eddies about appendages and sharp corners.

Righting arm: The horizontal distance between the center of gravity and the center of buoyancy.

Roll: The cyclical transverse tipping of a boat or ship from side to side, generally caused by wave action. A roll cycle includes two rolls, that is, from a starting point, over to the other side, and back to the starting point.

Rudder: The foil suspended from the stern of a vessel to control the direction of travel. Boats not having rudders include rowboats (usually), powerboats fitted with outboard motors or inboard/outboard drives, and the unusual Great South Bay (NY) Scooters.

Section: The cross section of a vessel, or of any other object, taken at any desired point for the purpose of showing its shape or its interior arrangement.

Shaft horsepower: The horsepower actually delivered to the engine's coupling and available for use.

Sheer: The upper edge of a hull, usually at the main deck level. A curvature of the sheer that is attractive when viewed from any vantage point is always admired, especially in yachts.

Span: The length of a foil measured perpendicular to the flow of the fluid, that is, perpendicular to the chord (*q.v.*).

Stability: The measure of ability of a vessel to remain upright. A boat with low stability heels easily and is described as "tender." A "stiff" boat resists heeling. A tender boat may be comfortable but unsafe, a stiff boat safe but uncomfortable; the naval architect endeavors to find the happy mean.

Station: The location of section used for drawing the hull lines. Stations are equally spaced over the designed waterline, normally with station 0 at the forward end and station 10 at the after end so there are 10 spaces and 11 stations. Some large vessels use 20 spaces instead of 10.

Stem: The vertical structural member at the bow extending from the keel to the uppermost deck.

Stern: The after part of a vessel. Rather indeterminate, it may refer only to the very last part of the hull or to the after quarter or so of the hull.

Surge: The fore-and-aft horizontal motion of a hull due to the orbital path of the water particles in waves. It is superimposed on the steady-state forward motion of the craft.

Sway: The lateral horizontal oscillations of the hull due to the orbital path of water particles in waves coming more or less on the beam.

Tonnage: There are a number of different ways of measuring tonnages, and it is important to know which one is being used. Refer to chapter 3 for detailed definitions of the most common tonnages.

Tons: *Always* in naval architecture the tons used are long or metric, never the short ton of 2,000 lb. The long ton is 2,240 lb = 35 ft^3. The metric ton is 1,000 kg (2,204 lb) = the weight of 1,000 liters of fresh water. Usually long tons and metric tons can be used interchangeably without conversion.

Trapezoidal rule: A simple method of finding the area, through measurement and simple arithmetic, of a figure of any size and shape. Accuracy is usually acceptable. See chapter 4 for a full description of the method.

Trim: The fore-and-aft level of a vessel. Trim "by the bow" indicates the bow is down, the stern up, "by the stern" the stern down and the bow up. Since the axis of rotation, the center of flotation, is close to the midpoint of the hull, the amount one end goes down is nearly the same as the amount the other end comes up.

Trimaran: A three-hulled sailing craft, with the center hull considerably larger than the side hulls.

Vector: An arrow representing the direction and intensity of a force or velocity. Any number of vectors can be added to give a resultant vector, that is, the net result of all the vectors.

Viscosity: The "stickiness" of a fluid, which causes frictional resistance. The molecules of a fluid in direct contact with the moving body are carried along by it; the resistance results from the attraction of these moving molecules on the hull to the stationary molecules farther out.

Wake: As far as the naval architect is concerned wake refers to the disturbance in the water caused by the passage of a watercraft. There are two types of wake disturbance: turbulence caused by friction on the hull and by the eddies set up by appendages, and waves created by the passage of the vessel through the water.

Waterline: An imaginary horizontal plane passed through the hull of a vessel. It can also refer to the intersection of the hull with the plane of flotation.

Water plane: The plane defined by the intersection of the hull with the water surface.

Weatherliness: The ability of a vessel to cope with sea conditions with respect to ease of motion, dryness of decks, ability to keep moving. A sea-kindly craft has good weatherliness, a crank vessel does not.

Work: The product of force times distance. Moving 1 lb 500 ft takes the same work as moving 500 lbs 1 ft.

Yaw: The departure of a vessel from its desired course. Yaw may be intermittent, as when turning or broaching in a quartering sea, or it may be relatively constant as in the leeway angle made by a sailing craft.

Bibliography

If my purpose in writing this book has been achieved, you will be able to complete your sketch design without the need to resort to any other sources of information. We are inquisitive beings, though, and a little knowledge, like peanuts, whets the appetite for more. This bibliography is for those who wish to delve further into the fascinations of naval architecture.

The literature on design, construction, operation, and actions of boats and vessels is extremely voluminous. The bibliography given here is a selection of the volumes I have benefited from during my career; those marked with an asterisk have been especially valuable. The list is by no means complete, many will seem old-fashioned, and another naval architect may have a completely different assortment of references. So I suggest that the reader, if he wants to pursue further any or all aspects of naval architecture, spend a couple of days at a library apt to have a broad collection in the field, and select those volumes to which he responds most positively.

There is one word of warning. It is very easy to access so much information—it is all out there waiting for you—that you may have difficulty resolving the ambiguities and contradictions you will encounter. So start small and expand deliberately and selectively. Be critical of all you read until you have convinced yourself of its validity. Instead of trying to read all that's written on this highly complex subject, find a few reliable sources and stick with them.

General:
Giesecke, Frederick E. et al. *Engineering Graphics.* New York: Macmillan, 1987.
Handbook of Ocean and Underwater Engineering, New York: McGraw Hill, 1969.
Packard, Robert T., ed. *Architectural Standards—AIA.* 7th ed. New York: John Wiley and Sons, 1981.
Sellers, Robert C. *Metric Transition for Managers.* New York: Thomas Y. Crowell, 1975.

General naval architecture:
* Barnaby, Kenneth C. *Basic Naval Architecture.* London: Hutchison's, 1967.
* Chapman, Charles F., revised by Elbert S. Maloney. *Piloting, Seamanship, and Small Boat Handling.* New York: Hearst Marine Books, 1981.
* Comstock, John P., ed. *Principles of Naval Architecture.* New York: Society of Naval Architects and Marine Engineers, 1967.
Liljgren, C.O. *Naval Architecture as Art and Science.* New York: Cornell Maritime Press, 1943.
Nicholson, Ian. *Boat Data Book.* 2d ed. Dobbs Ferry, N.Y.: Sheridan House, 1986.
* Rabl, S.S. *Practical Principles of Naval Architecture.* New York: Cornell Maritime Press, 1942.

Commercial craft design:

* Food and Agriculture Organization of the United Nations (Rome). *Fishing Vessels of the World,* Volumes I (1955), II (1960), III (1967). Farnham, U.K.: Fishing News Books, Ltd.

Fyson, John, ed., Food and Agriculture Organization of the United Nations. *Design of Small Fishing Vessels.* Farnham, U.K.: Fishing News Books, Ltd., 1987.

Hamlin, Cyrus and Ordway, John R. *Design Study: An Optimum Fishing Vessel for Georges Bank Groundfish Fishery.* Springfield, Va.: Bureau of Commercial Fisheries (now the National Marine Fisheries Service), National Technical Information Service, 1972.

Hamlin, Cyrus and Tupper, Christopher. *Elementary Naval Architecture for Workers in Marine Fields.* Rome: Food and Agriculture Organization of the United Nations, 1976 (unpublished).

Priebe, Paul D. *Modern Commercial Sailing Ship Fundamentals.* Centreville, Md.: Cornell Maritime Press, 1986.

Taggart, Robert, ed. *Ship Design and Construction.* 3d ed. New York: Society of Naval Architects and Marine Engineers, 1980.

Yacht design:

Baader, Juan. *The Sailing Yacht.* New York: W.W. Norton, 1965.

* Chapelle, Howard I. *Yacht Designing and Planning.* rev. ed. New York: W.W. Norton, 1971.

* Davis, Charles G. *The ABC of Yacht Design.* New York: Rudder Publishing Co., 1930.

* Henry, Robert G. and Miller, Capt. Richards T. (USN Ret). *Sailing Yacht Design.* Cambridge, Md.: Cornell Maritime Press, 1965.

* Illingsworth, John H. *Further Offshore.* 6th ed. London: Coles Ltd., 1969.

* Kinney, Francis S. *Skene's Elements of Yacht Design.* rev. ed. New York: Dodd, Mead & Co., 1981.

* Lord, Lindsay. *Naval Architecture of Planing Hulls.* New York: Cornell Maritime Press, 1946.

Rousmaniere, John, ed., Technical Committee of the Cruising Club of America. *Offshore Yachts.* New York: W.W. Norton, New York, 1987.

Fluid mechanics:

Abbott, Ira H. and von Doenhoff, Albert E. *Theory of Wing Sections.* New York: Dover Publications, 1959 (originally published 1949).

Marchaj, C. J. *Aero-Hydrodynamics of Sailing.* New York: Dodd, Mead & Co., 1980.

* Morwood, John. *Sailing Aerodynamics.* New York: Philosophical Library, 1954.

Prandtl, L. and Tietjens, O. G. *Applied Hydro- and Aeromechanics.* New York: Dover Publications, 1957 (originally published 1934).

Prandtl, L. and Tietjens, O. G. *Fundamentals of Hydro- and Aeromechanics.* New York: Dover Publications, 1957 (originally published 1934).

* Rouse, Hunter. *Elementary Mechanics of Fluid.* New York: Dover, 1978.

Saunders, Capt. Harold E. (USN, Ret). *Hydrodynamics of Ship Design,* Volumes I, II, III. New York: Society of Naval Architects and Marine Engineers, 1957.

Boat and vessel construction:

Bingham, Bruce. *Ferro-Cement Design, Techniques and Applications.* Centreville, Md.: Cornell Maritime Press, 1984.

* Bureau of Ships, Dept. of the Navy. *Wood: A Manual for Its Use as a Boatbuilding Material.* Kingston, Mass.: Teaparty Books, 1983.

* Chapelle, Howard I. *Boat Building.* New York: W.W. Norton, 1941.

Desmond, Charles. *Wooden Ship-Building.* 2d ed. Vestal, N.Y.: Vestal Press, 1984 (originally published 1919).

Gougeon Brothers. *The Gougeon Brothers on Boat Construction.* Bay City, Michigan, 1985.

* Hamlin, Cyrus. "Glued Strip Construction," *Yachting Magazine:* February 1954 (with later additions).

Roberts, John. *Fiber Glass Boats—Construction, Repair and Maintenance.* New York: W.W. Norton Co., 1984.

Steward, Robert. *Boatbuilding Manual.* 3d ed. Camden, Maine: International Marine Publishing Co., 1987.

Willis, Melvin D.C. *Boatbuilding and Repairing with Fiberglass.* Camden, Maine: International Marine Publishing Co.

Wind, wave, and seaworthiness:

* Bigelow, Henry B. and Edmondson, W.T. *Wind Waves at Sea, Breakers and Surf.* Washington, D.C.: Hydrographic Office, U.S. Navy, 1947.

* Coles, K. Adlard. *Heavy Weather Sailing.* 3d rev. ed. Clinton Corners, N.Y.: John de Graff Co., 1981.

* Marchaj, C.J. *Seaworthiness: The Forgotten Factor.* Camden, Maine: International Marine Publishing Company, 1987.

History and experiences:

Chapelle, Howard I. *The American Fishing Schooners.* New York: W.W. Norton, 1973.

Chapelle, Howard I. *The American Sailing Craft.* New York: Kennedy Bros., 1936.

Chapelle, Howard I. *The American Sailing Navy.* New York: W.W. Norton, 1949.

Chapelle, Howard I. *American Sailing Ships.* New York: Bonanza Books, 1935.

Chapelle, Howard I. *American Small Sailing Craft.* New York: W.W. Norton, 1951.

Chapelle, Howard I. *The Search for Speed Under Sail.* New York: W.W. Norton, 1984.

Davis, Charles G. *American Sailing Ships.* New York: Dover Publications, 1984.

Landstrom, Bjorn. *The Ship: An Illustrated History.* Garden City, N.Y.: Doubleday, 1983.

McMullen, R.T. *Down Channel.* London: Sheridan House, 1986 (first published in 1869).

Schoettle, Edwin J. *Sailing Craft.* New York: Macmillan, 1949.

Slocum, Capt. Joshua. *Sailing Alone Around the World.* New York: Dover Publications, 1956 (originally published 1900).

Stephens, William P. *Traditions and Memoirs of American Yachting.* Camden, Maine: International Marine Publishing Company, 1981.

Propulsion guides:

Elements of Marine Propulsion. Detroit, Michigan: Detroit Diesel Engine Division, General Motors Corporation.

GM Diesel Marine Manual—Propeller Selection. Detroit, Michigan: Detroit Diesel Engine Division, General Motors Corporation.

Hull Speed Estimator and Propeller Calculations. Peoria, Illinois: Industrial Division, Caterpillar Engine Co.

Marine Horsepower and Speed Calculator. Columbus, Indiana: Cummins Engine Company.

Buyer's guides:

"Yachting" Boat Buyers Guide (Annual), 5 River Road, Cos Cob, Connecticut 06807. Telephone: 203-629-8300.

Marine Catalog Buyers Guide (Annual), published by *Marine Engineering/Log International,* 345 Hudson Street, New York, New York 10014. Telephone: 212-620-1225.

Index

Carbon fiber composite. *See* Fiberglass/carbon fiber composite
Caribbean, 148
Cartesian graphs. *See* Graphs, Cartesian
Carvel planking. *See* Planking
Catamarans, 188–90, 196, 199. *See also* Multihulls
  as commercial craft, 225, 226, 230
Catboat. *See* Rig
Cavitation, 154
CB. *See* Buoyancy, center of
Centerboard craft, 207, 208
CF. *See* Flotation, center of
CG. *See* Gravity, center of
Chapelle, Howard, *Boat Building,* 125
  curator, 218
Charter boats, sail, 212–14
Chine. *See* Bilges, shape of
Clearwater, 199, 214, 218, 220
Clinker planking. *See* Planking
Coasters, 205
Coast Guard regulations. *See* Regulations, U.S. Coast Guard
Cockpit. *See* Deck space
Code of Federal Regulations (CFR), 214, 229
Coefficient, prismatic (C_p), 32, 33, 183
Coefficient, propulsive, 139
Coles, Adlard, *Heavy Weather Sailing,* 52
Color, use of, 88
Comfort and safety, 84, 180, 230. *See also* Stability
Commercial craft, 113, 114, 223–35
  dredges, 231, 232
  drilling rigs, 230
  fishing, 226, 227
  passenger, 227, 229, 230
  profitability, 223, 232, 269–75
  size, 223, 224
  special purpose, 230, 231
  tankers, 232
  towing, 226–28
Commissioning. *See* Vessel acceptance and commissioning

Computer aided design (CAD), 5, 6, 11
Concrete. *See* Ferro-cement
Construction, cost of, 167
  commercial craft, 169, 170
  estimating, 170, 171
  institutional craft, 169, 170
  pleasure craft, 168, 169
  variations, 169
Construction, hull. *See* Hull construction
Construction materials, 121–36, 198, 199. *See also* names of specific materials
  combinations of, 123, 132
  suitability of, 124, 184
Construction methods, wooden boats, 125–28
Construction plan. *See* Plans, construction (working)
Construction of vessel, inspection, 260, 261
Controls, mechanical, 163
Controversy design, 115–17
Corrosion
  allowance, 130
  galvanic, 130, 132
  oxidation, 130, 131
  prevention, 131, 132
Costs. *See* Economics; Hull construction, cost factors
Cousteau, Jacques, 147
C_p. *See* Coefficient, prismatic
Crew
  paid, 214, 225
  quarters, 210, 225
Cubic number (CUBE), 30, 32, 100, 224
  in estimating costs, 167, 170
Curve, speed/power, 138
Curves, drawing. *See* Instruments, drawing
Curves of form, 44, 45, 63
Custom-built craft, 122, 128
Cutter. *See* Rig

D

Datum plane. *See* Designed waterline

also specific types of craft, e.g.,
Power yachts
bilge, 131, 181
forebody, 180, 181
sketching, 102
and speed-length ratio, 182
water plane area, 70, 72
Hulls, planing. *See* Planing craft
Hulls, plan of, 24, 27
Hulls, unit (monocoque), 127
Human power, 139–41
Hurricane Island Outward Bound
(Rockland, Maine), 124
Hydrofoils, 226. *See also* Commercial
craft, passenger

I

Illumination. *See* Lighting
Indonesian shipbuilding, 22, 124
Inertia, moment of, 69, 70
Information sources, 12, 13, 218, 262–64
Inspection. *See* Construction of vessel,
inspection
Institutional craft, 114, 236–39
cost factors, 238, 239
function in design, 237, 238
Instruments, drawing, 9–11
Interior joiner work specifications. *See*
Specifications, interior joiner work
Invisible lines. *See* Ghost lines
Iorns, Michael (builder), 134
Iron, wrought, 129

J

Jacaranda, 196
Janthina, 189
John Leavitt, 218
Jones Act, 216, 217

K

Katumaran, 196
Keels, 207, 208. *See also* Underbody
Ketch. *See* Rig
Knockdown[90°], 194
Knots defined, 156

L

Laboratory. *See* Work space
Laminar flow. *See* Flow, laminar
Landing School of Boatbuilding and
Design, xviii
Lapstrake (clinker) planking. *See*
Planking
LCB. *See* Buoyancy, longitudinal center
of
LCF. *See* Flotation, longitudinal center of
Leeward Islands. *See* Caribbean
Leeway, 65, 144
Length overall (LOA), 29, 33, 100
Length, registered, 34
Length, waterline (LWL), 29, 81, 100
Lexcen, Ben, 206
Lifelines, 112
Lighting, 12, 87, 120
Lines plan, 17
List (heel), 65
Living quarters, 83–85, 186, 189, 190,
201, 210
eating/lounging, 89, 210, 229
sleeping, 90, 201, 215
Lobster boats 74, 227. *See also*
Commercial craft, fishing
Logarithmic graphs. *See* Graphs,
logarithmic
Logarithms, 42, 43

M

Machinery specifications. *See*
Specifications, machinery
Machinery systems, 105
Magnus effect, 147
Maintenance and repair, 122, 130
costs, 168
Maldives, Republic of, 148, 217
Marchaj, C. J., *Aero-Hydrodynamics of
Sailing,* 142
Mast. *See* Spars
Materials specifications. *See*
Specifications, materials
Mathematical calculations, 36–46

Sailing craft, 165, 191–222
  character, 202, 205, 206
  cruising, 202, 204, 205, 207, 208
  displacement, 198, 200, 202, 205
  hull form, 195, 202, 207
  monohulls, 196–99
  racing, 202, 206, 207
  working, 212–22
  yacht, 200, 202, 203
Sailing Directions, U.S. Government
    Printing Office, 221
Sail plan, 104, 107
Sails, 145–48
  mechanized, 220
  wing, 146, 147
Scales, of drawings, 11, 37, 101
Schematic sketches, 244, 245
School ships, 214, 215, 217. *See also*
    Institutional craft
Schooner. *See* Rig
Sculls. *See* Oars
Sea-kindliness, 184. *See also* Comfort
    and safety
Seamanship, modern, 85, 86
Seasickness, 84
Sea trials. *See* Trials
Sections. *See* Stations
Sheer, 3, 24, 118. *See also* Deck, top of,
    at side
  reverse, 115–17
Ship curves. *See* Instruments, drawing
SHP (shaft horsepower). *See* Horse-
    power, shaft
Shrimp vessel, 74
Sinking. *See* Stability, ultimate
Skegs, 76, 186, 207
Skene, Norman L., *The Elements of
    Yacht Design,* xvii
Sketch designs, 95, 96, 103
Sketch, "envelope," 95, 96, 99
Sketches, schematic. *See* Schematic
    sketches
Sketching exercises
  binocular box, 17
  hull lines, 19

Sketching, freehand, 14, 20, 102
  straight line, 15
  curves, 16
Sleeping space. *See* Living quarters,
    sleeping
Sloop. *See* Rig
SLR. *See* Ratios, speed-length
Sole, 104, 105
Spars, 205
  aluminum, 122, 133
Special purpose craft. *See* Commercial
    craft, special purpose
Specifications, 105, 243–51
  electrical, 248, 249
  equipment, 251
  hull, 246, 247
  interior joiner work, 247, 248
  machinery, 249–51
  materials, 245
  painting and finishing, 251
  plumbing, 248
  rigging, 251
Speed-length ratio. *See* Ratio,
    speed-length
Speed/power curve. *See* Curve,
    speed/power
Speed, vessel, 162, 164, 165, 178, 179
Splines. *See* Instruments, drawing
Spray, 181
Stability, 66, 68, 70, 71, 76, 189
  directional, 75
  operational, 77, 78, 192, 193, 224
  ultimate, 77–79, 194, 198, 225
Staterooms. *See* Living quarters, sleep-
    ing
Stations, 18, 19, 26, 28
Steel, structural, 123, 129–31
  material thickness, 104
  strength (tensile), 128
Steering systems, 208–11
Steward, Robert, *Boatbuilding Manual,*
    125
Stock boat, 122
Strip planking. *See* Planking
Subchaser, WWI, 31

US $34.99

ISBN: 978-0-87033-621-8